Screening World Cinema

Screening World Cinema: A Screen *Reader* brings together a selection of key articles on world cinema published over the past two decades in the internationally renowned journal *Screen*.

This new collection allows readers to cross-reference the wide-ranging debates on world cinema that have been pursued and developed across many issues of the journal. Themes addressed include: the problem of defining 'World Cinema'; the relationship between 'First' and 'Third' cinemas and criticisms; issues of modernity and modernization; and melodrama as a national and transnational cinematic mode. *Screening World Cinema* also features chapters on important contemporary world cinemas – New Iranian, Latin American and Chinese cinemas among them – as they negotiate issues of globalization and cultural and political modernity; as well as a complete listing of articles and other items on world cinema published in *Screen* since 1976.

Contributors: Julianne Burton-Carvajal, Shohini Chaudhuri, Nezih Erdoğan, Howard Finn, Teshome H. Gabriel, Lalitha Gopalan, Catherine Grant, Annette Kuhn, Ning Ma, Scott MacKenzie, Andrea Noble, Alastair Phillips, Laura Podalsky and Ravi Vasudevan.

Catherine Grant is Senior Lecturer and Director of Film Studies at the University of Kent. She has published widely on international cinema and culture in journals and anthologies. In 1997 she co-edited a special issue of *Screen* on Latin American cinema.

Annette Kuhn is Professor of Film Studies at Lancaster University, where she directs an undergraduate course on international cinema. She is an editor of *Screen* and a Fellow of the British Academy. Her many publications include *The Women's Companion to International Film* (1989).

Screening World Cinema

A *Screen* Reader

**Edited by Catherine Grant
and Annette Kuhn**

Routledge
Taylor & Francis Group

LONDON AND NEW YORK

First published 2006
by Routledge
2 Park Square, Milton Park, Abingdon, Oxon OX14 4RN

Simultaneously published in the USA and Canada
by Routledge
270 Madison Ave, New York, NY 10016

Routledge is an imprint of the Taylor & Francis Group, an informa business

Editorial selection and material © 2006 Catherine Grant and Annette Kuhn
Individual chapters © 2006 Chapter authors

Typeset in Perpetua by Keystroke, Jacaranda Lodge, Wolverhampton
Printed and bound in Great Britain by The Cromwell Press, Trowbridge, Wiltshire

British Library Cataloguing in Publication Data
A catalogue record for this book is available from the British Library

Library of Congress Cataloging in Publication Data
Screening world cinema : the screen reader / edited by
Catherine Grant and Annette Kuhn.
    p. cm.
  Includes bibliographical references and index.
  1. Motion pictures. I. Grant, Catherine, 1964– II. Kuhn, Annette.
PN1994.S435 2006
791 .43–dc22

                                                              2005029278

ISBN10: 0–415–38428–1 (hbk)
ISBN10: 0–415–38429–X (pbk)

ISBN13: 978–0–415–38428–5 (hbk)
ISBN13: 978–0–415–38429–2 (pbk)

Contents

Illustrations

Editors' acknowledgments

We are grateful to Rebecca Barden, who responded with great enthusiasm to the *Screen* editors' proposal for a new Routledge series of *Screen* Readers, and made it possible for us to move forward swiftly on *Screening World Cinema*, the first volume in that series and the fifth *Screen* Reader. Previous *Screen* Readers were: *Cinema/ Ideology/Politics* (Society For Education in Film and Television, 1977); *Cinema and Semiotics* (SEFT, 1981); *The Sexual Subject* (Routledge, 1991); and *Screen Histories* (Oxford University Press, 1998).

For their valuable input into this project, thanks are due also to *Screen*'s publishers, Oxford University Press, and in particular to Clare Morton and James Munro. Natalie Foster, Aileen Irwin and Annamarie Kino at Routledge have been a pleasure to work with, as have the contributors to *Screening World Cinema*: we thank them for their hard work and patience. We have been fortunate in enjoying encouragement and practical support from everyone at *Screen*: the journal's other editors (John Caughie, Simon Frith, Karen Lury, Jackie Stacey and Sarah Street) and its editorial assistants (Caroline Beven and Emily Munro). We also have pleasure in acknowledging each other's contribution to what has been an enjoyable and productive collaboration.

In addition, Catherine Grant would like to thank James S. Williams, Elizabeth Cowie and Michele Aaron.

Catherine Grant
Annette Kuhn

Publisher's acknowledgements

The publishers gratefully acknowledge permission to reprint articles from *Screen* journal.

Chapters 1, 2, 3 and 7 reprinted by kind permission of the John Logie Baird Centre and the authors.

Chapters 4, 5, 6, 8, 9, 10, 11 and 12 reprinted by kind permission of the John Logie Baird Centre, Oxford University Press and the authors.

Further details on the volumes of *Screen* journal in which each chapter originally appeared can be found in the Appendix.

Contributors

Julianne Burton-Carvajal is Professor of Literature at the University of California–Santa Cruz, and her interests include Latin American visual culture, particularly film, and melodrama as a transnational form. She is editor of *Cinema and Social Change in Latin America* (1986) and *The Social Documentary in Latin America* (1990).

Shohini Chaudhuri is Lecturer in Contemporary Writing and Film at the University of Essex. Her articles have appeared in *Camera Obscura, Strategies: Journal of Theory, Culture and Politics* and *Screen*. She is the author of *Contemporary World Cinema: Europe, the Middle East, East Asia and South Asia* (2005).

Nezih Erdoğan teaches semiotics and film sound at Bilgi University, Istanbul. He has published articles and chapters on Turkish cinema in, *inter alia, Companion Encyclopedia of Middle Eastern and North African Film* (ed. Oliver Leaman, 2001) and *Hollywood Abroad: Audiences and Cultural Exchange* (ed. Melvyn Stokes and Richard Maltby, 2005).

Howard Finn teaches film and literature at Queen Mary, University of London, and has published widely on modernism, cinema and critical aesthetics.

Teshome H. Gabriel teaches in the Department of Theatre, Film and Television at the University of California–Los Angeles. His books include *Otherness and the Media: the Ethnography of the Imagined and the Imaged* (1993, coedited with Hamid Naficy) and *Third Cinema in the Third World: the Aesthetics of Liberation* (1982). He is the founding director of several journals, including *Emergencies* and *Ethiopian Fine Arts Journal*.

Lalitha Gopalan teaches Film Studies at Georgetown University, where she is Associate Professor in the School of Foreign Service and Department of English. She is the author of *Cinema of Interruptions* (2002) and *Bombay* (2005). Her current research project explores the formation of spaces in contemporary Asian cinemas.

Catherine Grant is Senior Lecturer and Director of Film Studies at the University of Kent. She has published on international cinema and culture in journals such as *Screen, Journal of Latin American Cultural Studies, Feminist Theory, Film Studies: An International Review*, and *Revista Iberoamericana*, and in numerous anthologies. In 1997 she co-edited a special issue of *Screen* on Latin American cinema.

Annette Kuhn is Professor of Film Studies at Lancaster University, an editor of *Screen* and a Fellow of the British Academy. Her publications include *Family Secrets: Acts of Memory and Imagination* (1995 and 2002); *An Everyday Magic: Cinema and Cultural Memory* (2002); *Screen Histories: A* Screen *Reader* (1998, co-edited with Jackie Stacey); she also edited *The Women's Companion to International Film* (1989).

Ning Ma has taught Film and Media Studies in Australia at Griffith University, the University of Newcastle and the University of Western Sydney; and is currently Visiting Professor in the School of Film and Television, Shanghai University.

Scott MacKenzie is Senior Lecturer in Film Studies at the University of St Andrews. He is the author of *Screening Québec: Québecois Moving Images, National Identity and the Public Sphere* (2004) and co-editor of *Cinema and Nation* (2000) and *Purity and Provocation: Dogma '95* (2003).

Andrea Noble is Reader in Latin American visual culture at the University of Durham. She is author of *Tina Modotti: Image, Texture, Photography* (2001) and *Mexican National Cinema* (2005); also co-editor, with Alex Hughes, of *Phototextualities: Intersections of Photography and Narrative* (2003).

Alastair Phillips is Lecturer in Film Studies in the Department of Film, Theatre and Television at the University of Reading. He is author of *City of Darkness, City of Light: Emigré Filmmakers in Paris 1929–1939* (2004) and co-editor, with Ginette Vincendeau, of *Journeys of Desire: European Actors in Hollywood Cinema* (2006), also, with Julian Stringer, of *Japanese Cinema: Texts and Contexts* (2006).

Laura Podalsky is Associate Professor in the Department of Spanish and Portuguese at Ohio State University. She is author of *Specular City: Transforming Culture, Consumption, and Space in Buenos Aires, 1955–1973* (2004) and has published articles in *El ojo que piensa; Screen; Studies in Latin American Popular Culture*; and *Cinemais*. Her current research project deals with contemporary Latin American cinema, the politics of affect and the public sphere.

Ravi Vasudevan works at the Centre for the Study of Developing Societies, in Delhi, where he co-directs Sarai, a research programme on media experience and urban history. He is Visiting Professor in the Department of Film Studies, Jadavpur University, Kolkata; in the Mass Communication Research Centre, Jamia Millia Islamia, Delhi; and in the Film and Television Institute of India in

Pune. He serves on the editorial advisory board of *Screen*, is an adviser to the Public Service Broadcasting Trust, India, a member of the editorial collective of the Sarai Reader series, and editor of *Making Meaning in Indian Cinema* (2000).

1   Screening world cinema

Annette Kuhn and Catherine Grant

'World cinema' is today a strenuously promoted brand that endows cultural and commercial endeavours, such as film festivals and DVD collections,[1] with a degree of scholarly respectability. It also lends a commercial edge to a range of educational and academic initiatives – many new courses, and even degree programmes, on world cinema have been launched in recent years, for example, and there has been an explosion in academic publishing in the field.

Part of the attraction of the world cinema brand must lie in its twofold promise of inclusivity and distinctiveness. While the term can refer specifically to Third World cinemas which embody non-mainstream or alternative approaches to film content and/or style, it can equally well cover all non-Hollywood or all non-First World cinemas, from the most mainstream to the most experimental. And in what is perhaps an older usage, world cinema can stand simply for a global cinema that embraces all films, including those of the First World.[2] In a Euro-American university context, 'world cinema' might recall the idea of *Weltliteratur*, a 'world canon' of great cultural texts; but outside that institutional sphere, and in its guise as a marketing tool, the term tends to cover territory similar to that embraced in the widespread coinage 'world music'. This denotes a 'protected' or circumscribed space for the circulation and critical consideration, in the West, of cultural products from non-western, and often non-mainstream or counterhegemonic, national and regional traditions. World cinema, then, is not so much a contested term as, frequently, a perfunctory, contradictory and catch-all one.

Nonetheless, within screen studies, world cinema constitutes a distinctive, if shifting, object of study with a complex history that is informed not only by critical–theoretical debates across the discipline as a whole but also by the institutional, and even the technological, conditions of existence of screen studies as an independent discipline within the academy. In turn, these local conditions are intertwined with ongoing changes in the world order of media.

In her recent book on contemporary world cinema, Shohini Chaudhuri argues:

> Film now belongs to an enormous multinational system consisting of TV networks, new technologies of production and distribution, and international

co-productions. It is no longer a separate art but part of the digital convergence with other media. Through these transnational processes of film production, financing and distribution, it increasingly makes sense to think in terms of 'world cinema'.[3]

Other writers, including most of the contributors to the present volume, would agree that the transnational aspects of the medium – that is to say its *inter*national interconnectedness and interdependence rather than simply its *multi*national manifestations – merit greater comparative attention.

It would be misleading, however, to think of world cinema in the academic context solely in terms of an object, or a set of objects, of study: it is important as well to consider the field in terms of the approaches it takes to its objects – its methodologies, in other words. Writing on issues that arise in the teaching of international cinema in a US university, Dudley Andrew notes:

> Any study of world cinema [. . .] should [. . .] be ready to travel more than to oversee, should put students inside unfamiliar conditions of viewing rather than bringing the unfamiliar handily to them. This is the pedagogical promise of *world cinema*, a manner of treating foreign films systematically, transcending the vagaries of taste; taking the measure of 'the foreign' in what is literally a freshly recognized global phenomenon.[4]

Andrew proposes that courses, and indeed books, on world cinema should be neither 'gazetteers' nor 'encyclopedias', 'futilely trying to do justice to cinematic life everywhere'. Instead, they should 'model a set of approaches, just as an atlas opens up a continent to successive views'.[5]

Andrew's five 'views' (political, demographic, linguistic, 'orientation', topographical) offer the key virtue of opening up films and cinemas that will at first be unfamiliar to his students to a broad-based and systematic study undertaken on these cinemas' own terms. His approach, like Chaudhuri's, suggests interesting possibilities for transnational research and pedagogy in screen studies. In different ways, both writers adopt a conceptualization of 'world cinema' that is informed by a 'world systems' theory developed in the fields of social, political and economic science. A key concern of this approach is the mechanisms through which capitalism functions as a 'world system', maintaining itself through ever-evolving 'core/periphery' relations.'[6] In the screen studies context, notes Andrew, 'a world systems approach . . . demands a[n] . . . analogy . . . of "waves", which roll through adjacent cultures whose proximity to one another promotes propagation that not even triangulation can adequately measure'.[7]

This may seem uncontroversial today; and indeed, neither Andrew nor Chaudhuri see any need to defend such global (or 'globalized') perspectives in their work. And yet, in the 1980s – before the end of the Cold War and before the prominence of discourses of globalization – the world systems approach was among the sites of fierce polemic concerning the study, in the West, of 'marginal' or 'non-mainstream' cinemas. Although *Screen* had previously touched on world cinema, with articles on Japanese director Ozu Yasujiro's films and reports on contemporary Chinese cinemas,[8] it was not until the early to mid 1980s that the journal began in earnest to tackle questions arising from western scholars' 'seemingly recent discovery of "otherness" with regard to film practice and theory'.[9]

This quotation is taken from Robert Crusz's contribution to a 1985 double issue of *Screen* on 'Other Cinemas, Other Criticisms', the second of two special issues of the journal treating racism, Eurocentrism, colonialism, and 'difference' in global film and audiovisual media, as well as in western film and media studies.[10] Both were published against a backdrop of growing debate and scholarship on these topics. Books such as Teshome Gabriel's 1982 *Third Cinema in the Third World* and Michael Chanan's 1983 *Twenty-Five Years of the New Latin American Cinema* had succeeded, perhaps for the first time, in making the western academy take note of theories of cinema that had not originated within a specifically Euro-North American context.[11] The most prominent of these theories was associated with 'Third Cinema', and followed a 1969 manifesto by Argentine filmmakers Fernando Solanas and Octavio Getino which called for a revolutionary, collectivist practice in the Third World and elsewhere of 'a cinema of decolonization, which expresses the will to national liberation, anti-mythic, anti-racist, anti-bourgeois, and popular'.[12]

'Other Cinemas, Other Criticisms' led with a polemical article by US-based Latin Americanist scholar Julianne Burton. 'Marginal cinemas and mainstream critical theory' (reproduced as Chapter Two of this volume) is in part a critical review of Teshome Gabriel's book on Third Cinema, in that Burton attacks what she calls his '"mythical" vision' that Third World cinema is the 'site of a unitary and autonomous oppositional cinematic practice'.[13] However, the main objective of Burton's contribution was to explore the relationships between Third World cinema and 'First World criticism'; to examine the points of intersection between US and European film theory and Third World attempts to forge, and to explore, national identity and cultural autonomy through film practice. Above all, and against the grain of most theorizing on Third Cinema, Burton argued for approaches to Third World, or 'marginal', cinemas which took up aspects of film theory developed in *Screen* over the preceding decade, referring in particular to 'cinesemiotics', to theories of spectatorial pleasure, and to feminist theories.

In arguing against the somewhat adversarial quality of encounters between First World theory and Third World practice, between the 'mainstream' and the 'marginal', Burton wrote:

> Mainstream cultural manifestations appropriate marginal creativity without acknowledging (while often actively concealing) the source. Oppositional cultural practice defines itself as a denial of, and alternative to, dominant

practice, a stance which requires constant monitoring of its adversary. Dominant or mainstream cultures thus establish the terms of oppositional or marginal cultures to a significant degree. In this sense, oppositional culture is necessarily reactive. Culture can be marginal without being oppositional but cannot be mainstream without being in some degree dominant. The terminology is relational, requiring the articulation of both poles of the antithesis. It also allows for varying degrees of dominance and oppositionality. Most importantly, the terms presuppose a global focus, a 'world systems' approach.

Teshome Gabriel's response, published in *Screen* a year afterwards (and forming Chapter Three of the present volume), was 'mortifying in likening Burton's suggestion that Third (World) Cinema differed only in degree and not in kind from other cinemas to what he perceived as the First World intellectual arrogance of Immanuel Wallerstein's "World System Theory" which subsumed Socialism within all forms of non-capitalism and denied the possibility of post-capitalism.'[14] Gabriel attacked what he saw as Burton's own subsumptions and conflations. He also refuted Burton's hopes for a productive dialogue between the 'mainstream' and the 'marginal':

> Critical theory is not an innocent discipline, nor is it an 'objective' phenomenon. Like any theory of social change, it has blind spots and limits. It is today a battleground. The pivotal question should rather be, to what end is 'mainstream' critical theory directed? Of what use are such analytic tools? To what degree are they tools of oppression rather than liberation?

Twenty years on it is clear that, despite their shared situations as US-based academics teaching and researching Third World cinemas, Burton and Gabriel were staking out very different battlegrounds. In contributing to *Screen*, Gabriel wanted to convince 'progressive western voices' to ally with 'Third World progressives to bring about . . . the overthrow of "the world cinematic language"'.[15] Burton wanted a less adversarial, more mutually informing relationship between Third World film practice and First World critical theory: 'the selective appropriation and transformation of "appropriate critical technologies" is a strategy capable of enhancing the practice and theory of both marginal and mainstream, metropolitan and peripheral, cultures and societies'.

Burton's article and Gabriel's response betoken the considerable political importance attached, at the time they were written, to theoretical practice and practical theory. However, if First World film theory seemed hegemonic from one standpoint, from another it remained very marginal. In the UK, as indeed elsewhere in the western academy, film studies had yet to establish itself as an academic discipline, and the version of film studies espoused by (and in considerable measure created in) *Screen* saw itself as allied with a range of oppositional film practices, at home and abroad. But although the fortunes of both film studies and oppositional cinemas have fluctuated somewhat since the mid 1980s,[16] Burton's and Gabriel's articles continue to be pertinent and valuable for their vigorous flagging of political and ethical issues which ought still to be central to the treatment of international cinema in the western academy.[17]

Unfortunately, such issues are seldom raised today in discussions around world cinema, in part because the rise of world systems and global capitalism has tended to place issues of exploitation, dependency and power differences between regions outside the discursive frame. Indeed, the decline in usage of terms like Third World and Third Cinema is revealing in this context; as, relatedly, is the rather greater attention given in recent studies of world cinema to Asian, and especially Chinese, cinemas as against those of, say, Latin America or Africa. It is surely no coincidence that those areas of the world most prominently involved in transformations in the global cultural economy are precisely the ones that have given rise to many of the debates on transnational film cultures that figure so prominently in current studies of world cinema.

Screen has continued to publish work on international cinema that reflects, politically and ethically, on its own objectives and methodologies; leaning, perhaps, towards Burton's rather than Gabriel's approach to critical–theoretical engagement with non-western cinemas, and also taking on board wider shifts of focus in screen studies scholarship. The editorial in *Screen*'s special millennial issue noted the rise in submissions to the journal of theoretically-informed (rather than 'theory-led') empirical work in screen studies, especially in cinema history.[18] In the same issue, in a discussion of shifts in the discipline, Indian scholar Ravi Vasudevan concurs:

> Looking back at Screen Studies over the past ten years or so, there emerges a strong impression of the ways in which historical analysis has provided the armature for several focuses. . . . [F]ilm scholars have begun to explore many different histories as these are played out across the world and as they interact in complex ways. Here, the question of national film cultures has provided a crucial way of disaggregating wider theorizations of film. Initially this was often posed in a defensive way in order to highlight patterns of distinction and difference, emphasizing particularity against hegemonic norms of narrative filmmaking associated with Hollywood cinema. Today, however, it is possible to pose another future for Screen Studies, one which might look to a more intricate cultural history of identity: to the web of exchanges, flows and translations that underlie cultural identity; to the negotiations of territoriality, in markets and geolinguistic spaces, that govern its changing terms.[19]

The beginning of this new approach to the study of international cinemas can be dated roughly to the late 1980s and early 1990s. During this period *Screen* moved its editorial base from London to Glasgow, and it was also at this time that significant shifts in the ecology of UK higher education were beginning to gain momentum. The latter (if not the former) would ultimately be instrumental in bringing about the institutionalization of screen studies across all areas of the academy – and, arguably, at the same time, the depoliticization of the discipline. It is salutary to consider the rise in – and the attendant transformation of – studies of world cinema against this background.

In 1989, the last London-produced volume of *Screen* included an article on Hindi cinema by Ravi Vasudevan which in effect pioneered the emergent approach signalled in his later article.[20] In 'The melodramatic mode and the commercial Hindi cinema', Vasudevan looks at classics of Indian popular cinema through the lens of theories on film melodrama developed by Anglo-North American scholars.[21] While finding that key features of the 'melodramatic imagination' are observable in these films (the Manichean moral universe, moral and ethical dilemmas acted out through familial relationships, music and dance as expressive of emotion, and so on), he shows that they also draw on nationally and/or culturally specific forms – folktales and legends, traditions of storytelling, music-making and performance.

Two aspects of Vasudevan's article mark it out as different from *Screen*'s other 1980s contributions to debates on world cinema. First, while Vasudevan is clear about the critical–political issues at stake, there is no sense that the terrain has to be fought over. Second, his argument is grounded in detailed reference to actual films, while at the same time drawing on informed understanding of their cultural–historical contexts. It is this distinctive and productive interweaving of textual interpretation and informed contextual explication that marks the bulk of the fifty or more articles on world cinema published in *Screen* since the early 1990s (see Appendix for details).

'The melodramatic mode and the commercial Hindi cinema', which forms Chapter Seven of this volume, is part of a thread of argument which has pervaded scholarly work on world cinema, and which surfaces repeatedly throughout *Screening World Cinema*. This has to do with genres in world cinema, both in their original contexts and in their manifestations and transformations across different national cinema cultures. Arguably, it is on this point that Vasudevan's 'web of exchanges, flows and translations' pivots. Two film genres emerge as particularly prominent in this web of cultural exchange: the action picture and the melodrama. Both draw on elements of local folk and popular performance and storytelling traditions, traditions that typically have to do with speech, music, song and the body rather with than the written word – traditions that possess the wide accessibility and appeal of the folktale.

In world cinema studies, attention to the action film has focused largely around Chinese cinemas, above all on the Hong Kong martial arts picture, arguably one of the earliest transnational genres, and the object of considerable scholarly attention in recent years.[22] But it is melodrama, or rather the melodramatic imagination, that emerges as the most pervasive, and the most thoroughly scrutinized, of generic modalities across world cinemas.[23] In the West, the melodramatic mode is historically associated with the revolutions in eighteenth- and nineteenth-century Europe that ultimately gave rise to a new social class, the bourgeoisie; and here and elsewhere it has also become associated with the recruitment of pre-existing popular cultural forms and traditions in the service of modern mass media such as cinema. Among the main issues around the melodramatic mode that arise in world cinema studies is the instrumentality of the genre across a wide range of cultural and national cinema contexts as a kind of demotic, or vernacular, engagement with modernity;[24] and sometimes, through their address, as linking modernity with national identity.

In Chapter Nine, for example, Nezih Erdoğan traces the operations of the melodramatic mode through a form of Turkish commercial cinema, Yeşilçam, that had its heyday in the 1960s and 1970s.[25] Like many expressions of the melodramatic in popular media, Yeşilçam has been critically derogated; and yet, argues, Erdoğan, a close reading of the films and an understanding of their contexts of production and reception reveal that they express and negotiate contradictions around national identity in a time of uneasy modernization in Turkey. In Chapter Six, Alastair Phillips looks at how the postwar films of Ozu Yasujiro engage traditional forms of domestic drama to address issues of modernity in postwar Japan.[26] And both Andrea Noble (Chapter Five) and Laura Podalsky (Chapter Twelve) note that certain Mexican film melodramas of the 1940s, with their characteristic appeal to the emotions, address – and so produce – the national 'subject' as a family member.[27]

Among the key features of the melodramatic as a transnational modality is the play of universality and contextual specificity through which themes and issues around gender – and specifically around female desire and its potential for trans-gressiveness in a patriarchal family setting – are engaged. However, in recent, often deliberately transnationally pitched, examples of world cinema – *Crouching Tiger, Hidden Dragon* (Ang Lee, China/Taiwan/US, 2000) is a case in point – gender issues are often played out in themes and settings that combine features of both the major transnational genres, the melodrama and the action picture; sometimes with the twist that the action 'hero' is female. In Chapter Eight, Lalitha Gopalan discusses the 'vengeful woman' film, a significant subgenre of 1980s Indian cinema that potently combines action and the melodramatic in woman-centred narratives.[28]

A hallmark of many of the contributions to this volume is an aspiration to attend, very much in *Screen* style, to the organization and operations of films as texts; whilst at the same time bringing to bear careful and informed attention to the historically and culturally specific contexts of their production and reception. One of *Screen*'s earliest ventures onto the terrain of world cinema took the form of two articles on Ozu, published in 1976.[29] These include detailed analyses of passages in films by the

Japanese director, analyses undertaken in the service of an argument centred on the films' highly distinctive organization of narrative space. Behind this argument lie two unspoken agendas: an assumption, first of all, that Ozu's films belong to a directorial canon in what Dudley Andrew calls the 'foreign art film', one of the pedagogical predecessors of world cinema;[30] and secondly – and much more significantly in terms of the trajectory of screen studies – that Ozu's work repays critical–theoretical attention from a western standpoint and using methods of film analysis developed by western scholars precisely because it differs so radically from the 'mainstream', in that its distinctive organization of narrative space constitutes an alternative, even a challenge, to the dominant model of classical Hollywood cinema.

In this regard Thompson and Bordwell might argue that it is in the formal organization of filmic space that the modernism, if not the modernity, of Ozu's *oeuvre* lies. Writing on Ozu in 2003, Alastair Phillips references this earlier work on the films' 'aesthetic strategies' and recognizes the distinctiveness of the formal qualities of Ozu's films, while urging the necessity, if we want to understand them more fully, of also taking on board their deployment of pre-existing Japanese cultural forms and dramatic genres, and setting this encounter within its social and historical milieux. The new approach, then, builds on the earlier work.

Reflecting key areas of *Screen*'s engagement with scholarship on world cinema, *Screening World Cinema* is divided into four parts: 'Views from here and there'; 'Modernity and modernization'; 'Melodrama as a national and transnational mode'; and 'Contemporary world cinema and critical theory'. Part I comprises the exchange between Julianne Burton and Teshome Gabriel discussed above, on the politics and ethics of articulating, from the privileged spaces of the western academy, critical theories about non-western, 'marginal', or non-dominant cinemas (Chapters 2 and 3). Both of these contributions turn on discussions of Third Cinema, and both also engage directly, though from opposing positions, with critical, theoretical and methodological issues that had become associated with *Screen*.

The three chapters in Part II examine instances of world cinema in which discourses and practices of modernity and modernization are, in various ways, prominent. All these contributions are marked by selfconsciousness as regards their methodologies; and all draw on archival research and bring to bear highly developed and sensitive 'local' knowledge as well as close acquaintance with canonical and contemporary film and critical theory.

In his essay on early cinema in Québec (Chapter 4),[31] Scott MacKenzie builds on the innovative work of Miriam Hansen and other leading film historians on early American and German cinema, adapting methods developed in the historical study of 'mainstream' early cinemas to a detailed historical study of a 'marginal', non-anglophone cinema. His work scrutinizes the relationship, at an important moment in the histories of both cinema and modernity, between national identity, cinema, and the francophone public sphere in Québec. A significant piece of historical work in its own right, MacKenzie's work also highlights new directions for critical theory as it addresses itself to 'marginal' or 'non-mainstream' cinemas.

Andrea Noble's 'If looks could kill: image wars in *María Candelaria*' combines Mexican and Latin Americanist theories of the modernization of visual culture with 'mainstream' theories of film spectatorship to construct an illuminating account of the specificities of Mexican film spectatorship at a particular time: the 1940s, the first true decade of Mexican cinema's 'Golden Age'. Noble's study is part of a growing trend in world cinema studies to take popular cinema, as well as art films and overtly political films, seriously. Her close analysis of the 1940s melodrama *María Candelaria* (Emilio Fernández, 1944) exposes the historically specific mechanisms of the colonial(ist) and nationalist 'gazes' during an intense period of social and political modernization.

In Chapter 6, as already noted, Alastair Phillips revisits the much studied work of Japanese filmmaker Ozu Yasujiro, proposing that the director's postwar films be understood as an engagement with the depiction of social change and its effect on gendered cultural milieux and social relationships. Phillips deploys film analysis alongside cultural historical methods in an important contribution to the study of national identity as it is constructed through a set of cultural texts at a particular historical moment.

Part III addresses the issue of genre in world cinema, focusing especially on the key transnational film mode of melodrama. Each chapter examines the figuration and instrumentality of the melodramatic in a different national or regional cinema culture; suggesting that the melodramatic is a generic modality that has a certain universal quality, while specific instances of the melodramatic are capable of embodying and expressing the local in highly accessible ways. Here, studies of the melodramatic in very different instances of popular cinema suggest that 'national cinema' is never a 'pure', nor indeed even a discrete, entity.

Ravi Vasudevan's groundbreaking study of the melodramatic mode in popular Hindi cinema forms Chapter Seven. As noted above, he proposes, heuristically, the use of a framework evolved in relation to western melodrama; and discovers that the Hindi film melodrama embodies structural features similar to those of western melodramas while at the same time articulating culturally distinctive modes of address. Here, critical theory developed by western scholars initially to shed light on western cultural texts is harnessed and adapted to help reveal the aesthetic, cultural and historical specificity of a 'non-mainstream', but in its own way 'dominant' nonwestern, filmmaking practice.

In Chapter 8, Lalitha Gopalan – like Vasudevan – reflects on and makes use of western methodology, drawing on Anglo-North American feminist film theory in her analysis of the Indian rape-revenge film cycle of the 1980s. While critiquing this body of theory for its overwhelming Hollywood focus, she notes that her 'reading strategies [. . .] are indelibly shaped by [a] feminist film theory that argues for formal textual analysis as a means to understand the articulation of sexual difference in cinema'. Besides its theorization of spectatorship, feminist film theory is also of use precisely because it helps her to explore points of contact between Hindi cinema and international filmmaking practices – in particular rape-revenge narratives produced in Hollywood. In this way, interrogation of a monolithic conception of 'national cinema' is made possible.

In Chapter 9, as already noted, Nezih Erdoğan looks at an instance of the melodramatic in Turkish cinema in relation to issues around national identity. He draws on postcolonial theory's formulation of the ambivalent nature of colonial discourse to explore how this identity both mimics, and at the same time resists, dominant western models. Neither nationalism, nor any other sort of non-western practice, suggests Erdoğan, can easily avoid reproducing colonial discourse and its derivatives.

Part IV of *Screening World Cinema* focuses on the ways in which contemporary world cinema finds forms that enable it to circulate beyond its original production contexts. These forms and contexts raise old, as well as new, issues concerning (neo)colonial mimicry and cultural specificity, returning us to some of the issues around politics and ethics in cultural theory and practice posited by Burton and Gabriel.

In Chapter 10, Shohini Chaudhuri and Howard Finn discuss New Iranian Cinema, the internationally successful low-budget art cinema that came to prominence at film festivals from the mid 1990s.[32] They show how it has developed elements drawn from the stylistic and political practices, and associated existential–phenomenological critical theories, of European cinema of the 1940s to the 1960s, Italian Neorealism and the French New Wave in particular. Engaging closely with a number of important films, the authors conclude with the provocative contention that the appeal of New Iranian Cinema in the West may have less to do with 'sympathy' for an exoticised 'other' under conditions of repression than with self-recognition: 'the open images of Iranian film remind us of the loss of such images in most contemporary cinema, the loss of cinema's particular space for creative inter-pretation and critical reflection.'

Writing on Chinese fifth-generation cinema in Chapter 11,[33] Ning Ma asks, 'how should we analyze the form and meaning of genre films whose claim to authentic representation rests less on a manifestation of the national psyche or the collective unconscious than on what Fredric Jameson calls the "logic of impersonal capital"? What role can locally produced genre films play in the global cultural economy characterised by what Arjun Appadurai calls "disjunctures and flows"? And what kind of subjectivity, if any, do genre films, which often assume a simulated hybrid and fractal form, construct for a global audience?' In a Foucauldian historical and aesthetic analysis of the internationally prominent film melodramas of the post-1989 generation of filmmakers in the People's Republic of China, Ning Ma argues that, even as the Fifth Generation has turned Chinese culture and history into a marketable generic product for global consumption, these 'new crosscultural melodramas' have forged a highly positive, intersubjective discursive space – an 'effective history' – for the national and international articulation of democratic politics.

Laura Podalsky's consideration of politics and form in contemporary Latin American cinema (Chapter 12) covers terrain similar to Ning Ma's – national and international politics and culture under globalization – but comes to less hopeful conclusions. In the context of recent discussions of the death of social and political utopias, Podalsky analyses a number of films, including the huge international success *Amores perros/Love's a Bitch* (Alejandro González Iñárritu, Mexico, 2000), that deal with the legacies of the radical and revolutionary political projects of the 1960s and 1970s. She argues that these films can be seen as attempts to reinscribe revolutionary projects in the light of the dominant neoliberal paradigm in contemporary Latin America. Yet the way these films evoke and deploy emotion suggests an alternative, more culturally and politically pessimistic, reading. In a further example of the productive use of theories and methodologies developed by western critics for other contexts (here, Thomas Elsaesser and Raymond Williams), set alongside those developed by Latin Americans and Latin Americanist scholars (Tomás Gutiérrez Alea; Ana López), Podalsky sets out to understand how these films carry out emotional work as well as, or *as part of*, their political work. In this regard, 'Affecting legacies' offers a positive response to Julianne Burton's call for a wider use of 'screen theories' in relation to non-dominant cinemas.

With the partial exception of the polemical pieces by Burton and Gabriel, which attempt to tackle, head-on, notions of the global and ideas about the 'worlds' of cinema, all the contributions to this volume emerge from close study of national and regional cinemas and films in transnational contexts. This initial rootedness in the local or the national, albeit at times highly critical of the valence and function of the latter concept, keeps alive the possibilities for greater engagement with the matters of epistemological and formal difference, and even of resistance, with which Gabriel is concerned. While attention is paid to the place of individual cinemas in their global context, each of the chapters in *Screening World Cinema* can be seen to work against the desire that Gabriel notes in some critical theory 'to globalise and homogenise world cinema and cultures'.

All of the contributors to this volume, then, are highly conscious of, and are well informed about, the present and the historical limits of such possibilities for local or national difference and resistance, whether these be in colonial, neocolonial, or 'postcolonial' situations. This is why their work, individually and collectively, contributes significantly to the study and the understanding of world cinema.

Notes

1   To cite two recent examples: the Cape Town World Cinema Festival and the 13th Annual Denver International World Cinema Independent Fall Film Festival 2005. Also, the World Cinema Fund of the Berlin International Film Festival aims to 'help the realisation of films which otherwise could not be produced, i.e. feature films and creative feature-length documentaries with a strong cultural identity. Another important goal is to strengthen the profile of these films in German cinemas.' http://www.berlinale. de/en/das_festival/world_cinema_fund/wcf_profil/index.html [27 June 2005].

2   The latter category includes Geoffrey-Nowell-Smith (ed.), *The Oxford History of World Cinema* (Oxford: Oxford University Press, 1997) and John Hill and Pamela Church Gibson (eds), *World Cinema: Critical Approaches* (Oxford: Oxford University Press, 2000). World cinema is treated in terms of its difference from the cinemas of the First World in Teshome Gabriel, *Third Cinema in the Third World: the Aesthetics of Liberation* (Ann Arbor, MI: UMI Research Press, 1982) and in Jim Pines and Paul Willemen (eds), *Questions of Third Cinema* (London: British Film Institute, 1989).

3   Shohini Chaudhuri, *Contemporary World Cinema: Europe, The Middle East, East Asia and South Asia* (Edinburgh: Edinburgh University Press, 2005), p. 2.

4   Dudley Andrew, 'An atlas of world cinema', *Framework*, vol. 45, no. 2 (2004), pp. 9–23, p. 9. A version of this article will also appear in Stephanie Dennison and Song Hwee Lim (eds), *Remapping World Cinema: Identity, Culture and Politics in Film* (London: Wallflower Press, 2006).

5   Andrew, 'An atlas of world cinema', p. 10.

6   Immanuel Wallerstein, 'World-systems analysis', in Immanuel Wallerstein (ed.), *The Essential Wallerstein* (New York: The New Press, 2000).

7   Andrew, 'An atlas of world cinema', p. 12.

8   See Kristin Thompson and David Bordwell, 'Space and narrative in the films of Ozu', *Screen*, vol. 17, no. 2 (1976), pp. 41–73; Edward Branigan, 'The space of *Equinox Flower*', *Screen*, vol. 17, no. 2 (1976), pp. 74–105; Rosalind Coward and John Ellis, 'Hong Kong–China 1981', *Screen*, vol. 22, no. 4 (1981), pp. 91–100; John Ellis, 'Electric shadows in Italy: a retrospective of Chinese film', *Screen*, vol. 23, no. 2 (1982), pp. 79–83.

9   Robert Crusz, 'Black cinemas, film theory and dependent knowledge', *Screen*, vol. 26, nos. 3–4 (1985), pp. 152–6, p. 152.

10 The first was 'Racism, Colonialism and the Cinema', *Screen*, vol. 24, no. 2 (1983).

11 Gabriel, *Third Cinema in the Third World*; Michael Chanan, *Twenty-Five Years of the New Latin American Cinema* (London: British Film Institute/Channel Four, 1983). See also Anthony Guneratne, 'Introduction', in Guneratne and Wimal Dissanayake (eds), *Rethinking Third Cinema* (New York: Routledge, 2003), pp. 1–28, p. 7. In Britain, the journal *Framework* began its longstanding programme of publication in this area in the late 1970s: http://www.frameworkonline.com/backissues.htm [14 September 2005].

12 Table ronde avec Fernando Solanas et al, 'Cinéma d'auteur ou cinéma d'intervention?', *CinémAction*, no. 1 (1978), p. 66. Cited and translated by Michael Chanan, 'The changing geography of Third Cinema', *Screen*, vol. 38, no. 4 (1997), pp. 372–88, p. 379. Chanan's article provides a useful overview of debates about Third (World) Cinema, in practice and in theory. See also Guneratne and Dissanayake (eds), *Rethinking World Cinema*; Roy Armes, *Third World Film Making and the West* (Berkeley, CA: University of California Press, 1987); John D. H. Downing (ed.), *Film and Politics in the Third World* (Westport, CN: Praeger, 1987); Pines and Willemen (eds), *Questions of Third Cinema*.

13 Julianne Burton, 'Marginal cinemas and mainstream critical theory', *Screen*, vol. 26, nos.3–4 (1985), pp. 2–21. Both Burton and Gabriel had published articles in the 'Racism, Colonialism and the Cinema' issue: Julianne Burton, 'The politics of aesthetic distance: *São Bernardo*', *Screen*, vol. 24, no. 2 (1983), pp. 30–53; Teshome Gabriel, 'Teaching Third World cinema', *Screen*, vol. 24, no. 2 (1983), pp. 60–4.

14 Guneratne, 'Introduction', p. 13. Gabriel's article, 'Colonialism and "law and order" criticism', was originally published in *Screen*, vol. 27, nos.3–4 (1986), pp. 140–7.

15 Ibid, citing Glauber Rocha, *Revolução do Cinema Novo* (Rio de Janeiro: Alhambra/ Embrafilme, 1981), p. 467.

16 'Millennial editorial', *Screen*, vol. 41, no. 1 (2000), pp. 1–6.

17 Though Ella Shohat and Robert Stam (eds), *Unthinking Eurocentrism: Multiculturalism and the Media* (New York: Routledge, 1994) should have made it impossible to evade political and ethical reflection in media and cultural studies. For a more recent exception, see Guneratne and Dissanayake (eds), *Rethinking Third Cinema* for its spirited revival of these issues. In *Screen*, see Felix Thompson, 'Metaphors of space: polarization, dualism and Third World cinema', vol. 34, no. 1 (1993), pp. 38–53; Michael Chanan, 'The changing geography of Third Cinema'.

18 *Screen*, 'Millennial editorial', p. 2.

19 Ravi S. Vasudevan, 'National pasts and futures: Indian cinema', *Screen*, vol. 41, no. 1 (2000), pp. 119–25, p. 119.

20 Ravi Vasudevan, 'The melodramatic mode and the commercial Hindi cinema', *Screen*, vol. 30, no. 3 (1989), pp. 29–50. Vasudevan pursues the debate in 'Addressing the spectator of a "Third World" national cinema: the Bombay "social" film of the 1940s and 1950s', *Screen*, vol. 36, no. 4 (1995), pp. 305–24.

21 The key texts include Peter Brooks, *The Melodramatic Imagination: Balzac, Henry James, Melodrama, and the Mode of Excess* (New Haven, CT: Yale University Press, 1976 and 1995); Thomas Elsaesser, 'Tales of sound and fury: observations on the family melodrama', in Christine Gledhill (ed.), *Home Is Where the Heart Is: Studies in Melodrama and the Woman's Film* (London: British Film Institute, 1987), pp. 43–69.

22 In *Screen* by Hector Rodriguez, 'Hong Kong popular culture as an interpretive arena: the Huang Feihong film series', vol. 38, no. 1 (1997), pp. 1–24; Julian Stringer, '"Your tender smiles give me strength": paradigms of masculinity in John Woo's *A Better Tomorrow* and *The Killer*', vol. 38, no. 1 (1997), pp. 25–41; See Kam Tan, 'Chinese diasporic imaginations in Hong Kong films: sinicist belligerence and melancholia', vol. 42, no. 1 (2001), pp. 1–20. See also David Bordwell, *Planet Hong Kong: Popular Cinema and the Art of Entertainment* (Cambridge, MA: Harvard University Press, 2000); Esther Yau, *At Full Speed: Hong Kong in a Borderless World* (Minneapolis, MN: University of Minnesota Press, 2001).

23 See, *inter alia*, Wimal Dissanayake (ed.), *Melodrama and Asian Cinema* (Cambridge: Cambridge University Press, 1993); Julianne Burton-Carvajal, 'Mexican melodramas of patriarchy: specificity of a transcultural form', in Ann Marie Stock (ed.), *Framing Latin American Cinema: Contemporary Critical Perspectives* (Minneapolis, MN: University of Minnesota Press, 1997).

24 On vernacular modernism, see Miriam Bratu Hansen, 'The mass production of the senses: classical cinema as vernacular modernism', *Modernism/Modernity*, vol. 6, no. 2 (1999), pp. 59–77.

25 Originally published as 'Narratives of resistance: national identity and ambivalence in the Turkish melodrama between 1965 and 1975', *Screen*, vol. 39, no. 3 (1998), pp. 259–71.

26   Originally published as 'Pictures of the past in the present: modernity, femininity and stardom in the postwar films of Ozu Yasujiro', *Screen*, vol. 44, no. 2 (2003), pp. 154–66.
27   Originally published as Andrea Noble, 'If looks could kill: image wars in *María Candelaria*', *Screen*, vol. 42, no. 1 (2001), pp. 77–91; Laura Podalsky, 'Affecting legacies: historical memory and contemporary structures of feeling in *Madagascar* and *Amores perros*', *Screen*, vol. 44, no. 3 (2003), pp. 277–94.
28   Originally published as 'Avenging women in Indian cinema', *Screen* vol. 38, no. 1 (1997), pp. 42–59.
29   Thompson and Bordwell, 'Space and narrative in the films of Ozu'; Branigan, 'The space of *Equinox Flower*'. See also David Bordwell, *Ozu and the Poetics of Cinema* (London: British Film Institute, 1988).
30   Andrew, 'An atlas of world cinema', p. 9.
31   Scott MacKenzie, 'A screen of one's own: early cinema in Québec and the public sphere 1906–28' originally appeared in *Screen*, vol. 41, no. 2 (2000), pp. 183–202.
32   Shohini Chaudhuri and Howard Finn, 'The open image: poetic realism and the New Iranian Cinema', *Screen*, vol. 44, no. 1 (2003), pp. 38–57.
33   Ning Ma, 'Signs of angst and hope: history and melodrama in Chinese fifth-generation cinema', *Screen*, vol. 44, no. 2 (2003), pp. 183–99.

Part I

Views from here
and there

2 Marginal cinemas and mainstream critical theory

Julianne Burton-Carvajal

Beginning in the mid 1950s and continuing up to the present day, individuals and groups throughout the Third World have embraced the film medium as an essential tool for forging a sense of national identity and cultural autonomy. Works produced over this thirty-year span have commanded considerable recognition in the metropolitan countries. During this same period, there has been an unprecedented elaboration of film theory and critical methodology in the developed sector. Despite ideological and programmatic affinities which derive from the essentially oppositional nature of both spheres of activity, from their embattled challenge to dominant modes of making and looking at films, these two spheres of activity have remained – until now – remarkably separate. My purpose here is to inquire why this has been the case and to consider some recent works which attempt either to ratify or to bridge this cultural–critical divide.

If the concept of *la politique des auteurs* as articulated in *Cahiers du cinéma* in the mid-1950s can be construed (however heuristically) as marking the inception of the development of modern film theory, it is instructive to contrast its evolution in the dominant and dependent sectors. Andrew Sarris's (mis)translation of the term as 'auteur theory' underlines the nature of its application in the English-speaking world in general, and to Hollywood production in particular. In these applications the term was used as the conceptual foundation of a critical perspective which hypostatised the determining role of a single individual (the director or 'author') in the shaping of a film. In Latin America (as in other regions of the Third World), *la política de los autores* was more directly translated and translatable as a practical–strategical position (simultaneously a 'policy' and a 'politics') from which to combat the actual or putative norm of a hierarchical studio-based production system in which the director was relegated to subordinate managerial status. The articulation of a *politique des auteurs* offered a theoretical and practical justification – and, in the careers of the French New Wave directors, a living precedent – for the directors' declaration of independence from the tyranny of the producers. The self-proclaimed reinfranchisement of Third World independents as the ultimate artistic and ideological authority for their films was a fundamental step in both the appropriation of the film medium to non-commercial ends and the consequent transformation of modes of filmic production in Latin America specifically, and in the Third World in general. The application of this concept in the Third World context retained the 'plurality' of the original term, in that it was used to foster the collaborative purposes of more or less unified groups of creative artists working towards similar political goals. (Brazil's Cinema Novo and the Cuban Film Institute are the outstanding examples here).[1]

This example is symptomatic of a more generalised disparity. In the more disadvantaged and consequently more embattled and politicised arenas of the Third World, emphasis falls on the practical application of theoretical concepts, while the relative shelter and security of the developed world encourages theoretical elaboration without any mandate for practical application outside the realm of the theorists and critics. The same theoretical construct that evolved into a critical methodology for examining existing films in the developed sector formed the basis, in regions of the Third World, for a programmatic practice which simultaneously produced new categories of films and transformed the structures and relations of film production and dissemination.

Concrete conditions in the Third World have not supported the division of labour which has occurred in the developed sector between action (in this case, filmmaking) and reflection (in this case, theory and criticism). Emphasis falls on practical theory, refusing the idea that the elaboration of theory can itself constitute a kind of praxis. As Fernando Birri, pioneer of the New Latin American Cinema movement, expresses it, 'Theory and practice must go hand-in-hand, [but] practice must be the key, with theory as its guide and interpreter.[2] The major theoretical essays to emerge from the Latin American film movement – 'The aesthetics of hunger', 'Towards a Third Cinema', 'For an Imperfect Cinema', 'Problems of form and content in revolutionary cinema'[3] – have all been written by filmmakers whose theoretical propositions derive from the concrete practice of attempting to make specific films under specific historical conditions. This fact has been the source of both their strengths and their weaknesses. Film criticism in the region suffers from a similar imbalance, in that the vast majority of Latin American film journals have been founded and edited by people who are also directly involved in producing and promoting independent national cinema. In practice, the most significant exchanges of ideas tend to take place in festivals and other public forums, while the magazines are reserved primarily for informational and promotional purposes rather than serving as sites of sustained critical–theoretical dialogue.

In Latin America, as elsewhere in the developed and underdeveloped world, filmmakers have often dismissed the operations performed by the critic as intrusive, arbitrary, superfluous. In what is regarded as the foremost manifesto of the New Latin American cinema, Cuban Julio García Espinosa declared quite categorically that 'Imperfect Cinema rejects whatever services criticism has to offer and considers the function of mediators and intermediaries anachronistic'.[4] The echoes of this rejection reverberated widely. In the Manifesto of Popular Unity Filmmakers (Chile, 1971), for example, article nine reads: 'We maintain that a cinema based upon our objectives necessarily implies a different kind of critical evaluation; and we affirm that the greatest critic of a revolutionary film is the people to whom it is directed, who have no need for mediators to defend and interpret for them.[5]

   This defensive attitude is no doubt partially responsible for the ongoing 'development of critical underdevelopment' in many Third World film sectors. The dearth of critical approaches specific to the film medium and cognisant of worldwide trends is pervasive in Latin America and in other regions of the Third World. In large degree this dissociation between marginal cinematic practices and 'mainstream' critical theory is another instance of the asymmetrical nature of cultural exchange between the developed and underdeveloped spheres, since the metropolitan sector imports and consumes the 'raw materials' produced in the Third World (films, in this case) more easily than peripheral sectors can import and consume the 'manufactured products' of the developed sector (in this case, theoretical and critical writings). Since specialists in film history, theory and criticism have only recently begun to be produced in significant numbers by metropolitan universities, it is not surprising that Third World societies have not yet found a means of supplying themselves with such a 'luxury product'. Translation is another specialised and expensive skill which has been rendered 'superfluous' by the crisis in the Latin American publishing industry – the combined product of repressive political conditions and a regional economic crisis which has severely curbed publishing activity throughout the hemisphere. These conditions have meant that the chronic cultural lag between 'First World' cultural production and Third World cultural reception has become in this case a cultural gap.

   Third World film study outside the Third World bears the mark of a double marginality – one inevitable, one voluntary. As products of Third World countries, the films which are the object of its inquiry are by definition marginal rather than mainstream outside their national context, whatever their status within it. This first level of marginality can be a source of influence to the degree that films from the Third World expose or subvert the more mystifying and alienating operations of dominant cinema, or declare their autonomy from them by returning to precolonial modes of signification. In their explicit and implicit contestation of mainstream culture in the developed world, marginal cultural products may, under certain conditions, exert an impact disproportional to their marginality, despite the efforts of the culture industry in the dominant sector to preclude this.

   But in order to exert such an impact outside their domestic sphere, Third World films have to rely on a mediating agency – an advocate in the guise of a film critic, historian, scholar, or other certified 'expert' with media access. To the degree that they wish their films to be viewed outside their own immediate geographical-cultural context, Third World filmmakers must enlist the services of those they have dismissed as superfluous.[6] Though the object of these critics' concern – oppositional film production in the Third World – is marginal by definition, the nature of their critical approach is only marginal by choice. Why have advocates of Third World film from the developed sector been so remiss in exploring the potential applications of mainstream critical theory to the oppositional cinemas of the Third World? And why have they (we) failed to make a compelling case for Third World film practice as a transformative prism through which the limitations of mainstream critical theory can be displayed and transformed?

Promotion and defence of Third World film practice in the dominant sector has generally been undertaken in terms of traditionally hegemonic critical discourse (liberal humanism) rather than in terms of what were initially more marginal, oppositional critical discourses (film-as-ideology and cinesemiotics, for example). Critics of Third World cinema who operate in a First World context have been motivated by the contradictory impulse to win recognition for their object of study within the very institutions which also serve to endorse and perpetuate dominant, colonising, hierarchical cinematic discourses. Given the crosscultural nature of such an enterprise, there has also been a predictable tendency for the articulation of the culturally specific to take precedence over the articulation of the cinematically specific, to the degree that these can be construed as separate.

The question of ideological identifications and allegiances also figures prominently here. A sense of solidarity with movements promoting greater political and cultural autonomy in the Third World has restrained many critics from undertaking a rigorous examination of the ideological contradictions lodged in the films and movements for which they seek recognition. Maintenance of the illusion of ideo-logical consistency within and among the products of oppositional film movements in the Third World – what might be called the myth of the monolith – has blocked the enlistment of some of the most viable methodological and critical propositions generated in the developed sector.

This essay grows out of the recognition that the present moment is one of transition. In both the film movements of the Third World and the theoretical–critical articulations of the developed sector, one senses a pause, a plateau, which provides an opportunity to take stock of past and future directions. This 'slowing down' is both the product and the portent of a 'broadening out', a pluralism of practical and theoretical discourses.[7] Critical theory faces the challenge of testing its claims to generality, if not universality, of application against instances of historical and cultural specificity. There is a clear and pressing mandate, articulated most insistently and constructively to date by Western European and North American feminists, to isolate and articulate modes and effects of differentiation in the production and reception of meaning through cinema. To date, independent and avant-garde practices have provided the instances of otherness against which existing theories and methodologies are to be tested. In both these cases, the degree of otherness is relativised by the fact of co-existing in the same sphere as the dominant practices that both are seeking to contest or displace. Third World film practices provide another locus of cultural and historical specificity, a 'new frontier' which, while extraordinarily promising in its extension, scope and variety, is also potentially intimidating in its resistance to assimilation.

Teshome Gabriel's *Third Cinema in the Third World*[8] is the first book to undertake a comprehensive analysis of Third World cinema as a tricontinental phenomenon. The study's most obvious virtue is also its principal weakness. In order to consider Third World cinema as a unified historical and political phenomenon, Gabriel feels compelled to posit the Third World over the past thirty years as the the site of a unitary, autonomous, ideologically transparent cultural practice. The distortions required to perpetuate this 'mythical' vision of an internally consistent cultural practice across oceans and decades and vastly disparate cultural heritages and social formations are multiple, beginning with the very term 'Third Cinema', an appellation widely questioned by many Third World filmmakers and flatly rejected by others, whose problematic genesis and history Gabriel declines to discuss.

The term 'Third Cinema' was in fact coined by Argentine documentarists Fernando Solanas and Octavio Getino to designate a kind of filmmaking which opposes both dominant-industrial ('first') and independent-auteurist ('second') cinema. Since their essay did not appear until 1969 and did not receive wide circulation until the early 1970s, 'Third Cinema' could not and did not designate the emerging film movements of the Third World from their inception. The term has an historical link with General Juan Perón's 'third option' for Argentine politics, a form of non-aligned developmentalism.[9] (Solanas and Getino were closely associated with Perón, both during his exile and after his return to Argentina.) The political connection to Peronism moved a large number of Latin American filmmakers to reject the term 'Third Cinema' in favour of other designations. The term has not enjoyed broad currency in other regions of the Third World, though some Western critics have adopted it.[10]

Throughout his 97-page text, Gabriel seems to be groping for a conclusive definition of 'Third Cinema'. In some instances, he cultivates specificity at the expense of broad applicability: for example, Third Cinema is 'moved by a concern for the fate of Third World man and woman threatened by colonial and neo-colonial wars' (p. 1). In others, he offers generality at its most diluted: as in, 'Inherent in this cinema . . . are the social life, ideologies and conflicts of the times' (p. 1), and Third Cinema 'corresponds to the cultural tasks and political needs of the society it represents' (p. 2). Gabriel claims that Third Cinema is developing a 'new language' (p. 2). The critical demonstration of the particular codes and component structures of this language would provide a more effective point of entry into the fundamental problem of definition. Gabriel's inability to articulate these compels him to fall back on attempted 'definitions' which are inductive and, as such, inevitably partial and frequently conflicting.

Third Cinema, for Gabriel,

> represents a significant alteration in the parameters of film form and in the
> critical and theoretical categories necessary for an explanation of its significance
> and effect. The aesthetics and ideology of Third Cinema pose a radical and
> singular challenge to existing or traditional categories of film scholarship, even
> to the universalistic claims of contemporary film semiotics (p. 5).

But rather than indicate how theoretical and critical categories bear redefinition in
light of Third World cinematic practice, Gabriel tends instead to suggest the
superfluousness of critical theory by positing the ideological transparency of
the Third World film (to the properly sensitised viewer):

> Cine-structuralism strives to find immanent meaning in works whose deeper
> meaning is concealed. The films under discussion in this study do not try to
> hide their true meaning. The burden of search, therefore, will be across a
> different terrain. (p. 5).

Yet, he acknowledges, 'more than an aesthetic of transparent reflection is needed.
. . . Represented reality is not simply a direct translation of empirical relations but
its filtering reconstruction' (p. 6). Repeatedly, he explicitly calls for 'a method
whereby the films can be viewed in an evolving aesthetic and social context', and
maintains that 'any theory and criticism within the context of Third Cinema cannot
be separated from the practical *uses* of film' (p. 6). In practice, however, Gabriel
ends up subsuming aesthetics, hermeneutics and the psychodynamics of textual
reception under the rubric of ideology, which he construes as specific, autonomous,
non-deceptive and non-illusory, exerting a material force in that it is governed by
its own system of representation (pp. 8–12). Gabriel's idea of ideological analysis
hinges on the assumption of equivalence rather than disparity, contradiction, or
incompleteness. Since only bourgeois or colonised filmmaking endeavours to
conceal the processes by which it produces meaning, the role of the interpreter of
Third World film is simply 'to place Third Cinema in its proper socio-aesthetic
context and to appraise its achievements in terms of its own cultural/ideological
outlook' (p. 2).

Conjunctural specificity is indeed one of the defining characteristics of oppositional art. Because of their hegemonic status, dominant cultural products (and the
institutions through which they circulate) tend to take the universality of their appeal
for granted. Oppositional art must recognise itself as a product of particular
historical/political/cultural circumstances. Yet no matter how particularised, no
matter how tendentious, no work of art – film, novel or other cultural product –
can sustain the kind of privileged claim to transparency and unity of meaning which
Gabriel attempts to make for Third World cinema (even in the eyes of those viewers

who are properly versed in Third World culture). Meaning in any communicative medium is never direct and complete; it is instead oblique, selective, mediated. The fact that a work of art may overtly acknowledge an ideological dimension does not exempt it from examination in search of inadvertent or unacknowledged ideological operations. Invisible, unconscious, uncontrollable factors intervene both at the point of production and at the point of reception.

Gabriel's assumption of such ideological unity and transparency is challenged by concrete examples of ideological suppressions and contradictions in countless Third World film texts. The four-part Bolivian feature *Chuquiago* (Antonio Eguino, 1977) attempts to examine class differences while suppressing the fact of history; but the absence of an historical perspective distorts the class analysis.[11] The Cuban feature *Retrato de Teresa/Portrait of Teresa* (Pastor Vega, 1979) undercuts the presentation of the heroine in ways which call into question the film's explicit claims to support women's equality.[12] Feminists have criticized *Lucía* (Humberto Solas, Cuba, 1968) for using women as historical symbols rather than genuine agents of history,[13] but the deep patriarchal bias of a subsequent Cuban film, Sara Gómez's *De cierta manera/One Way or Another* (1974/1977), has escaped the attention of a number of feminist critics whose enthusiastic assessments have established this particular film as a kind of paradigm of feminist signifying practice in a Third World context.[14] Films like *La hora de los hornos/The Hour of the Furnaces* (Fernando Solanas, 1968) and *Los traidores/The Traitors* (Raymundo Gleyser, 1972), both made in Argentina prior to Juan Perón's return to power, elicit a significantly different reading from the historical vantage point of the subsequent decade.[15]

Gabriel refers to all these films as examples of the unity of Third World texts. His commitment to presenting Third Cinema as a unified and unitary signifying practice thus leads him to ignore or suppress contradictions within the texts themselves and within and between the film movements which produce these texts. It also leads him to posit a kind of barrier of cultural impermeability between dominant and dependent cultures which does not exist. This container theory of culture conceives of a finite substance which can be spent and therefore requires that the remainder be 'conserved': 'Since the Third World should not continue to dissipate its culture and national identity, Third Cinema attempts to check this and conserve what is left' (p. xi). This notion leads Gabriel to posit pristine cultural integrity and autonomy as one of the criteria for distinguishing the genuine article: 'Films made in the Third World that show dependency on an external or alien culture cannot . . . be characterized as Third Cinema' (p. 2). Yet it can be persuasively argued that the very adoption of the film medium in a Third World context inevitably imports and/or perpetuates relations of technological dependency and risks introducing and/or perpetuating mechanisms of cultural dependency as well. The desire to return to a state of precolonial innocence and integrity, to strip off alien layers until the pure essence of national culture reveals itself, is a pervasive but illusory goal of proponents of 'cultural decolonisation' throughout the underdeveloped world. In a paper which meditates on the cultural impact of the Nicaraguan revolution, Uruguayan writer Eduardo Galeano posits an alternative to this view as it has been espoused in one particular Third World context:

> National culture is defined by its content, not by the origin of its elements. Alive, it changes incessantly, it challenges itself, it contradicts itself, and it receives external influences that at times increase it, and that are wont to operate simultaneously as a threat and a stimulus. It would be a delusion and an act of reactionary stupidity to propose the rejection of European and North American cultural contributions already incorporated into our heritage and into the universal heritage, arbitrarily reducing those vast and complex cultures to the machinery of imperialist alienation implicit in them. Anti-imperialism also is prey to infantile disorders. The lack of what is denied to us need not imply the refusal of what nurtures us. Latin America need not renounce the creative fruits of cultures which have flowered in great measure thanks to a material splendor not unconnected to the pitiless exploitation of our people and our lands.[16]

The very proliferation of names which have been used to designate Third World filmmaking – new cinema, alternative cinema, revolutionary cinema, Imperfect Cinema, anti-imperialist cinema, among others – testifies to a certain elusive indefiniteness in the object itself. Definitions of the nature of this activity, as Gabriel's *Third Cinema in the Third World* indicates, are no less multiple and indeterminate and no less problematic. I have adopted the terms marginal and oppositional because they are capable of designating the vast proportion of Third World film practice without being geographically confined to that area. Marginal and oppositional forms can and do exist in the developed world as well, and this fact, far from constituting a limitation, has the virtue of enhancing the viability of the terminology. Third World cinema has not been satisfactorily named or defined until now because those who have made the attempt have regarded it as a geographically and ideologically circumscribed activity. It must be recognised that the film products and practices of the underdeveloped world cannot be understood in isolation from those of the developed world. One of the major strengths of Third World film criticism (and Third World cultural criticism in general) has been its insistence upon the impossibility of severing any specific cultural product from its sociohistorical, geocultural context. One of the major weaknesses of Third World criticism has been its inability to recognise the impossibility of severing the oppositional (and collaborationist) cultural practices and ideologies of the dependent world from the dominant (and contestational) cultural practices and ideologies of the developed world.

Dominant and oppositional, marginal and mainstream cultures are not independent but interdependent phenomena. Antithetical to one another, that very adversarial quality locks them together in the hostile embrace of embattled wrestlers. Mainstream cultural manifestations appropriate marginal creativity without acknowledging (and often actively concealing) the source. Oppositional cultural practice defines itself as a denial of, and an alternative to, dominant practice, a stance which requires constant monitoring of its adversary. Dominant or mainstream cultures thus establish the terms of oppositional or marginal cultures to a significant degree. In this sense, oppositional culture is necessarily reactive. Culture can be marginal without being oppositional, but cannot be mainstream without being in some degree dominant. The terminology is relational, requiring the articulation of both poles of the antithesis. It also allows for varying degrees of dominance and oppositionality. Most importantly, the terms presuppose a global focus, a 'world systems' approach.

To point to the Third World as the site of a unitary and autonomous oppositional cinematic practice is to promote a deception for the reasons I have outlined above, and for another reason as well. In a very fundamental sense, 'Third World' is a signifier without a signified, a term without a referent. The debate over which countries are and are not to be included spans the life of the term itself. Even those who question its validity continue to use it for want of a more satisfactory term to designate those portions of the world characterised by economic underdevelopment which is the lingering heritage of colonial subjugation and exploitation. Given the patent arbitrariness and contradictions of the attempt to construe some three-quarters of the surface of the globe as a unified geopolitical entity, there is no reason to expect the cultural production of this heterogeneous amalgam of nations to be less blessed or cursed by difference and exception.

Transitional and intraconflictural cultural formations are just as typical of Third World societies as transitional social formations. The Third World must be analytically approached 'as a social formation which is dominated by an articulation of two modes of production – a capitalist and a non-capitalist mode – in which the former is, or is becoming increasingly, dominant over the other'.[17] The resulting 'restricted and uneven' forms of development characteristic of Third World political economies presuppose two or more modes of production whose very interdependence is a function of their eventual incompatibility. Until this interdependence of 'incompatible' elements is recognised as inherent to both the cultural products of the dependent sector and the process of their production, with full acknowledgement of the creative, as well as the restrictive, consequences of this dynamic tension, we cannot hope to understand the cultural products and practices of the Third World.

Any viable accounting of Third World film practices must therefore posit a relationship to dominant cinema which is continuous and contingent even in its will to discontinuity and differentiation. This interrelationship is present on several levels which range across language, technology and the entire cinematic apparatus.

Attempts at transforming the legacies of cultural domination are not confinable to the categories of form or content or even to the articulation of the interactive relationship between the two. A third term is essential: context, the social/ historical/cultural/political/economic milieux out of which any particular film is generated and into which it is received. More than their determination to give expression to new forms and new contents, the most significant aspect of oppositional film movements in the Third World has been their fundamental commitment to transforming existing modes of film production, diffusion and reception. These transformative strategies range from the apparently atavistic recourse to artisanal modes, to the anticipation of more socialised industrial ones. Where the dominant cinema prioritised exchange value, oppositional filmmakers have emphasised use values. Where dominant procedures turned filmmakers into virtual piece workers, oppositional procedures sought a reintegration of creative personnel at all levels of the process. Where dominant practices required large amounts of capital and infrastructure, oppositional filmmakers sought to strip the process down to its barest essentials – a camera in hand and an idea in mind, in Glauber Rocha's oft-quoted phrase. Where the structures and conventions of traditional cinema required an anonymous, passive and socially fragmented audience who did their viewing in the impersonal and ritualised space of the conventional movie theatre, oppositional filmmakers sought physical spaces and organisational formats which emphasised communality in order to encourage audience participation and feedback. The common thread linking all these efforts is the will to 'de-alienate' alienated and alienating social relations, based on a dual recognition: that social change has its deepest roots in self-realisation, and that the creative process provides a quasi-utopian space in which more ideal social relations may develop.

Oppositional filmmaking in the Third World is therefore best described not as a 'new language' but as a new practice or set of practices in constant evolution in response to the evolution of dominant practices. Whether or not they acknowledge the inevitable symbiosis produced by these relations of (inter)dependency, Third World filmmakers have only three basic textual strategies open to them. These strategies constitute a dynamic and flexible typology of Third World film.

On the formal level, in the present as in the past, dominant cinematic practices promote the phenomenon of cinema-as-spectacle. Third World filmmakers can mimic that spectacle, attempt to substitute a non-spectacular cinematics in its place, or aggressively subvert the cinema-as-spectacle phenomenon. In the first case, they can only make a claim to oppositional status based upon their attempt to infuse indigenous content into borrowed forms, adapting the cinema-spectacle to their own national/ideological ends. (*The Traitors*, a political thriller made clandestinely in Argentina in 1972, is a notable example of this mimetic strategy, as is *Bye Bye Brazil* (Carlos Diegues, 1980), a road movie *à la brasileira*.) Alternatively, Third World filmmakers can attempt to supplant the spectacle with the non- (or pre-) spectacular by substituting some indigenous/autonomous discourse whose 'otherness' is almost inevitably one of degree rather than kind. (The Brazilian feature *Como era gustoso o meu francês/How Tasty Was My Little Frenchman* (Nelson Pereira dos

Santos, 1971), an 'anthropological reconstruction' which scrupulously and humorously turns the normative assumptions of Western civilisation on their heads, is an intriguing example of this substitution strategy. Ousmane Sembene's *Emitai* (Senegal, 1971), discussed in detail by Gabriel (pp. 25–7), would be another.) After *Yawar Mallku/Blood of the Condor* (1969), criticised by its own director as being compromised by its conventional narrative structures and mimetic language, Bolivian Jorge Sanjinés has dedicated himself to filming historical reconstructions of actual events in collaboration with peasants and miners in various Andean countries, a practice which fits within this second category. Finally, Third World filmmakers can adopt an anti-spectacular strategy based on a process of re-spectacularisation/de-spectacularisation. This third strategy, a composite of all three possibilities, involves the critical adaptation of forms of dominant cinematic discourse in a three-part process of mimesis, negation or subversion, and substitution. (Cuban filmmakers have been particularly drawn to this third strategy, making a number of 'deconstructive' films which critique the very genre they adopt. *One Way or Another* subverts the Hollywood romance; *El otro Francisco/The Other Francisco* (Sergio Giral, Cuba, 1975) critiques the historical melodrama; *Girón/Bay of Pigs* (Manuel Herrera, Cuba, 1973) simultaneously imitates and subverts the blood-and-guts war movie.)

Though inclusive of all oppositional Third World film practice, it should be noted that the three strategies outlined above are only relatively, rather than absolutely, discrete. Does the Cuban trilogy *Lucía*, for example, belong in the first category or in the third, or does it upon closer examination also participate in the second strategy? It could be argued that each of its three segments bears a particular affinity to one of the three categories: Part II, in its patent nostalgia for classical Hollywood-style romance, corresponds to the mimetic strategy; Part III, with its voice-over narration in sung folk verse, represents a quest for substitute indigenous forms; while the operatic exaggeration of Part I can be seen as subtly deconstructive in its parodic impulse. Alternatively, it can be argued that the three-part assemblage, because of the formal diversity of its component parts, is implicitly deconstructive in its revelation of the historicity and artificiality of cinematic forms. Like *Lucía*, *Chuquiago* is made up of multiple 'discrete' segments. Yet because the formal distinctions between the four sections are not systematically marked, the Bolivian film inhabits the first, mimetic, category with much more docility.

Moving from the level of discrete practice (texts) to the level of cinema as a sociopolitical practice (regional or national cinema movements), it is important to note that rather than becoming more cohesive over the past two decades, Third World film practice has become more 'diffuse', demonstrating varying degrees of marginality and oppositionality. In many Third World countries, the state, pursuing a policy of 'import substitution' in the cultural sphere, has entered into film production, distribution and sometimes exhibition. Brazilian and Indian national film production now qualitatively rivals Hollywood's output. Production in the Asian country is regionally decentralised, while the largest of the Latin American film producers has pursued a more centralising strategy. In both countries, a crop of new independents challenges 'dominant' filmmakers like Satyajit Ray and the exponents of Cinema Novo, whose own practice represented the apex of oppositionality only two decades ago. Independents who choose for whatever reason to remain outside the system of state support assume a double marginality and a double oppositionality: *vis-à-vis* the developed sector outside their country, and *vis-à-vis* the state sector within it. Technological advances and the rise of the electronic media have also contributed to a growing diversity among Third World producers of moving images who increasingly have the option of working in Super-8 or video or a combination of filmic media unknown a decade ago. A counter-tendency, the quest for the Third World superproduction, has figured prominently in the recent history of Latin American filmmaking.[18]

A brief look at a specific national film movement should illustrate how modes of cinematic production and consumption in the Third World continue, even in the socialist sector, to be shaped by both industrial and anti-industrial, commercial and anticommercial, traditional and innovative tendencies; displaying – even within a single institution in a single country varying degrees of oppositionality and marginality. On the level of content, Cuban films continue to display a consistently and aggressively oppositional stance *vis-à-vis* western capitalist ideologies, but on a formal level the past decade has seen a return to the transparency of traditional, 'classic' film style and the decline of the deconstructive approach which characterised many notable films from the 1960s through to the mid 1970s. On a contextual level, with reference to the organisation and relations of production, ICAIC, the Cuban Film Institute, has been reorganised along more 'rational' and 'productive' lines with heightened attention to profitability. (Salary scale among directors is now differentiated according to productivity; they can be financially penalised for exceeding their estimated production schedules, or rewarded for completing a film in less than the time allotted. The distribution sector now purchases films outright from the production sector, and the finances of the two units have been formally separated. Economic constraints influence decisions about which proposals will be realised to an unprecedented degree.) Exhibition, on the other hand, has been increasingly decentralised in recent years, as the policies and operation of most cinemas around the island have been ceded to local control. Although ICAIC allows a high degree of diversity in the form and content of the films it produces, Cuba has done relatively little to promote filmmaking activity outside the ranks of the Institute, thus passively discouraging 'infra-oppositional' impulses which might derive from amateur independent cinema and/or video activity. Finally, a good deal of effort has been directed towards diversifying modes of reception and critically empowering viewers through prime-time television programmes and other events which demystify cinematic language and technique, while the level of film criticism in the Cuban print media remains deplorably low. Such conflicting tendencies must be analysed within the dynamics of both the domestic and the international political process, since even the most 'independent' Third World countries must constantly contend with constraints generated by external actions and interests over which they have little, if any, control.[19]

For Teshome Gabriel, the exploration of the psychodynamics of signification in Third World films is just as unnecessary as ideological interrogation, for Third Cinema 'does not function on a psychological or mythic level but rather takes up an explicit position with respect to an ideological or social topic' (p. 7). Yet a number of leading critics of socially committed art, from Georg Lukács to Annette Kuhn, have posited the social-historical component of character *in addition to* rather than *in place* of the psychological.[20] To question the applicability of western mythic paradigms in Third World cultural contexts is justifiable; to deny a mythic dimension in Third World cultural products is incomprehensible. What is needed is not the (continued) exclusion of psychoanalytical considerations from the critical discourse regarding Third World film, but the expansion or modification of those considerations to accommodate a less westernised, individually-based, notion of being-in-the-world.

In the conclusion to *Pictures of Reality*, Terry Lovell makes the following observations *à propos* a Brechtian model of politicised art:

> Despite his insistence on the importance of art as entertainment, [Brecht] was a rationalist. Political action . . . was to be mediated by thought, not feeling. . . . Similarly, progressive or revolutionary texts are essentially texts which make us think rather than texts which indulge us in pleasures. The rhetoric of making the . . . audience/reader into a producer of meanings . . . is a rhetoric based upon one kind of work, the intellectual labour of thinking. Resistance to this particular strand of puritanism is not to be conflated with anti-intellectualism. It is simply to deny that pleasure is or ought to be always at the service of knowledge, and that politics is only served by pleasure through the mediation of knowledge.
>
> This leaves an area in which little work has been done, which touches upon questions of pleasure of a kind which neither the psychoanalytic nor the Brechtian approach touch: social pleasures. The pleasures of a test may be grounded in pleasures of an essentially public and social kind. For instance pleasures of common experiences identified and celebrated in art, and through this celebration, given recognition and validation; pleasures of solidarity to which this sharing may give rise; pleasure in shared and socially defined aspirations and hopes; in a sense of identity and community. Like the desires of the unconscious, they are not in themselves either progressive or reactionary; but a political aesthetics . . . ignores this dimension at its peril.[21]

Current research into the psychology of infant perception and cognition emphasises the profoundly social, interactive nature of human beings from the first hours and days of life. Capacities for bonding and initiating communication and exchange with both adults and peers are increasingly recognised as predating language acquisition. Psychoanalysis has emphasised the process of individuation, the formation of an isolated and isolating subjectivity. Critical theory based on a psychoanalytical model which postulates the pivotal role of language acquisition has attempted to expose the belief in the autonomy of the individual ego as the deception through which ideology enlists our complicity.[22] But what of the hypothesis that in certain non-western societies, however similar or distinct the process of subject differentiation in infancy, there is a concomitant process of socialisation which fosters the social, psychological and emotional integration of the individual into the group? The result of such a process would be a more integrative interactional concept of being-in-the-world and a consequent absence or diminution of the extreme forms of individualisation which are assumed in the West to be one of the essences of human nature.

Bolivian director Jorge Sanjinés tells the story behind his group's nearly failed attempt to shoot *Blood of the Condor* in a remote Andean village as a lesson in the inapplicability of western assumptions about social hierarchies and the relationship of the individual to the group:

> Finally we realized where we had gone wrong. We had judged the community by the same standards with which one analyzes people and groups within bourgeois society. We had thought that by mobilizing one man who was powerful and influential we could mobilize the rest of the group, whom we assumed to be vertically dependent on their leader. We had not understood . . . that the Indians gave priority to collective over individual interests. We had failed to grasp that for them, as for their ancestors, what was not good for all of them could not be good for a single one.[23]

Sanjinés also remarks upon the fact that, in contrast to a certain western inclination to bask alone in the limelight, he could not persuade any Indian to act as cinematic spokesperson without sharing the frame with a number of his peers. Ousmane Sembene's films based on African tribal tradition – *Emitai* and *Ceddo* (1977) – similarly portray collectivised rather than individual action as the customary social mode. Such examples suggest another concept of being-in-the-world which has far-reaching implications for notions of creativity, meaning production, and the relationship between culture and society. Such a social concept of being or unity allows for and explains precisely the kind of 'social pleasures' emphasised by Terry Lovell – those pleasures which derive from and generate a sense of ethnic, community, class, national, or gender-based rather than purely individual identity, as well as a sense of common goals and progress towards them. In such circumstances, cinema assumes a kind of auto-ethnographic impulse: it becomes a tool in the discovery and expression of previously unrepresented or underrepresented aspects of the 'self' as a social and cultural being.

Gabriel's dismissal of cine-semiotics, a terminological umbrella which arguably shelters the greater portion of what is currently regarded as mainstream critical theory, represents a scepticism common to a number of Third World film critics, but no longer to all. 1982, the year Gabriel's *Third Cinema in the Third World* was published, also saw the completion of another doctoral dissertation by a Third World critic on a Third World film topic. The contrast in approaches is striking. Brazilian Ismail Xavier's *Allegories of Underdevelopment*[24] is much narrower in its focus, concentrating on 'the trajectory of the Brazilian independent film in the 1960s' (p. 4), but it is the richly syncretic nature of the work which I want to emphasise here. Xavier performs a series of textual analyses which coalesce into a kind of national intellectual, cultural and political metahistory capable of illuminating not only the period under study but subsequent developments as well.

Xavier's study differentiates itself from cinematic historiography as customarily practised in Brazil. Where his predecessors have emphasised plot structures or the thematics of specific directors, Xavier places the concept of mediation at the core of his analysis, and the articulation of cinematic specificity at the centre of his method: 'Cinematic storytelling is a multilevelled process and the analysis of *mediation* in films entails a detailed account of the combination of such specifically cinematic procedures as camera work, editing strategies, off-screen narration, dialogue, mise-en-scene, image/sound relationship' (p. 2). His theoretical framework consequently 'draw[s] upon the . . . basic descriptive categories of film theory and criticism: montage theory as founded in Eisenstein's work, the characterization of classic *découpage* (Bazin, Burch), work on modern narrative cinema (Christian Metz, P. P. Pasolini) and the theory of identification concerning the cinematic "apparatus" inflected contemporary psychoanalytic research' (p. 2). From the Anglo-European literary critical tradition, Xavier adopts the ancient hermeneutical figure of allegory as the principal focus of his study, borrowing from work by Angus Fletcher, Erich Auerbach, Jean Pepin, Walter Benjamin and Paul de Man. According to his interpretation, the metaphors of hunger and garbage with which Brazilian filmmakers of different generations have chosen to describe their cinematic project involve a recognition of film's direct involvement with advanced technology and a simultaneous act of resistance to this fact through the creation 'of a cinema that turns scarcity itself into a signifier' (p. 17). His synthesis of textual and historical approaches transcends the potential contributions of each approach in isolation, charting a new direction within Brazilian film studies and Third World film study in general.

Examples of other kinds of 'rapproachment' between the marginal and the mainstream have recently appeared in print. *Screen* has published three of these: Robert Stam's and Louise Spence's outline of a methodology for approaching the representation of colonialism and racism in the cinema; Homi K. Bhabha's theorisation of the ambivalent and contradictory stereotype as the major representational strategy in colonial discourse and my own interpretation of a particular Third World film text as a working out in practice of the most problematic areas of contemporary critical theory.[25] Robert Kolker's *The Altering Eye: Contemporary International Cinema*[26] is the first major contemporary history to give Third World films more than token attention. Kolker focuses on films 'made in a spirit of resistance, rebellion, and refusal', and more specifically on 'films made in Europe and Latin America . . . in reaction to American cinema, often to America itself, yet dependent upon . . . the conventions and attitudes of American films and culture . . .' (Preface). He argues that 'in fact no direct split between filmmaking in America and elsewhere exists. There is rather an interplay in which the dominant style (or styles) of American movies are always present to be denied, expanded upon, embraced, and rejected, only to be embraced again' (p. 5). Zuzana Pick's work on Chilean cinema in exile calls attention to a different zone of interplay between margin and mainstream. She argues that for many Chilean filmmakers, the fact of exile in countries throughout Europe and North America 'has provided the necessary distance to question some of the ideological elements that determine their political and cinematic perception of reality' because they have had to confront the 'personal paradox' of immersion in societies and cultures of the developed world which have historically colonised their own. The inevitable result is a questioning of the rhetorical and representational strategies characteristic of oppositional filmmaking in Latin America and a closer, though continually questioning, linkage to the metropolitan avant garde.[27] Roy Armes's study of filmmaking in the Third World[28] effectively situates African, Asian and Latin American cinema within the requisite context of an international political and cultural economy of film production.

What 'First World' critical theory brings to Third World film practices is, above all, the revelation of mediation as essential to any act of communication. The issue is not the elimination of mediators and intermediaries, as García Espinosa proposed, but rather the selfconscious assumption of the mediating role of the critic as one (meta-mediation) among many. Although the specific practical function of the critic is certainly open to ideological interrogation, particularly in the 'art marketplace' of the West,[29] the general role of criticism needs to be understood as (among other things) a more informed, specialised, public act of reception. Oppositional film-makers throughout the Third World have asserted, like Chilean director Miguel Littín, that 'There is no such thing as a film that is revolutionary in itself; it only becomes such through the contact that it establishes with its public and principally through its influence as a mobilizing agent for revolutionary action'.[30] This conception of the film as activated through viewer response is fundamentally inconsistent with a cultural politics which denies the links between reception and critical analysis. When should reception – the simultaneous viewing and interpreting of a film, the interaction of artifact and receiver which produces meaning – *not* be critical in the most fundamental sense? As in Paolo Freire's concept of education for critical consciousness, criticism presupposes the active enlistment of the subject as social agent.

Critical theory from the developed sector continues to develop methodologies and conceptual vocabularies which recognise reciprocal interaction (dialectics), acknowledge oppositionality as process rather than stasis, and purport to find ways of identifying and articulating gaps, discontinuities, fissures, fragmentations, opacity, ambivalence and other contradictory practices inevitably inscribed in acts of communication. Explicit methodological approaches and theoretical frameworks are simply means of making the mechanisms of reception manifest. Both are evolving rather than immutable constructs. The degree to which poststructuralist thought, for example, has incorporated the insights and concerns of feminist thinkers testifies to this evolutionary potential. Current critical emphasis on the mechanisms of gender differentiation in the cinema and the concomitant privileging of forms of male subjectivity demonstrate both the openness to, and the productivity of, more politicised approaches. A complementary emphasis on the effects of racial, ethnic and class differentiation, and on the dominant cinema's denial of history and the social tensions which fuel it, must also be made. The most logical source of this transformative feedback are the critics and historians whose theoretical and practical knowledge of Third World cultural expression provides the grounding for an informed assessment of the limitations and blind spots of critical–theoretical practices developed in the metropolis and exercised almost exclusively upon the products of metropolitan culture. Without cognisance of mainstream critical theory, critics of Third World film are inadequate to this task, and without modification in light of Third World realities and practices, western critical theory is also insufficient.

What, then, can Third World film practice bring to First World critical theory aside from simply a more 'otherly' sphere of otherness, and a mandate to recognise and articulate the modes of representation of that otherness in both colonial and anti-colonising discourse? The introduction of instances of greater cultural and historical specificity asserts the need for a broader contextualisation which would include a more effective sociology and political economy of cultural production, applicable – and essential – to the dominant as well as the dependent sector.

Third World cultures offer 'living museums' where four stages of world culture (collective art and ritual, the unique 'masterpiece', mass culture in an age of mechanical reproduction, and mass culture in an era of electronic dissemination) exist simultaneously and often remarkably discretely. This fragile cultural heterogeneity points up multiple categories of cultural-historical specificity: intracultural (subcultural variations of race, class, gender, ethnicity, and so on, within a given national culture), crosscultural (between contemporary cultures), and transhistorical (within and between cultures across historical markers).

Third World film practice emphasises and requires *practical theory*, functional vocabulary and skills which, in contrast to a restricted discourse of initiates, are transferable across lines of social stratification. The corollary emphasis on concrete uses over abstract essences demands an ability to recognise and account for transformative practices in the spheres of production, diffusion, reception. The study of the production of meaning cannot be limited to the film text, but must theorise that text as process as well as product. Third World cultural practices require a model which recognises a world outside individual subjectivity, a world in need of improvement, and affirms the social possibility of transforming it. In challenging cultural critics to recognise and articulate pleasure and desire as social rather than as exclusively individual experiences, oppositional cultural practices from the Third World bear the promise of unifying the presently polarised view of culture as either a 'privatized realm of personal enrichment' or a 'socializing realm of ideological significance'.[31] A view of culture in which the realm of ideological significance is not incompatible with the realm of personal enrichment (because personal enrichment is also viewed as a social phenomenon) would free western critics from the onerous role of 'diagnostician of pathologies', reaffirming instead their function as guide and celebrant. For these reasons, the selective appropriation and transformation of 'appropriate critical technologies' is a strategy capable of enhancing the practice and the theory of both marginal and mainstream, metropolitan and peripheral, cultures and societies.

Notes

1 The majority of my examples derive from Latin America, the site of the most sustained and concerted oppositional cinematic practice in the Third World and the principal area of my own expertise.

2 In Julianne Burton, *Cinema and Social Change in Latin America: Conversations with Filmmakers* (Austin, TX: University of Texas Press, 1986).

3 All four essays are included in Michael Chanan (ed.), *Twenty-five Years of the New Latin American Cinema* (London: BFI and Channel Four, 1983). Authors and dates are, in order: Glauber Rocha, 1965; Fernando Solanas and Octavio Getino, 1969; Julio García Espinosa, 1970; Jorge Sanjinés, 1976.

4 In ibid, p. 32.

5 Written by Miguel Littín. The English version appears in Michael Chanan (ed.), *Chilean Cinema* (London: BFI, 1976), pp. 83–4.

6 This need is a function of commercial and/or crosscultural ambitions. Super-8 and video makers who direct themselves to restricted, homogeneous audiences and harbour no ambitions outside this intended radius are arguably exempt.

7 See Terry Eagleton, *Literary Theory: An Introduction* (Minneapolis, MN: University of Minnesota Press, 1983), pp. 201–2; and Bill Nichols (ed.), *Movies and Methods*, vol. 2 (Berkeley, CA: University of California Press, 1985), Introduction.

8 Teshome Gabriel, *Third Cinema in the Third World: The Aesthetics of Liberation* (Ann Arbor, MI: UMI Research, 1982).

9 For more on this 'non-aligned developmentalism', see Juan Corradi, cited in Ronald Chilcote and Joel Edelstein (eds), *Latin America: The Struggle with Dependency and Beyond* (Cambridge, MA: Schenkman, 1974), p. 375.

10 See Zuzana Pick (ed.), *Latin American Filmmakers and the Third Cinema* (Ottawa: Carleton University 1978); and Guy Hennebelle, 'L'influence du "Troisième Cinéma" dans le monde . . .', *Revue Tiers Monde*, vol. 20 no. 79 (1979), pp. 615–45.

11 See my review in *Cineaste*, vol. 9, no. 3 (1979), pp. 50–3.

12 See my essay, 'Seeing, being, being seen: *Portrait of Teresa or* the contradictions of sexual politics in contemporary Cuba', *Social Text*, no. 4 (1981), pp. 79–95.

13 See Anna Marie Taylor, '*Lucía*', *Film Quarterly*, vol. 28, no. 3 (1975), pp. 53–9.

14 This patriarchal substratum goes unnoticed in Julia Lesage, '*One Way or Another*: dialectical, revolutionary, feminist', *Jump/Cut*, no. 20 (1979), pp. 20–3; as well as in Annette Kuhn, *Women's Pictures: Feminism and Cinema* (London: Routledge and Kegan Paul, 1982), pp. 162–6; and E. Ann Kaplan, 'The woman director in the Third World: Sara Gomez' *One Way or Another*, *Women and Film: Both Sides of the Camera* (New York: Methuen, 1983), pp. 189–94.

15 See Robert Stam, '*The Hour of the Furnaces* and the two avant gardes', *Millenium Film Journal*, nos 7/8/9 (1980–1), pp. 151–64; and Mark Falcoff, 'Original sin and Argentine reality: Peronist history and myth in *The Traitors*', *Proceedings of the Pacific Coast Council on Latin American Studies*, vol. 6 (1977–9), pp. 217–30.

16 Eduardo Galeano, 'The revolution as revelation', trans. Walter I. Bradbury, *Socialist Review*, no. 65, (1982), p. 14.

17 John G. Taylor, *From Modernization to Modes of Production: A Critique of the Sociologies of Development and Underdevelopment* (London: Macmillan, 1979), pp. 101–3.

18 Most notably in the work of exiled Chilean director Miguel Littín; most disastrously in *Cecilia* (Humberto Solas, 1981), which greatly exceeded its budget and demoralised the Cuban Film Institute.

19 For a fuller discussion of the organisation and administrative changes affecting the Cuban Film Institute, see Julianne Burton, 'Film and revolution in Cuba: the first twenty-five years', in John M. Kirk and Sandor Halebsky (eds), *Cuba: Twenty-Five Years of Revolution, 1959–1984* (New York: Praeger, 1985).

20 See Kuhn, *Women's Pictures*, pp. 140–2.

21 Terry Lovell, *Pictures of Reality: Aesthetics, Politics and Pleasure* (London: BFI, 1980), pp. 94–5.

22 For useful explanations and applications of these intricate arguments, see Bill Nichols, *Ideology and the Image: Social Representation in the Cinema and Other Media* (Bloomington, IN: Indiana University Press, 1981) and Kuhn, *Women's Pictures*.

23 Jorge Sanjinés, 'Cine revolucionario: la experiencia boliviana', *Cine Cubano*, nos 76/77 (1972), pp. 9–12 (my translation).

24 Ismail Xavier, *Allegories of Underdevelopment: Aesthetics and Politics in Modern Brazilian Cinema* (Minneapolis, MN: University of Minnesota Press, 1997).

25 Robert Stam and Louise Spence, 'Colonialism, racism and representation: an introduction', *Screen*, vol. 24, no. 2 (1983), pp. 2–20; Homi K. Bhabha, 'The Other question – the stereotype and colonial discourse', *Screen*, vol. 24, no. 6 (1983), pp. 18–36; Julianne Burton, 'The politics of aesthetic distance: the presentation of representation in *São Bernardo*', *Screen* vol. 24, no. 2 (1983), pp. 20–53.

26 Oxford: Oxford University Press, 1983.

27 Zuzana M. Pick, 'Chilean cinema in exile (1973–1983)', *Framework*, no. 34 (1987), pp. 39–57.

28 Roy Armes, *Third World Film Making and the West* (Berkeley, CA: University of California Press, 1987).

29 For a provocative consideration of these questions in the realm of the fine arts, see Carol Duncan, 'Who rules the art world?', *Socialist Review*, no. 70 (1983), pp. 99–119.

30 Michael Chanan, *Chilean Cinema*, p. 84.

31 Bill Nichols (ed.), *Movies and Methods*, vol. 2, Introduction.

3   Colonialism and 'law and order' criticism

Teshome H. Gabriel

Among the Ewe people of Southern Ghana, the High God is an androgynous figure called Mawu-Lisa, 'Mawu' being the female principle and 'Lisa' the male. In translating the Bible into the Ewe language, the female component was severed from the androgynous name. The Ewe rejected this concept of a one-sided High God, and despite the most brutal acts of 'law and order' visited on them by the 'civilising mission', have to the present time remained predominantly animist.

The legacy of colonialism has not only defined the Third World as non-western but it has also made the West non-Third World. This has given the western person a worldview and a readiness to regard his or her activities as the 'mainstream'. In the USA, the 'Super Bowl' and the 'World Series' reinforce a worldview governed by an obsession for superlatives in all spheres of life; one can easily characterise this era as the age of hyperbole. What is culturally specific is viewed as a phenomenon engulfing the globe. Even when noble causes with good intentions and positive results are involved, with implications far greater than cultural specificity, global annexation is obvious. Such is the case, for instance, with the all-star fundraising hymn for hunger, 'We Are the World' where 'we are' functions as a determinant, thus turning into a borderland the very people that are being aided. The Third World continues to be viewed as 'dependent', 'peripheral' or 'marginal', not because the Third World is marginal per se, but because it is marginalised in, and by, colonial discourse.

In this era when even mosquitoes have adapted to DDT it is understandable that the intellectual heirs of colonial ideology have readjusted their rhetoric, too. Nowadays, First World intellectuals enthuse over their global focus, and this idea is not new. Ten years ago, Immanuel Wallerstein made it a mark of his 'World System theory'. For Wallerstein there is only one World capitalist system, whose principal categories are 'core' and 'periphery', where the 'core' is the determinant of relations of exchange. He quotes Karl Marx, trying to enlist him in his interpretation. But for Wallerstein, besides pre- and non-capitalism there is no post-capitalist formation. For him 'socialism' is subsumed under the general category of 'non-capitalisms'. Accordingly, no Third World country can become socialist.[1] Third World countries can move from one peripheral status to a semi-periphery within the capitalist mode; change can only be of degree rather than of kind.

In *Screen's* special issue, 'Other Cinemas, Other Criticisms', the lead article by Julianne Burton, 'Marginal cinemas and mainstream critical theory', proposes a most troubling example of critical theory along the lines of Wallerstein's core and periphery. There is a perfect fit here between Wallerstein's 'World System theory' and Burton's cinema-as-spectacle':

> Third World filmmakers can attempt to supplant the spectacle with a non- (or pre-) spectacular by substituting some indigenous/autonomous discourse whose 'otherness' is almost inevitably one of degree rather than kind.[2]

Just as 'socialism' is not only non-capitalism but 'Socialism', so also is Third World cinema not only non-spectacle but Third World cinema. The 'otherness' is not only one of degree but also of kind. 'Third Cinema' attempts to draw attention to this fact. To hold on to the modes of operation and discourse of dominant cinema is counter to Third Cinema practice. The discourse strategy of Third Cinema has a more political and ideological social focus. This Julianne Burton seems unable to understand – not all Third World film texts qualify as 'Third Cinema'. The territory is *not* the map. Third Cinema in the Third World is anti-imperialist, militant and confrontational cinema. It is neither pre- nor non- cinema–as–spectacle; it is, as Fernando Birri puts it, 'an active cinema for an active spectator' – it is 'a cinema of and for liberation'.[3]

In her essay, Burton argues that the 'claim to transparency and unity of meaning' of Third Cinema texts is not only unattainable but impossible. She denies this ideological transparency in Third Cinema practices not because they have any hidden or 'unconscious' agenda but precisely because, as she suggests, 'they are potentially intimidating in their resistance to assimilation.' Such arguments tend to obscure the proven resistance of the Third Cinema text.

The issue of transparency should be looked at within a specific cultural–historical context. What is not transparent for a western viewer is transparent enough in its own context. For instance, Third World ethnographic films tend to be viewed as political in the country of their origin, while they are viewed as exotica outside it. Similarly, an American fiction film seen overseas may be regarded as a documentary on American life. First-time visitors to the USA often have a strange nostalgic feeling about the New York skyline or the Statue of Liberty. They have never been there before but they have 'already seen it' in their past. Folks, it's the movies! Obviously, the West is more than the Third World's exotica. Similarly, the Third World is also 'already read' as a lack by the West.

A dialogue between the West and the Third World is always a welcome endeavour. But what blocks such efforts is the historical mishap they suffered and are locked into, namely colonialism and imperialism. This has made reciprocity and peaceful coexistence difficult to achieve. The Third World has always tried to incorporate the West in its cultures and developmental schemes. The fact that more Third World people speak European languages than westerners speak Third World languages is a case in point. But it is the conflictual onesidedness of the West that defeats and frustrates meaningful communication, because of its unceasing desire for colonial enclaves as well as cultural synchronisation with itself. The barrier to real dialogue is thus the terms of dialogue itself. Consequently, in its desire to globalise and homogenise world cinemas and cultures, critical theory is also implicated.

Burton's inability to understand the specific ideological predicaments of the Third World's cultural politics undermines the basis of her criticism of Third Cinema. If it is agreed that the Third World is characterised by underdevelopment and the 'lingering heritage' of colonial exploitation, cannot unequal economic exchange carry over into unequal symbolic exchange? For instance, Burton sets up proponents of 'cultural decolonisation' in the Third World as though their only desire is a return to 'precolonial innocence'. This, of course, denies them any awareness of their history. Burton uses a selective quotation from Eduardo Galeano to legitimate her assertion that 'cultural decolonisation' is 'a pervasive but illusory goal'. She would have been fairer to the spirit of Galeano's article had she also quoted the following, which speaks the opposite of what she claims:

> In general, it can truly be said that many education centers and almost all the massive communication media radiate translated messages, fabricated outside and designed to drain the Latin American memory and prevent it from recognizing its own reality and capacity: they induce it to consume and passively reproduce the symbols of the very power that humbles it.[4]

Likewise, Julio García Espinosa comments on a similar misunderstanding of his idea of an 'Imperfect Cinema': 'Many people thought it was about making bad films'. According to Espinosa, this does not set up an either/or situation in terms of good and bad films, but judges from a cultural–ideological perspective that encompasses the ideology of the work and the artistry of the maker.[5] As Glauber Rocha has intimated, 'technique is closer to ideology than to aesthetics'. A critic brought up in a tradition which extols artistry above all else would assume that 'an Imperfect Cinema' was about making bad films. And if the critic belonged to the so-called 'mainstream critical theory' group, he or she would try to support that assumption with selective quotations.

In her eagerness to explicate a 'critical theory' based on a vague form she calls 'psychodynamics', Burton misquotes and misrepresents *Third Cinema in the Third World*. Her appropriation and (mis)use of the original text is presented here:

> For Teshome Gabriel, the exploration of the psychodynamics of signification in Third World films is just as unnecessary as ideological interrogation, for Third

Cinema 'does not function on a psychological or mythic level but rather takes up an explicit position with respect to an ideological or social topic'. (p. 29)

Here I provide the original text as it appeared in *Third Cinema in the Third World*:

In Third Cinema point of view does not function on a psychological or mythic level per se but rather takes up an explicit position with respect to an ideological or social topic.[6]

Burton then goes on to say that leading critics of socially committed arts, 'posited the social-historical component of character *in addition to* rather than *in place of* the psychological' (p. 29) – the very point that, but for her deletions, I made.

This misquotation/misrepresentation is not merely the result of a basic difference between the two texts shown above. The root cause is ideological and lies in the incompatibility of stated approaches to the 'aesthetics of social pleasure'. As Terry Lovell points out in the paragraphs following those quoted by Burton, 'aesthetic sensibilities are class- and sex-linked, and the politics of aesthetic pleasure will depend on the particular ways in which that sensibility has been appropriated and developed along lines of sex and class.'[7] The question then is: *Whose aesthetics? Whose pleasure?* It is not transhistorical or transcultural. Rather, it is a question of who develops it, for whom, under what conditions and along what lines? Burton would rather the West define it for the Third World. Third Cinema insists that the people of the Third World do it for themselves.

More than 'the aesthetics of pleasure', therefore, the issue is one of activist aesthetics and the conditions for it. The question of social pleasure for the Third World filmmaker is not a theoretical question but a practical one; more than a condition of psychological alienation, it is a political issue of bread and butter.

To say, as Burton does, that 'oppositional cultural practices from the Third World bear the promise of unifying the presently polarised view of culture' by '*challenging* cultural critics to recognise and articulate pleasure and desire as social rather than as exclusively individual experiences' (p. 34, emphasis added) is to credit Third World film language and practice with what it does not do. Third Cinema, presents 'an other' film practice that cannot be adequately explicated by western critical theory of 'pleasure' and 'desire'.[8] This Third World filmmakers have said time and time again. As the Cuban director Jorge Fraga puts it, 'We are not in favor of firing merely for the pleasure of hearing the shot. We shoot in order to hit the target'.[9]

As the honorary president of the Centro de Capacitación Cinematográfica in Mexico City, I once went to visit the school and was introduced to several professors, including a young man in a suit and tie who blushed a good deal.

When I asked him what he taught, he replied, 'The Semiology of the Clonic Image.' I could have murdered him on the spot. By the way, when this kind of jargon (a typically Parisian phenomenon) works its way into the educational system, it wreaks absolute havoc in underdeveloped countries. It's the clearest sign, in my opinion, of cultural colonialism.[10]

It is indeed a sad commentary, particularly coming from such a prominent director as Luis Buñuel, but it is precisely when Third World intellectual activity is *solely* European-flavoured that it runs the risk of being obtrusive, obscure and irrelevant. This kind of semiotic intellectual of the Third World is of course more at home in a European atmosphere than in his or her own. Buñuel's scepticism is shared by Third World filmmakers, but it should be regarded as an opposition to 'ivory tower semiotics' and not as a dismissal of semiotics. As Marshall Blonsky tartly observed, 'the reason the discourse has never "taken" – never become, itself . . . – is that action would be threatened by it.'[11]

This issue brings out in force the reason why Third World filmmakers/scholars should not be forced always to think in a sign system that is not theirs. The question is whether the categories that inform western semiotics are fully relevant to the analysis of non-western sign systems. Western semiotics has presumed that its categories can travel across cultures and languages. But language is saturated with the values of its own culture. To think in a language other than one's own is to experience a peculiar form of alienation – a kind of self-exile. Besides, western semiotics has not developed a strategy to explain the specific mode of transformation required by the Third World context where semiotics should be an instrument of political action. This has been largely ignored and underdeveloped. It is now imperative to formulate Third Cinema semiotics in terms of its relation between Third World concepts and its own artistic mode and to develop forms of explanation that account for its specificity.

The position of the spectator in the western cinema is different from the position of the spectator in Third Cinema. The theorisation of the western spectator within the Althusserian framework views the subject as passive and mystified. This has been the cornerstone of the ideological critique of western cinema. Western cinema represents and replays these mystified social relations. Third Cinema by contrast maintains that the relation between the Third World audience in Third Cinema is one of *immediate* ideological lucidity. As the exiled Chilean filmmaker Miguel Littín states, 'We maintain that a cinema based upon our objectives necessarily implies a different kind of critical evaluation; and we affirm that the greatest critic of a revolutionary film is the people to whom it is directed, who have no need for mediators to defend and interpret for them.' Indeed, the politicised spectator of the Third World film who has an ideological and semiotic grip on the text does not need, as Burton suggests, 'a mediating agency – an advocate in the guise of a film critic . . . or other certified "expert"' (p. 19), because this spectator, as an agent of the historical process, sees in films the concrete realisation of his or her political and material circumstances.

The issue at stake here is ideological – it disclaims value-free semiotics. Littín's statement should therefore be read as a call for ideological mediation which is sensitive to the cultural and ideological needs of both the filmmaker and the audience. Third Cinema practices maintain that the Third World audience has an active and essentially constructive relation to the sign systems of Third World cinema. The spectator activates the sense of the text. When Julio García Espinosa, quoting Marx, intones 'in the future there will no longer be painters but rather men who, among other things, dedicate themselves to painting',[12] he is proposing the mission of Third Cinema – to make every spectator/reader ideologically astute.

Why is it that, structurally, semiotics underplays history and everyday existence? Because, as Blonsky observes:

> Semiotics has been a futile gaze at the world's seeming pleasures, its drunken stupidities; and it may all the while have been imaginary, the way in which we, semiotic intellectuals, have wanted to be loved and respected. No, a critic will answer me, semiotics can also be *unpolitical, unideological*. It can yield up a renewed joy every time we see the functioning of the world's semantic organization. Studying poetry, painting, narrative and so on, we learn that the world is an immense message, we enjoy all the intelligence of everything that is intelligible. To which we can respond: but *spying out the world's meanings, you have spied out its misery once more. Meaning is an instrument, a conduit of power.*[13]

Why is it that a cinestructuralist variant of the semiotic inquiry is a calculated affront to common sense? When meaning is readily accessible, it seeks answers elsewhere; and in the process the subject, the lives and struggles of human beings, gets lost in the shuffle. The issue is whether to regard structure or structuring absences as the meaning of a text or to consider the significance of the text by its place in the social context. Western semiotics, as a deciphering operation, not only dismisses the 'obvious' and the 'habitual' as false consciousness, but also sets out to marginalise competing ideological interpretation. The question is not whether one can escape semiotics, but rather to understand that all sign systems are implicated in ideology.

What, then, is Third Cinema semiotics? The following, inasmuch as they can shed more light on the current debate, should be regarded as the main concerns of Third Cinema semiotics.

1. To explicate and interrogate the kinds of intuitive knowledge spectators bring to the process.
2. To clear the ideological confusion that surrounds semiotic inquiry into crosscultural studies.

3.   To wed political economy of the signifier to critical theory of the text and, above all, to emphasise the 'ideological' as opposed to the 'psychological' spectator.

Here you have it: semiotics of everyday life, crosscultural semiotics, the political economy of the social sign and, finally, a semiotics rooted in the dialectics of struggle. Semiotics can no longer afford to overlook these concerns of Third Cinema and to alienate, or be alienated by, those who act in it.

Perhaps the greatest challenge to the realisation of the semiotic project is those texts of Third Cinema that are resistant to the absorption tendencies of 'mainstream' critical theory. Third Cinema texts exist within both ideology and history and thus need the application of a bonded historiography and semiotics for meaningful explication.

The concept of 'Third World' has been strongly attacked by scholars both from the USSR[14] and the USA due to its non-differentiation between one superpower and the other in their relation to the Third World. Burton also dismisses the concept by calling it 'a signifier without a signified, a term without a referent' (p. 25). This is a neither/nor situation and is, at best, agnostic thinking. Once she has dismissed the term, she nevertheless continues to use it, equating it with 'less westernised', 'dependent', 'non-western' and 'marginal', as if all these terms of analysis are the same. If Burton does not acknowledge that the concept exists, what then is her article about?

What is one to make of the Third World alliance within the United Nations in which these countries quite frequently take a unified stand on issues of mutual concern? So long as we recognise 'First World' and 'Second World' there will always be a 'Third World'. These labels are relational: they have an instrumental value, not an absolute one. The real reasons for denying the term legitimacy lie in its connotations of 'power' and 'united front' as the basis of global differentiation.[15]

Burton's dismissal of the concept of 'Third Cinema' is, therefore, quite understandable, because it too connotes power and united front. 'Third Cinema' challenges the hegemonic hold of cinema-as-spectacle. Indeed, the concept of Third Cinema is unified in its difference from Hollywood or mainstream cinema. For Burton to allege that the term has been 'widely questioned by many Third World filmmakers and flatly rejected by others' (p. 21), because of its Peronist associations, is guilt by association. It would have been useful to have a relevant reference for her allegation at this point.

According to Burton, 'cultural impermeability between dominant and dependent cultures . . . does not exist' (p. 23). Have you ever watched a Third World film with native viewers of that culture? To do so is to find the 'untranslatable' and 'unparaphraseable' nuances of culture foregrounded by two distinct responses: from those following the subtitles and from those following the direct address. While one group struggles to fashion a linear narrative, the other is engaged in intellectual and emotional involvement, be it in chuckles, choruses of laughter or other forms of response. Cultural impermeability cannot be simply wished away.

Mythical consciousness and folk narrative poetics are specific elements of Third World film texts. The specificities of each Third World culture are unities in their own settings, but they are also unities measured against differences within a Third World context. This relationship is a dialectical one: rather than oppositional it is a relationship marked by differences of strategies for development. The 'mainstream' paradigm, on the other hand, is measured by production values and the trajectory of technical brilliance. If, as it currently seems, mainstream cinema needs forty million dollars plus for the sheer quality of its productions, Third Cinema practices can live without it. The unifying impulse that originally spurred Third Cinema was, and is, a need for the primacy of subject matter over material considerations. To know this is to acknowledge the energy of social commitment and vision concentrated or lodged within it. Consequently, as I have suggested elsewhere,[16] we need to attend to a new critical theory that takes into account cultural resistance to domination as its prime rhetorical strategy. A genuine crosscultural system of exchange, a cross-fertilisation of ideas, can only occur if the notion that there cannot be discourse without metadiscourse or message without metamessage is reconsidered in light of text and context.

To imply that mainstream critical theory should dominate and assimilate all others because of its position of power, is to speak only in economic terms and to collapse everything else, including social concerns, into it. As Buñuel has observed:

> It seems clear to me that without the enormous influence of the canon of American culture, Steinbeck would be an unknown, as would Dos Passos and Hemingway. If they'd been born in Paraguay or Turkey, no one would ever have read them, which suggests the alarming fact that the greatness of a writer is in direct proportion to the power of his country.[17]

In this period of world hunger, nuclear threat, ideologised racism, the Debt Trap and violent conflicts in Central America and natural disasters in Mexico and Colombia, the 'great' film directors of the West would have been mere footnotes in history, had it not been for the economic power of their countries, and such notables as Nelson Pereira dos Santos of Brazil, Ousmane Sembene of Senegal, Tomas Gutiérrez Alea of Cuba, Mrinal Sen of India, Fernando Birri and Fernando Solanas of Argentina, Miguel Littín of Chile and several North American and European progressive filmmakers, active in Nicaragua, El Salvador, the Middle East and South Africa, would have been the actual luminaries of this era.

Of course, mainstream critical theory operates under the 'myth of the monolith' and tends to forget that there is another West, whose main concern is also social and political and whose struggles to liberate cinema compares with that of the Third

World. Too often these filmmakers are also ghettoised in just the same way as the Third World filmmakers. As Peter Steven has observed:

> Variety magazine and its rave reports of 'box office magic' represent the voice of dominant cinema. . . . But at the same time there are other, different voices – different languages – calling for radically new types of films, and for a new approach to cinema. These voices don't have the backing of Wall Street and Madison Avenue but they are present nevertheless and very active in parallel nooks and crannies in North America and beyond, and especially in the Third World.[18]

If anyone should claim credit for ushering in, and popularising, Third World film in western universities and cinemas, it is this progressive voice, and not, as Burton implies, the academic institutions per se. Progressive faculty, students and film journals in the US and Europe have played an important role. However, the claim to be allied with this movement is not in itself an indication of solidarity with the goal of cultural liberation. What is called for, above all else, is a more coherent and constructive understanding and practice than that espoused in Burton's concluding remarks:

> A view of culture in which the realm of ideological significance is not incompatible with the realm of personal enrichment (because personal enrichment is also viewed as a social phenomenon) would free western critics from the onerous role of 'diagnostician of pathologies', reaffirming instead their function as guide and celebrant. (p. 34)

Progressive western voices that have grasped the ideological agenda of decolonisation and liberation of Third Cinema have allied in co-productions and other forms of critical solidarity with Third World progressives to bring about, in the words of Glauber Rocha, the overthrow of 'the world cinematic language' under 'the dictatorship of Coppola and Godard'.[19] In this spirit, Julio García Espinosa has said, 'Cinema can be constructed on the ashes of what already exists. Moreover, to make a new cinema is, in fact, to reveal the process of destruction of the spectacle. . . . We have to make a spectacle out of the destruction of the spectacle'.[20] When this is accomplished, it is then and only then that Burton's hopes would be realised and, using her own words, western critics, would be freed 'from the onerous role of 'diagnostician of pathologies', reaffirming not 'their function as guide' (whose guide?) but as co-celebrants of the social institution of cinema and the human arts.

Critical theory is not an innocent discipline, nor is it an 'objective' phenomenon. Like any theory of social change, it has blind spots and limits. It is today a battleground. The pivotal question should rather be, to what end is 'mainstream' critical theory directed? Of what use are such analytic tools? To what degree are they in fact tools of oppression rather than liberation? Critical theory cannot be a method of perpetual alienation, but a guide a tool for liberation. Critical theory perhaps, as never before, is symbiotically linked to the propositions of political economy:

> In its concept of an ultimate goal, critical theory did not intend to replace the theological hereafter with a social one. . . . It only makes explicit what was always the foundation of its categories: the demand that through the abolition of previously existing material conditions of existence the totality of human relations be liberated. . . . In the theoretical reconstruction of the social process, the critique of current conditions and the analysis of their tendencies necessarily include future-oriented components.[21]

This then is the theory–praxis nexus that Third World film practice suggests. Today, it bears a clear signal of power relations within a given society. But it cannot, and should not, be opaque to that power, or it will cease to be. The expressed desire of the western intellectual, touristing in Third World discourse, is that the Third World abdicate or surrender its theoretical concerns and responsibilities to the West. This Third Cinema filmmakers understand all too well. To them filmmaking has always been a political act. They have been incarcerated, exiled and killed not because of the lack of their own critical theory but, in fact, precisely because of it.[22]

To think of 'Other Cinemas' in terms of the spectacle only is disastrous. To dismiss the social and/or revolutionary functions of 'Other Criticisms' as 'defensive' is an even graver error. To belittle the efforts of Third Cinema practitioners, by design or default, leads too quickly to the temptation to speak for them by constructing one's own fictions. This cultural negation, this mechanism of confinement and totalisation, and this system of unequal cultural and symbolic exchange, are evidence not of a theory of liberation, but rather of 'law and order' criticism.

Marx's letter to Arnold Ruge, September 1843, remains the last word on the subject:

> Nothing prevents us therefore from starting our criticism with criticism of politics, with taking sides in politics hence with *actual* struggles, and identifying ourselves with them. Then we do not face the world in doctrinaire fashion with a new principle, declaring, Here is truth, kneel here! We develop new principles for the world out of the principles of the world. We do not tell the world, Cease your struggles, they are stupid; we want to give you the true watchword of the struggles. We merely show the world why it actually struggles, and the awareness of this is something which the world *must* acquire even if it does not want to.

Acknowledgements

I would particularly like to thank Martin Blythe, Scott Cooper, Ronnie Serr and Billy Woodbury for their critical comments on this paper. I have also appreciated the insightful remarks of I.N.C. Aniebo, David Iyam, Naguib Ktiri, Hamid Naficy, Ramiah Shanker and Esther Yau.

Notes

1   Immanuel Wallerstein, *The Modern World-System* (New York: Academic Press, 1974).
2   Julianne Burton, 'Marginal cinemas and mainstream critical theory', *Screen*, vol. 26, nos. 3–4 (1985). Burton's essay forms Chapter 2 of the present volume, in which this quotation appears on p. 26. Page references for all passages from Burton's essay cited in this Chapter refer to the present volume; with subsequent references given in the text.
3   Fernando Birri, 'For a nationalist realist, critical and popular cinema', ibid, p. 90.
4   Eduardo Galeano, 'The revolution as revelation,' trans. Walter I. Bradbury, *Socialist Review*, no. 65 (1982), p. 9.
5   Julio García Espinosa, 'Meditations on Imperfect Cinema', *Screen*, vol. 26, nos. 3–4 (1985), pp. 93–4.
6   Teshome Gabriel, *Third Cinema in the Third World: The Aesthetics of Liberation* (Ann Arbor, MI: UMI Research Press, 1982), p. 7.
7   Terry Lovell, *Pictures of Reality: Aesthetics, Politics, Pleasure* (London: BFI, 1980), p. 95.
8   The quest for 'pleasure' and 'desire' within the Lacanian rereading of Freud suggests the notion of sexual difference. There is, however, no cultural reading of either Freud or Lacan in film texts in the Third World. Here, the social paradigm stands for the sexual paradigm as the generator of excess. In Third Cinema 'pleasure' and 'desire' are set forth as revolutionary agencies. For further reading on this issue, see Richard Lichtman, *The Production of Desire* (New York: The Free Press, 1982), and Gilles Deleuze and Felix Guattari, *Anti-Oedipus* (New York: The Viking Press, 1977).
9   Quoted in Peter Steven (ed.) *Jump Cut: Hollywood, Politics and Counter-cinema*. (Toronto: Between the Lines Press, 1985), p. 351.
10   Luis Buñuel, *My Last Sigh: The Autobiography of Luis Buñuel* (New York: Alfred A. Knopf, Inc., 1983), p. 222.
11   Marshall Blonsky (ed.), *On Signs* (Baltimore, MD: Johns Hopkins University Press, 1985), p. 36.
12   Quoted in Michael Chanan (ed.), *Twenty-five Years of Latin American Cinema* (London: BFI and Channel Four, 1983), p. 29.
13   Blonsky, *On Signs*, p. 35, emphasis added.
14   See Y. Zhukov et al, *The Third World* (Moscow: Progress Publishers, 1970).
15   For an introduction to the term and concept of 'Third World', see S.D. Muine, 'The Third World: concept and controversy', *Third World Quarterly*, vol. 1, no. 3 (1979), pp. 118–28.
16   Gabriel, 'Towards critical theory of Third World films', *Third World Affairs 1985* (London: Third World Foundation for Social and Economic Studies, 1985), pp. 355–69.
17   Buñuel, *My Last Sigh*, p. 222.
18   Steven (ed.), *Jump Cut*, p. 15.

19 Glauber Rocha, *Revolução do Cinema Novo* (Rio de Janeiro: Alhambra/Embrafilme, 1981), p. 467.
20 Quoted in Steven (ed.), *Jump Cut*, p. 357.
21 Herbert Marcuse, 'Philosophy and critical theory', in *Negations* (Boston, MA: Beacon Press, 1968), p. 145.
22 For a partial list of Latin American filmmakers jailed, exiled or killed, see 'In Latin America they shoot filmmakers', *Sight and Sound*, Summer 1976, pp. 160–1.

Part II

Modernity and modernization

4   A screen of one's own: early cinema in Québec and the public sphere, 1906–1928

Scott MacKenzie

This essay seeks to address the relationship between national identity, the cinema, and the alternative public sphere in Québec between 1906 and 1928. I argue that the advent of early cinematic screening spaces allowed new discursive spaces to emerge which were intrinsically tied to developing moving picture culture. Such spaces allowed French Canadian viewers to reimagine themselves and their society. These alternative public spheres – which can be traced back to the beginnings of film in Québec – formed points of resistance to bourgeois publics and official culture. Although the emergent cinematic space in Québec was not explicitly defined in terms related to notions of publicness, the fact that the cinema could be seen as a potentially counterhegemonic public space within culture was not only demonstrated by the provincial government's and the Catholic Church's fear of the thematic content of films, but also in the concern these institutions had about the large publics which were formed through film screenings. Films were seen not only as 'entertainment' but as providing the means to enable audiences to reimagine their community and their national identity.

The relationship between Church and state in Québec in the early twentieth century is worth examining. From the mid nineteenth century onwards, the Catholic Church in Québec virtually co-managed the State with the elected governments of the time. The Church ran both the educational system, from primary schools to the universities, and the healthcare system.[1] Québec's political leaders, from the Mayor of Montréal to the Premier of the Province, all wished to maintain positive relations with the Church because of the strength that the pulpit afforded members of the priesthood. Therefore, unlike the role played by the Church in the USA, in Québec Church and state were quite inseparable when it came to laws that mandated the policing of the 'public good'. Both institutions used legalistic and discursive means in an attempt to limit the effects of urbanization and modernity in Québec in general, and in Montréal in particular. If anything, the rise of a new, urbanized public sphere in Montréal came about through the radical juxtaposition of the traditional views of the Catholic Church (which quite explicitly recalled the Catholicism of pre-Revolutionary France) and the rise of modernity in the urbanized centres of

North America. If, as Michel Foucault argues, power relations must be understood as a multiplicity of force relations that are variant, reversible and in conflict, and which contain a variety of forms of resistance which ebb and flow within them,[2] we can begin to see how the cinema space itself became not only a contested space, but also a space of concurrent emancipation and repression. Indeed, the politics of space came to the forefront in the battle between modernity and religion in Québec in the 1900s to the 1920s.

The possibility of the cinema functioning as a counterhegemonic space within the public sphere was a primary concern of the Catholic Church in Québec from the 1900s to the 1930s. This concern originated because the cinema offered large groups of individuals a place to congregate outside the confines of the Church. The roots of the belief that the cinema was both emancipatory for the people and a perceived threat to the established order can be traced back to the advent of cinema in Québec in 1906 and to the first movie theatres of Léo-Ernest Ouimet. While many theorists have argued that political and social action in Québécois cinema emerged with the advent of *cinéma direct* in the 1950s and the Challenge for Change/*Société nouvelle* programme in the 1960s, I shall argue here that these practices began much earlier, and that the latent potential of an alternative public sphere has been at the heart of French Canadian and Québécois cinema since the *fin de siècle*.[3]

As the cinema developed in Québec, the images on the screen quickly shifted from the presentation of the 'exotic' images of the Lumière brothers' travelogues to the presentation of locally shot actualities. Similar to the trajectory followed by the emergent cinema in other urban centres, this fostered a sense of community which was previously found – in the context of Québec – in either Churches or taverns.[4] The cinema, in a relatively short period of time, became a place to gather, debate and discuss images and experiences.[5] For these and other reasons I shall discuss, early film in Québec offered its audiences a place to negotiate their national (if not nationalist) identity, to reimagine their history, and to envision an egalitarian future, even if these practices can only be understood as the postulation of utopian ideals, created through a dialectic between the repressive Church and state and the development of 'leisure time' on the part of urbanized working classes. Because of these factors, of interest here are both the discursive practices and the legalistic issues surrounding the cinematic text and the extradiegetic film culture in Québec at this time: the interpretations, appropriations, contextualizations and contestations that aid us in understanding the larger role played by cinema in Québec culture and its relation to the institutional discourses of Church and state.

The *cinématographe* came to Montréal six months after the Lumière brothers premiered their invention in Paris. On 27 June 1896, at the *café-concert* Le Palace at 78 rue Saint-Laurent, Louis Minier and his assistant Louis Pupier presented the Lumière brothers' *cinématographe*; this was the first film screening in Canada and the first North American screening of the Lumière brothers' invention.[6] The event was primarily for dignitaries, journalists and the Mayor of Montréal. From the descriptions found in the Montréal daily *La Presse* on 29 June 1896, it is apparent that *L'Arrivée d'un train* (France, 1895) was screened, as were *Démolition d'un mur* (France, 1895), *Partie écarté* (France, 1895) and *Baignade de mer* (France, 1896), among others. According to some accounts, Léo-Ernest Ouimet was one of the spectators present at this screening.[7] While there is some doubt as to whether he was actually in the audience, there is no doubt that Ouimet was interested in moving pictures soon after their arrival in Montréal. The son of a farmer, Ouimet was born in St-Martin, Laval, Québec, on 16 March 1877. He was a young electrician working at the Théâtre Nationale when he began attending film screenings at Parc Sohmer, an amusement park near the port of Old Montréal. In 1902, the proprietors of Parc Sohmer – Joe Lajoie and Ernest Lavigne – decided to screen films on Sundays. It was here that Ouimet first learned how to use Edison's kinetoscope; he was trained by Edison projectionist Bert Fenton. Ouimet was able to attend these early screenings because provincial byelaws required, in deference to the Catholic Church, that theatres such as the one he worked at were closed on Sundays.

By 1903 Fenton was facing problems with Canadian customs officials. He was told that he could no longer bring films across the border to project himself; instead, he was to send the films via express mail, so that import taxes could be collected. In light of this development, Fenton asked Ouimet to receive the films and project them for him.[8] When Georges Gauvreau, the owner of the Théâtre Nationale, decided to add films to his bill, it was again Ouimet who was asked to project them. Here, Ouimet's entrepreneurial skills became apparent. At the beginning of each projection, Ouimet flashed his name on the screen through a stereopticon. This self-promotion quickly made Ouimet's name as synonymous with the cinema in Montréal as Edison's was in the USA and the Lumières' was in Paris.

As the popularity of the cinema grew, Ouimet realized that it could become one of the key technological revolutions of the century and, hence, highly profitable. In 1904 he did publicity work for the Tarte brothers of the newspaper *La Patrie*, by projecting films on a screen attached to their building, which was under construction at the time.[9] Also in 1904, he acquired the franchise for Walters' Kinetograph Company of New York, bought two Edison projectors, and worked as a travelling projectionist, exhibiting films in and around Montréal. By 1905 this venture had become so successful that Ouimet opened the Ouimet Film Exchange, the first film exchange in Canada.[10]

While Ouimet was successful as a travelling projectionist, there was greater profit to be found in the burgeoning storefront *graphes* – the term derived from *cinématographe* – similar in format to the American nickelodeons. With fifty dollars – all his available capital – Ouimet was able, on 1 January 1906, to open his first Ouimetoscope in the Salle Poiré, by the Klondike Bar located on rue Ste-Catherine. This first Ouimetoscope could accommodate approximately six hundred people and was in the style of the nickelodeons of the time. The admission price ranged from ten cents for matinees, to fifteen cents for evening screenings and twenty-five cents for reserved seating. At first Ouimet screened Pathé films, actualities from Europe and America, and Edison products, along with the only available francophone material in Montréal, *chansons illustrés*, silent films which illustrated popular French songs, allowing audiences, and usually a *chansonnier*, to sing along.[11] The range of his selection, however, quickly increased. By February Ouimet was screening 'colour films'; by July along with his Pathé product, he was showing Selig, Kamen, Biograph and Méliès films; and by November he was shooting his own actualities.[12]

By the summer of 1907, Ouimet had generated enough capital to renovate the Ouimetoscope. Faced with competition from Gauvreau – who opened the Nationoscope at the corner of rue Ste-Catherine and rue St-André in 1907, after failing to buy Salle Poiré – Ouimet bought the property for $70,000 and the liquor licence for $30,000 more. He then razed the Ouimetoscope over the summer – traditionally a period when theatres closed because of the heat, as there was no air conditioning. He then invested $50,000 more to rebuild, and opened the new, improved Ouimetoscope on 31 August 1907.[13]

This new Ouimetoscope, along with the Nationoscope, were the first movie palaces in North America, seating 1,200 and 1,100 people respectively (the next comparable palace was The Strand, which opened in New York in 1915).[14] Ouimet was not only trying to compete successfully in the burgeoning *scope* market; for a number of reasons he was also trying to attract a middle-class, bourgeois audience. To this end, he attempted to modify the class composition of his clientele not only through a change in emphasis in the programming, but through decor and the press. He also changed the emphasis of his programmes: the nickelodeon format was replaced with two two-and-a-half hour shows a day. His top admission price went up to fifty cents. He also emphasized the 'refined' nature of his programmes: on the opening night of the renovated Ouimetoscope, Ouimet screened an actuality which was appropriately 'cultured': *Marriage du roi d'Espagne* (France, 1905).[15] The announcement of the grand opening in *La Presse* on 31 August 1907 also mentions the 'superb spectacle' of the Victoria Falls in Africa.[16] As Germain Lacasse notes, Ouimet wished to 'draw to the cinema the bourgeois client, who paid more and frequented the theatre'. This was the policy that Ouimet gradually established,[17] initiating a process of gentrification which is also readily apparent in the comments describing the decor of the new Ouimetoscope. An article in *La Presse* – probably a press release written by Ouimet himself – goes into great detail about the marble floors, the ceramic patterns in the walls, the framed screen and the smoking room. Finally, the article mentions the appearance of 'aristocrats' at the Ouimetoscope, a concept which was totally foreign in Québec.[18]

Miriam Hansen's groundbreaking work on the silent cinema as an alternative public sphere is of some relevance in the examination of the role played by the Ouimetoscope in the Montréal social horizon. Hansen's use of the term 'public' denotes 'a discursive matrix or process through which social experience is articulated, interpreted, negotiated and contested in an intersubjective, potentially collective and oppositional form'.[19] Hansen, drawing on the work of Alexander Kluge and Oskar Negt, argues that American silent cinema offers a horizon on which an emergent new public sphere can be hypothesized; one which is, in its conceptualization, proletarian in nature, unlike the bourgeois public sphere posited by Jürgen Habermas in *The Structural Transformation of the Public Sphere*.[20]

Negt's and Kluge's conceptualization of the proletarian public sphere is not an autonomous part of the social horizon; instead, it is constituted at the intersection of the decaying bourgeois public sphere and the market economy of twentieth-century capitalism. The term 'proletarian', in this instance, goes beyond a simple working-class orientation; instead, it embraces the position of marginality that is inevitably constructed by dominant forces:

> Even if there were nothing in the history and living situation of the working class that corresponded to a proletarian public sphere, Negt/Kluge argue this category would have to be – and could be – developed in its negative determination: on the basis of hegemonic efforts to suppress, repress, destroy, isolate, split or assimilate any formation of potential proletarian public sphere and to approximate its material substance, experience, in the interest of private profit-maximization.[21]

In the context of US silent film, Hansen sees the attempt to consolidate a middle-class audience in the shift from the diversity of early cinema styles to the dominant style of Classical Hollywood cinema. She further claims that this transformation of the movie house from a working-class to a middle-class social space is not as linear a trajectory as many film historians have argued. In lieu of a Rankean model of historical progression, Hansen contends that the history of film spectatorship should be looked upon from a different angle:

> Rather than emphasize historical parallels in the cinema's integration into the dominant public sphere, one might consider the potential of the gap created by a historically changed constellation, i.e. the possibility that early silent cinema – *because* of and *counter* to its commercial orientation – may have contained elements of a public sphere radically different in kind.[22]

The need to regulate and negate, then, is not simply the act of a censor; it is an attempt to appropriate emergent, and possibly contestatory, spaces on the social horizon and subsume them under the dominant spheres of power and influence. In doing so, however, what is new and perhaps radical about the space gains strength through its negation, as negation only serves further to define its boundaries and power. Even if the new public space is not, in the first instance, used as a place of critique, the attempts at assimilation or negation will necessarily place it in this position. While this process of negation may create new spaces for democratic possibilities to emerge as an ideal, it was not the articulated desire of movie theatre owners and managers that these ideals develop.

Hansen contends that the last thing on the minds of movie theatre owners was the creation of democratic public spaces in which the working class, immigrants and the bourgeoisie could gather.[23] This certainly applies to Ouimet who, more than any of his competitors, wished to attract a bourgeois, affluent clientele and, if possible, transform his movie palace into a legitimate theatre. Indeed, his drive for a bourgeois audience led him into direct competition with the local theatres, especially with the Théâtre Nationale, whose clients frequented middle-class theatres and not working-class nickelodeons.[24]

Nevertheless, through the 1910s the main audience of the *scopes* remained working class. As Dane Lanken points out, 'the two main movie house streets in Montréal were Notre-Dame and St-Laurent, both in solidly working-class areas, the latter long the starting point in the city for immigrants'.[25] Despite his attempt to change the social class of his audience, Ouimet must have realized who filled the seats in his theatre, especially on Sundays. As time progressed, however, the audience did become more heterogeneous, even when Ouimet abandoned the 'prestige format', which was an obvious attempt to replicate the middle-class milieu of the theatre, and returned to the 'grind house' screenings of the nickelodeons. Indeed, one of the key ways to understand the diversity of Ouimet's audience is to consider the location of his theatre, and indeed, that of the other *scopes*: all were in the heart of the city, where English and French, working and middle class came together. The crowds, therefore, that gathered at the Ouimetoscope were diverse in terms of both their class backgrounds and their mother tongues, and in turn-of-the-century Montréal this in itself was a new phenomenon. And while it is impossible to empirically reconstruct who composed Ouimet's 'real' audience, it is interesting to map out the kinds of tensions that surrounded the nature of the cinema's audience at the time.

Through the creation of this new space where different classes could mingle outside the confines of the Church, the Ouimetoscope became a highly contested space in Montréal, fought over, celebrated, derided and denounced by the state, the clergy, the press and the people. In the context of French Canadian cultural life in the early twentieth century, the Ouimetoscope, and the numerous 'scopes' which followed, offered the possibility of creating a space outside the dominant social horizon of the state, the family and, most profoundly in Québec, the Catholic Church. Part of this has to do with the existence of the space itself, but there was more to it than that. Parks, for instance, had existed for years without the need for them to be unduly regulated or closed down, mainly because there was no reason – short of strikes and protests, which were quickly suppressed – to gather there in an organized fashion.

The creation of this new space arose from a variety of factors. The working classes only had one day off a week, which was Sunday. Historically, on this one day of rest, families attended Church and spent time within the private spheres of culture. Most forms of entertainment were closed on Sundays, and other forms of entertainment during the week were prohibitively expensive. The cinema, open on Sundays, not only provided an alternative to the Church which was often sought after in urban centres, but also provided a form of entertainment that was, for the most part, completely 'foreign' (unlike the theatre, which was at least performed in French).

The factor which brought about anxiety and debate in the dominant sphere was nevertheless linked to the nature of the attraction itself – the images on the screen – and the fact that the projection took place in a public, unregulated space. It was not only the specifics of a given film that bothered the state and the clergy, but the possibility that anything could appear to the screen and that there was no way to control the contingent actions and debates of the audiences. During the silent period, as Hansen points out, 'films were viewed differently, and were likely to have a wide range of meanings, depending on the neighbourhood and the status of the theatre, on the ethnic and racial background of the habitual audience, on the mixture of gender and generation, on the ambition and skills of the exhibitor and the performing personnel'.[26] Further, as both Hansen and Tom Gunning have pointed out, the structure of the films themselves was not as rigid as it became with the advent of Classical Hollywood cinema. Early cinema was characterized by the power to astonish over the ability to narrate; by its greater intertextuality; by the alternation of live shows with films; and by the potential for the film to be commented on through the use of music, sound effects or an onstage narrator.[27] The cinema seemed to provide the social function once provided by the Church, but without the rigid control, and audiences of early cinema interacted both with the film and with each other. At the very least, this was how the Church perceived things to be. These claims as to the interactive nature of film spectatorship hold true in the context of the Ouimetoscope, and this interactivity developed even further once images of Québec made it to the screen.

While films had already been shot in Montréal by Americans and shown at the Ouimetoscope and other local theatres since the turn of the century, these films were scenics, shot because of the 'exotic' nature of snow and skating. Key examples which are still extant include: *Skating: Montréal* (Anon., 1898); *Duke of York in Montréal* (Edison, 1901); *Montréal Fire Department on Runners* (Edison, 1901); *After the First Snow* (American Mutoscope & Biograph, 1903); and *Logging in Québec* (Anon., 1903). André Gaudreault and Germain Lacasse contend that the films made by Edison, American Mutoscope, and others planted seeds leading to 'the development of a "local", if not "national", cinema. . . . Montréalers were not content for very long seeing their city as "scenics" shot by outsiders. They also wished to see their city as they defined it'.[28]

In order to attract both the working and the middle classes, one of the promises made by Ouimet when he reopened the Ouimetoscope was to present actualities of Montréal which he himself would shoot. He had begun this practice during the run of the first Ouimetoscope in 1906, and increased his rate of production with the advent of the new Ouimetoscope. These actualities were immediately popular, as they reflected the main passions and concerns of the Québécois working and bourgeois classes of the time. In this regard, Ouimet was a pioneer. As Hye Bossin notes: 'Ouimet made his own Canadian newsreels a year before Pathé came on the scene with the first on the continent in 1909'.[29] At the time Bossin was writing (the 1950s), it was believed that Ouimet began film production in 1908; it is now clear that Ouimet was producing actualities a full three years before Pathé's arrival in 1909. One of the key reasons for the early popularity of Ouimet's films was that there was no local competition of any significance. Furthermore, because of his penchant for self-promotion, Ouimet was a local celebrity and his films were therefore viewed as local, and consequently more authentic. Authenticity, of course, is a thorny issue, but the belief on the part of the public that locally produced actualities were more 'real' certainly held sway both in Montréal and in other urban centres during the course of early cinema.

One of earliest films shot by Ouimet himself, *Mes espérances* (Québec, 1908), superficially recalls Auguste and Louis Lumière's *Déjeuner de bébé* (France, 1895), as it is a film which features Ouimet's children. However, the film quickly foregrounds the tension between documentary and fiction film. At first the film is a straight-forward portrait of Ouimet's children as they play with a phonograph; in the second series of shots, though, one sees the little boy reading the newspaper as if after a hard day's work, while the little girl takes care of the 'feminine' chores such as child rearing, represented by her playing with a doll. The film quickly moves from documenting Ouimet's children to his staged fantasy of their future roles in culture.

In essence, *Mes espérances* resembles the latter-day image-making practices undertaken when one first acquires a Super-8 camera, or a camcorder: a document of one's immediate, private-sphere surroundings. Quickly, though, Ouimet and his cameraperson Lactance Giroux moved on to shooting actualities of fires, bridges and public events in Montréal. Ouimet's films, which are not included in most English-language histories of Canadian and Québécois cinema – or, at best, are mentioned in a cursory fashion, offer one of the earliest examples of the secular documentation and mediation of Québécois identity. As Gaudreault and Lacasse write: 'these productions represent the first significant effort to constitute a local – which at times took on the aim of being a national – production'.[30] These films were tied intrinsically to notions of local identity. And while the films at times represented national concerns, it would be premature to discuss them in terms of nationalism, as the nationalist discourses of the time were the highly conservative, if not reactionary, ones of Henri Bourassa and Lionel Groulx, who were concerned with the purity of the French language and the unquestioned authority of the

Church. The secular, popular imaginary of what it was to be Québécois in a modern, urban context was a quite different form of national identity and identification. Indeed, the cinema was one of the means through which the French language and the Church were supposedly being usurped.

Ouimet's films reflected and reported on the world in which the spectators lived. As Ouimet and his camerapersons developed their skills, they would film fires, disasters and parades which took place in the Montréal area – and, less frequently, in other parts of Québec – and have a one- to three-day turnover from event to projection. Spectators could then see the events that recently took place, and also, in the case of parades and festivities, go and see if they appeared in the image. This process meant that the Ouimetoscope, in a relatively short period of time, provided a space wherein the public could come and reexperience communally recent events.

On 17 November 1906, Ouimet and Giroux filmed a foot race at Carré Saint-Louis, a popular event at the time. The following Monday, 19 November, the film was playing at the Ouimetoscope.[31] This was successful, so Ouimet followed it up on 3 and 4 December by driving to fires and filming them, and then projecting the films in his theatre. The day after Ouimet filmed the first fire, *La Presse* covered Ouimet's filming, which necessarily built up anticipation for the filmed version of the event. By May 1907, the Ouimetoscope was screening a film shot by Giroux and Ouimet on snowshoe races in Montréal, another attempt to draw the local audience to the scope by evoking local practices and events. Ouimet's films, then, in a fairly short period went from simple actualities to films which were representative of the key events of the day. This practice culminated with the *course de sacs de sel*, organized by *La Presse* on 31 October 1907. Contestants in this race had to run with a hundred kilogram bag of salt on their back. A popular sport at the time, the press built up the event over the preceding month. Furthermore, as Lacasse writes: 'Every stripe of politician publicized the event as a nationalistic and patriotic demonstration'.[32] According to newspaper accounts – admittedly biased as they organized the event – over 300,000 spectators turned out. Within the week, *Le Concours de sac de sel* (Québec, 1907) was playing in the Ouimetoscope. The film played for two weeks, a very long run at the time, as only the annual presentation of *La Passion* had anywhere near as long an engagement.[33] *Le Concours de sac de sel* is a turning point in the development of French Canadian and Québécois cinema, as the circular relationship between profilmic event, filmic event and audience that was to become a key part in both the theory and practice of Québécois cinema was already present at this early stage. Films such as *Congrès eucharistique* (1910) reinforced this novelty of the 'quick turnover' into practice.

Film also began to play a role in the political sphere. During the federal elections of 1908, a great deal of interest was generated in Québec about the outcome of the vote, as the Liberal candidate, Sir Wilfrid Laurier, was a native of Québec. Ouimet had made a film earlier in the year entitled *Wilfrid Laurier: l'assemblée de Laprairie* (Québec, 1908). As Laurier passed by the Ouimetoscope during a campaign parade,

Ouimet projected the film on the building across the street from the theatre. The film was used again on the election night of 26 October 1908. *La Presse* projected the election results, riding by riding, onto the facade of a building on rue St-Jacques. Once Laurier was declared the winner, *Wilfrid Laurier: l'assemblée de Laprairie* was projected for the ecstatic crowd by Ouimet.[34]

All these examples point to the fact that the cinema played a highly charged role in Montréal during the early twentieth century. If one is to conceptualize the Ouimetoscope and Ouimet's films as the formation of a new or alternative public sphere, one is faced with a very different scenario from the one theorized by Hansen in the American context, but one just as filled with possibilities. The *scope*, in the Québécois context, did not offer the viewer the same kind of space which Hansen contends *The Corbett–Fitzsimmons Fight* (US, 1897) offered women in New York. To be more precise, the contested space which surrounded the *scopes* offered publics more than spectatorial pleasures that could be understood through dominant and alternative readings of the images on the screen. Instead, films like *Le Concours de sac de sel* offered the viewers images of themselves, projected back into a public space. Audiences were not going to see a film to find out what happened at a given event, as they were most probably present at the event itself. Instead this public space for the first time put 'the people' – an ill-defined but intuitive concept – on the screen and offered the working and middle classes a place to congregate, speak and share a communal experience outside the institutionalized hierarchies of the workplace and the Church. In sharing this communal experience, working-class audiences had the chance to imagine themselves as part of a community separate from both Church and state. And even this space did not arise, in the first instance, from the audiences themselves; it came into formation once the combined forces of the Church and state, through both discursive and legislative practices, attempted to control the space. Through negation, then, the images and the space itself became contested sites.

Michael Warner suggests that the advent of mass audiences, such as the one found at the Ouimetoscope, brings about a different relationship between the reader/viewer and the text, be it written or visual.[35] This position is one of imagining the self not just as an individual consuming a public text, but also one where the individual imagines a larger public of which she is a member. The imagining of a social and public horizon is as important as the comprehension of the information in the text, and this imagined horizon frames the responses one has to texts within the public sphere. The ability to imagine a community in such a way is magnified by the cinema: as one watches a film within a public space, the imagined audience and the real audience blur, accentuating the feeling of, in Benedict Anderson's much-used phrase, an imagined community. In the history of the cinema, this notion of community is manifested in many diverse instances, through the efforts of both film producers and film audiences. In the case of early Québécois cinema, this experience typically took place on Sunday, the one day the workers had off, a time typically relegated to a very different kind of congregating and social imagining: that of churchgoing.

Despite his financial success and his attempt to legitimize the *scopes* by appealing to the middle classes, the two forces which would plague Ouimet throughout his cinematic career first appeared on the horizon in 1907: the attempt of US companies to control distribution, and the goal of the Catholic Church in Québec to close movie theatres on Sundays. In September 1907, Ouimet was invited to attend the meeting of the United Film Service Protective Association and the Film Importers and Manufacturers of the United States in Chicago; he was the only Canadian to attend. As Hye Bossin notes, this meeting was the prelude to the Trust initiated by Edison in order to secure and protect his copyrights through protectionism and the monopolization of performance, production and distribution. While Ouimet was informed at this meeting that, as a Canadian distributor, he would be exempt from the requirements of the Trust, the pressure from American distributors never relented and their protectionist methods – along with the omnipresent rhetoric of the Church – eventually forced Ouimet out of film distribution in 1922.[36]

Ironically, the one fear shared by both Ouimet and the Catholic Church was the threat of US interventionism in the Québec film industry. This situation was paradoxical, as the films that the Americans made increasingly difficult for Ouimet to distribute were the same ones that the Church wished to keep out of Québec. But while the Church eventually became extremely critical of the content of American films, the debate about the cinema began over something entirely different: the question of Sunday closings. It was in December 1907 that the Catholic Church began to take note of the cinema in Québec. Theatres, concerts, horse races and sport competitions had been long closed on Sundays, but *scopes* and nickelodeons had been able to remain open by finding loopholes in the law: for instance, Ouimet sold candy at the Ouimetoscope. With each candy bar sold on Sunday, the purchaser could enter the theatre free. In the face of these actions, the archbishop of Montréal, Paul Bruchési, led the crusade to keep movie theatres closed on Sundays, claiming that the cinema had questionable moral values. Ouimet and other movie theatre owners resisted the edict of the Church, as they drew their largest audiences on Sundays.

The power of film had swept through Montréal incredibly quickly. Ouimet's press and publicity aside, it was the working classes of the East end of Montréal that went to the burgeoning *scopes* most frequently, especially as venues opened in the working-class East End of the city. Furthermore, the support felt for the cinema by the public was immense: when the Government of Canada introduced the 'Sunday observance' law on 13 July 1906 – adopted as law on 1 March 1907 – which would effectively close the *scopes* on the one day the working classes had off, more than ten thousand people turned out to protest against the law at Champ-de-Mars.[37] This led to a legal challenge by Ouimet which was referred to the Supreme Court of Canada (in 1912

Ouimet won his case; as many of his co-litigants had gone bankrupt, Ouimet had to pay the entire legal bill).[38]

Throughout 1907, the attacks on the *scopes*, particularly from the Catholic Church, increased dramatically. Because of his public renown, Ouimet was targeted for arrest and charged with opening illegally on Sunday on 1 December 1907. The battle with Ouimet was not solely over his actions, but also over what he represented; and this led to his problems with the clergy. As Lacasse points out:

> In rural and Catholic Québec, it was preached that the 'salvation of our race' (*salut de notre race*) resides in a profound attachment to the past, to values that the evolution of the world leaves further behind every day. Without a doubt, it took an upstart (*parvenu*) like Ouimet to take the step to liberate himself from the reactionary and semi-feudal ideology that dominated the French Canadian bourgeoisie and to dare to face down the restraints that the reactionaries were imposing everywhere.[39]

It is important to stress that, at this time, the threat posed by the cinema was not based on the content of the images themselves, but on their popularity and the massive publics that this popularity created, as evidenced by the protest of 1906. This popularity was seen as being in direct competition with the authority of the Church to disseminate information to the public: to use Kantian terminology, it was an attack on tutelage. This attack on the new public space of the cinema, however, quickly turned into an attack on the moral lessons of the films themselves, and this attack was led again by members of the Catholic Church. While the films screened by Ouimet helped build an alternative public sphere, a space outside those of Church and state, they did not promote a strong sense of nationalism. The Church, in fact, saw the cinema as an attack on the lifestyle and history of Québec.

It is important to stress in any discussion of the emergence of Québécois cinema as a potential site of an alternative public sphere that one is not solely advancing an abstract, theoretical proposition. In much the same way as the development of cinema technology had an effect on the kinds of films which could be produced in Québec and Canada, the discourses of the Church and state attempted to frame the kinds of films that could be distributed and to limit the cinema's role in constructing a national imaginary. If one takes to heart Negt's and Kluge's argument that negation is a means by which an oppositional site may be constructed, then the cinema in Québec can be seen as a site that has been negotiated, shaped and contested by the Church, the state, the forces of capital and various publics. And while, *pace* Foucault, the discursive and legalistic systems of power which structured the space of the cinema were both diverse and dispersed, the process of negation was nevertheless a key determining factor in the kinds of discourses which surrounded the cinema in Québec. This kind of negation is nowhere more apparent than in the actions of the Catholic Church from the 1900s to the 1920s.

The Catholic Church, especially the young, activist clergy, opposed the cinema and, indeed, most forms of popular communication as the tools of Americans, English Canadians and Jews, all of whom wished to obliterate the culture, history and traditions of the Québécois through the dissemination of prurient texts. The power of the Catholic Church in Québec was based upon maintaining a 'traditional' culture that took the symbols of Christianity as unmediated representations of the power and glory of God. The Church postulated that the culture of Québec ought to be composed of individuals who were religious, devout, self-sacrificing, mostly rural, and latently nationalistic. As mass media developed in North America, a fervent feeling that new communication technologies, exposing the populace to ideas in opposition to those of the Church, would erode both the French language and the power and authority of the clergy. The most apparent manifestation of this erosion is illustrated by the fact that in 1912 the Supreme Court of Canada finally ruled that movie theatres could remain open on Sundays. This enraged the Catholic Church, which then campaigned for total closure of the cinema in Québec, as they argued that the cinema was ruining the souls of the population. In response, Québec's first film censorship laws were passed on 21 December 1912.[40]

These debates grew with the advent of sound in 1928 which, in the eyes of the Church, forever determined the 'nationality' of a film through language. Father Lionel Groulx, Professor of History at the Université de Montréal, was one of the key figures to argue vehemently that French Canada had to be seen as a uniform collectivity and not as a collection of individuals existing in a culturally diverse community. Furthermore, Groulx claimed that the French Canadian collectivity was being attacked from all sides; that anyone outside it wished to 'contaminate' it with ideas and ideals that were 'foreign' to the Catholic way of life. For Groulx, one of the key examples of this 'contamination' was the cinema: its American ideology of secular life and loose morals was anathema to Catholicism. While the cinema was a convenient scapegoat, it is apparent that the cinema was only a symptom of larger changes taking place in Québécois culture. The Church was aggressively attempting to reaffirm a collective identity: one which could maintain the clergy's spiritual and economic control over a populace that, through urbanization, was slowly moving towards a secular existence.

The priests and writers associated with the journal *L'Action française* were the most vocal about the evils of the cinema.[41] Founded in 1917 as an offshoot of the Catholic, proto-nationalist group *Ligue des Droits du Français*, *L'Action française* was edited by Groulx. In a speech at the *Monument National* in 1918, Groulx proclaimed that the cinema was eroding the traditional culture of French Canada and referred to the cinema as an 'agent of denationalization'.[42] In Groulx's view, what was ailing French Canadian society was the influx of Anglo-American (read: Jewish) culture. This influx lead to a loss of a sense of one's own cultural history, language and identity. This collective identity, which was inextricably linked to the Catholic Church, had to be preserved in the face of the immorality of the mass media. It is important to note that discourses of anti-Semitism were in the minority in Québec in the 1920s. Nevertheless, the voices of anti-Semitism came from some of the most respected corners of French Canadian society: the nationalist daily *Le Devoir* (founded by Henri Bourassa) and *L'Action française*. Both Groulx's historical writings and his works of fiction reflect the desire for a racially pure, ahistorical French Canadian race.

In 1924, the attack on the cinema by Groulx and others reached the pages of *L'Action française*, which was an influential and widely circulated magazine in Québec. The magazine was very much the voice of the Catholic Church, especially for middle-class francophones; its publisher was the most austere of the francophone dailies, *Le Devoir*. Anti-anglophone, anti-American, and incredibly anti-Semitic, in its first ten years *L'Action française*, under the general directorship of Groulx, found villains and scapegoats lurking around every corner. These villains were constructed in order to preserve the racial and cultural purity of the French Canadian collectivity and to reassert the power and authority of the Church. As the cinema was seen to be beginning to eclipse the Church's place in the popular imaginary, it needed to be vilified. And the most expedient way to vilify the cinema was to create a 'counter-imaginary' by launching an attack against the 'Jewish conspiracy' to rule the world through the cinema.

In an essay entitled 'L'ennemi dans la place: théâtre et cinéma', Harry Bernard – who wrote the piece at the behest of Groulx – finds the faults of the cinema to lie in a 'Jewish conspiracy' to take over the world and destroy Christianity: 'The films they show us are, with rare exception, of American, or more precisely, Judeo-American, provenance'.[43] Bernard offers statistics to 'demonstrate' that Jews control eighty-five per cent of the American film industry – a figure which includes the works of 'the Jew Charlie Chaplin'. He then goes on to 'expose' the goals of the Hollywood Jews:

> The Jews, with their goal of dechristianization, have as their principal goal, to make money and to get their hands on the world's finances. To arrive at their goals nothing is negligible or too low. They exploit passion in all its forms and flatter the instincts. They have no anxiety about morals or order and the marvellous means of education offered by the cinema becomes in their hands, because of their love of gold and their quest for domination, a tool of depravity, a school of corruption and revolution.[44]

According to Bernard, the Jews were not satisfied with simply accumulating wealth; this was solely 'a means of arriving at their goal which is the domination of the civilized world'.[45] This propagandistic conspiracy was effective upon French Canada precisely because its culture and history had been obliterated through colonialization: it no longer had a collective imaginary in which to invest. The cinema, then, offered the people a comfortable imaginary which came from outside the morals and traditions of the collectivity: 'For the people, the cinema is some sort of conscious dream'.[46] According to Bernard, this 'Judeo-American' imaginary not only supplants the goals of the Church, it also impedes the progress of French Canadians who are attempting to build their national identity: 'The national feeling is what is missing the most with us and individuality is blooming around us; and the cinema, which is exclusive to Israeli-Americans, is favourable to its formation'.[47] It does not matter that '*le sens national*' that *L'Action française* proposed was anti-individual and anti-Semitic, to the extent that this doctrine supports the sublimation of the individual in a manner which parallels that of fascism. What this statement really means is that the individualism which may develop from the cinema is at odds with the kind of national identity proposed by Bernard, Groulx, and others: one of an undifferentiated, and profoundly ahistorical, collectivity. Bernard concludes by contending that the cinema is now such a part of the popular imaginary that it is impossible to rid Québec society of it. Therefore, fire must be fought with fire: 'we must fight the cinema with the cinema, opposing the good against the bad'.[48] The Church therefore required counterpropaganda to ensure the survival of the traditions of the collectivity.

Others did not believe even in the power of counterpropaganda. Whatever redeeming qualities the cinema possessed were there solely to seduce the innocent, as Father Phillipe Perrier argues, citing Father Archambeault in his essay '*Contre le cinéma, tous*': 'Do not let yourself be seduced by these common bribers who offer you the Jewish dechristianization even if they use, to convince us, a few of our compatriots who have forgotten their traditions and are infidels to the teachings of the Church'.[49] Around the same time, Hermas Bastien writes of how the cinema is the greatest evil that the Québécois have faced: 'Never, in our history, has our small people been victims of an agent as deadly as the cinema. This medium propagates an exoticism which disfigures our Christian and French soul and includes modes of thinking and acting that are the most barbarous of American civilization.'[50] Further on, he writes that the cinema 'develops the kind of brute-man who gets rid of the heavy weight of his soul in order to trust his base instincts . . . the cinema represents for society . . . a slavery more pernicious than gambling, alcohol or opium.'[51]

The anti-Semitism found in these seminal texts of French Canadian nationalism requires contextualization, as its meaning is continually contested. Authors such as Mordecai Richler and Esther Delisle have contended that there was a profoundly anti-Semitic overtone to certain key aspects of early nationalism in Québec.[52] Others have responded to these critiques by stating that anti-Semitism was a very small part of the nationalist agenda of Groulx and others of the 'nationalist elite', and that their work towards formulating a French Canadian national consciousness cannot be dismissed simply because of a few egregious statements that were voiced in many places other than Québec at the time.[53] Neither of these views offers sufficient insight into the Church's fears about the cinema or the context of *L'Action française*'s anti-Semitic stance. It seems obvious that the construction of 'the Jew and the cinema' in the writings of Groulx and other *L'Action française* writers plays an important role in developing the notion of a ethnically pure collectivity. This notion of a collectivity is central to the agenda of the early right-wing religious nationalists in Québec: at its heart lies the fear that a collectivity has to protect itself from outside encroachment in order to remain pure and to survive. Well after anti-Semitic slurs had fallen away from nationalist doctrines, this guiding principle remained at the heart of right-wing nationalism in both North America and Europe. Furthermore, by uniting the Jew and cinema, the Church's two most hated enemies, Groulx was able to demonize the potential alternative public sphere of the cinema by claiming that the community which formed around it was based on foreign and inherently evil, if not blasphemous, ideals.

The hyperbole of these texts demonstrates how threatened the Church felt by the popularity of the cinema. Until 1927, advocacy for the banning of the *scopes* by clergy remained at the level of rhetoric, but soon a real event would catalyze the movement. In 1927, the Laurier cinema caught fire, leaving seventy-eight children dead.[54] This gave *L'Action française* a physical manifestation of the moral destruction they had seen in the cinema. *L'Action française* was outraged at this tragedy, and redoubled its efforts to regulate the cinema. In the February 1927 issue, Father Phillipe Perrier outlined the recommendations of the journal to combat '*le cinéma meurtrier*': first, to restrict access to the cinema for children under the age of sixteen, whether accompanied by a parent or not; second, to close all cinemas on Sunday; and, third, to censor all films that promote prurient interests.[55] Eventually the provincial government, in response to the recommendations of the Boyer Commission, passed a law making it illegal for children under the age of sixteen to enter cinemas. While this law could easily be framed as a public safety issue, it also prevented children from being influenced by the pernicious nature of the cinema. In essence, to appease the Church, the government passed a law which was designed to save the souls of the next generation from the temptations of the screen. Significantly, the government never introduced legislation on any of these other recommendations. The following year marked the development of sound – and necessarily the arrival of 'national cinemas' determined by and through language – which forever changed the landscape of film in Québec.

This essay has traced the emergence, development and trajectory of a constellation of discourses on national identity and publicness as they pertain to French Canadian filmmaking and the emergence of a potential alternative public sphere. While I do not contend that the cinema, *a priori*, existed as a counterhegemonic space within French Canadian culture between the 1900s and 1920s, I do claim that the cinema's potential as a means of resistance is present as early as the screenings of Léo-Ernest Ouimet. It is important to stress the different levels of analysis that substantiate these claims, as I argue that the 'power' of the cinema lies at the intersection of: first, the public space; second, the audience; third, the cinematic text; and fourth, the public discourses which surround the cinema. I have posited that one of the roles played by early cinema in Québecois culture has been as a site where radically shifting notions of the nation and national identity have been publicly negotiated. One could claim that these different levels of analysis are incommensurable and that the public use of space, the representation of national identity in the cinema, questions of spectatorship, and the use of the cinema as a means of reconfiguring the public sphere are issues which need to be examined separately. Nevertheless, to examine how cinema developed as an alternative public sphere and how, for a brief period, the cinema was used as a means of cultural transformation necessitates examining the points at which these different levels intersect. The public sphere itself is fed by many different types of media and discourses. As Charles Taylor notes:

> What is a public sphere? I want to describe it as a common space in which the members of society meet, through a variety of media (print, electronic) and also in face-to-face encounters, to discuss matters of common interest; and thus to be able to form a common mind about those matters. I say 'a common space' because, although the media are multiple, as well as the exchanges taking place in them, they are deemed to be in principle inter-communicating. The discussion we may be having on television right now takes account of what was said in the newspaper this morning, which in turn reports on the radio debate of yesterday, and so on.[56]

In this theoretical framework, subjects are participants in the creation and dissemination of the cultural meanings of texts. Further, to position the cinema as a site of contestation allows one to avoid the pitfall of postulating a theory which is largely substantiated through a 'reading' of a given set of films that comprise a national cinema, making both film theory and national identity fit the parameters of the 'reading'. More importantly, it allows one to examine the variety of cultural, political and historical discourses which intersect in the public sphere of which image-making becomes a part. This, in essence, removes the cinema – and film theory – solely from the hermeticism of the screening room, and positions it as a shifting and dynamic aspect of the cultural landscape.

It is important to delineate what I take to be the cultural 'impact' of the cinema within the public sphere. Adapting the critical paradigms outlined by Warner, one cannot contend that the cinema, in a simple causal manner, changed the public sphere, as if through an agency of its own.[57] Furthermore, one cannot claim that the cinema is ruled by technological specificities that are unchanging through time. In relation to eighteenth-century print technology, Warner writes: 'The assumption that technology is prior to culture results in a kind of retrodetermination whereby the political history of a technology is converted into the unfolding nature of that technology'.[58] The same must hold true for the cinema. The history of the development, projection and distribution of film points to the fact that the uses of the technology and the institutional, ideological, and cultural paradigms within which it functioned were highly contingent; filmmaking was largely determined by the contextual practices of the cultures in which the technology circulated.[59] To give but one example, the relationship between the movie camera and the Catholic Church in Québec is a highly complex and culturally specific one: the cinema was both the work of the Devil (or the Jews) and a tool used by priests to build the beginnings of a properly Québécois national identity, from their yearly screenings of *La Passion* to the ethnographic documentaries shot from the 1920s to the 1950s by travelling projectionist Father Albert Tessier, without doubt one of the unsung forefathers of *cinéma direct*.[60] These relations need to be examined in a synchronic manner, and not strictly by a causalist view of technological overdetermination. Therefore, I contend that the cinema did not 'change' the public and the State; neither did the public and the State 'change' the cinema. Instead, I believe the best way to understand the relationship of the alternative public sphere to the cinema is in a dialogical, non-linear manner. Nevertheless, I would hesitate to state that the cinema *allowed* individuals to come together and debate the concerns of the day in a rational manner and on equal ground; I would, however, contend that, at times, the cinema held the promise of this possibility, and that this promise often motivated social intervention in the real world, be it in relation to Church, state, poverty or national identity. This development, in a culture that has so often been marginalized by the dominant public sphere is, if not revolutionary, a radical reconfiguration of the social fabric of Québec.

Notes

1   See John A. Dickinson and Brian Young, *A Short History of Québec*, second edition (Toronto: Copp, Clark Pitman, 1993), pp. 233–61.

2   Michel Foucault, *The History of Sexuality, Volume One: An Introduction* (New York: Vintage, 1980), pp. 92–102.

3   For overviews of the Challenge for Change / *Société nouvelle* programmes, see Ron Burnett, 'Video/film: from communication to community', in Nancy Thede and Alain Ambrosi (eds), *Video the Changing World* (Montréal: Black Rose, 1991), pp. 54–60; Janine Marchessault, 'Reflections of the dispossessed: video and the "Challenge for Change" experiment', *Screen*, vol. 36, no. 2 (1995), pp. 131–46; and Scott MacKenzie, 'Société nouvelle: the Challenge for Change in the alternative public sphere', *Canadian Journal of Film Studies*, vol. 5, no. 2 (1996), pp. 67–84.

4   The cinema also offered a space which was not defined by gender exclusion, as was the men-only tavern in Québec. The exclusion of women from taverns was legislated by the provincial government, and the law remained in force until 1979. See Dickinson and Young, *A Short History of Québec*, p. 255.

5   Similar practices have been documented by Miriam Hansen in her study of US silent cinema, *Babel and Babylon: Spectatorship in American Silent Film* (Cambridge, MA: Harvard University Press, 1991).

6   Germain Lacasse, '*Histoires de scopes: le cinéma muet au Québec* (Montréal: Cinémathèque québéçoise, 1988), p. 5; Lacasse 'Cultural amnesia and the birth of film in Canada', *Cinema Canada*, no. 108 (1984), pp. 6–7.

7 See Léon-H. Bélanger, *Les Ouimetoscopes: Léo-Ernest Ouimet et les débuts du cinéma québécois* (Montréal: VLB Editeur, 1978), p. 18; and Hye Bossin, 'The story of L. Ernest Ouimet, film pioneer', in Hye Bossin (ed.), *Canadian Film Weekly 1952–53: Yearbook of the Canadian Motion Picture Industry* (Toronto: Film Publications of Canada, 1953), pp. 28–9.

8 Arthur Larente, 'The beginning of the moving pictures in Montréal as narrated by pioneer L. Ernest Ouimet to Arthur Larente', unpublished MS, Bibliothèque nationale du Québec, 1964.

9 Ibid., p. 2.

10 British and Colonial Press Limited, 'Advance press service of L.E. Ouimet' (Toronto: British and Colonial Press Limited, 1918), pp. 2–3.

11 See Germain Lacasse, 'Du bonimenteur québécois comme practique résistante', *Iris*, no. 22 (1996), pp. 53–66.

12 Lacasse, *Histoires de scopes*, pp. 78–9.

13 Bossin, *Canadian Film weekly 1952–53*, p. 36.

14 For more on the battles between the Ouimetoscope and the Nationoscope, see Jean-Pierre Sirois-Trahan and André Gaudreault, 'Quand la Nationoscope dama le pion au Ouimetoscope', in André Gaudreault, Germain Lacasse and Jean-Pierre Sirois-Trahan, *Au Pays des ennemis du cinéma . . .: Pour une nouvelle histoire des débuts du cinéma au Québec* (Montréal: Nuit blanche éditeur, 1996), pp. 163–74.

15 Lacasse, *Histoires de scopes*, p. 17.

16 'Le Ouimetoscope: ouverture de la nouvelle salle aujourd'hui', *La Presse*, 31 August 1907.

17 Lacasse, *Histoires de scopes*, p. 19.

18 *La Presse*, 31 August 1907.

19 Miriam Hansen, 'Early cinema, late cinema: permutations of the public sphere', *Screen*, vol. 34, no. 3 (1993), p. 201.

20 Miriam Hansen, 'Early cinema: whose public sphere?', in Thomas Elsaesser (ed.), *Early Cinema: Space, Frame, Narrative* (London: British Film Institute, 1990), pp. 228–46.

21 Hansen, *Babel and Babylon*, p. 232.

22 Ibid., pp. 231–2.

23 Ibid., pp. 60–5.

24 Lacasse, *Histoires de scopes*, p. 19.

25 Dane Lanken, *Montréal Movie Palaces: Great Theatres of the Golden Era 1884–1938* (Waterloo: Penumbra Press, 1993), p. 11.

26 Hansen, 'Early cinema, late cinema', p. 209.

27 See Tom Gunning, 'The cinema of attractions: early film, its spectator and the avant garde', in Elsaesser (ed.), *Early Cinema*, pp. 56–62.

28 André Gaudreault and Germain Lacasse, 'Montréal cinématographie au début du siècle (première période: 1895–1906)', in Gaudreault et al., *Au Pays des ennemis du cinéma*, p. 61.

29 Hye Bossin, 'They led the way: the motion picture industry in Canada marks the golden anniversary of the silver screen', in Bossin (ed.), *Canadian Film Weekly 1953–54*, p. 23.

30 Gaudreault and Lacasse, 'Montréal cinématographie au début du siècle', p. 62.

31 Lacasse, *Histoires de scopes*, p. 17.

32 Ibid., p. 20.

33 Passion Play films were not only successful in Montréal, but throughout the USA as well, which makes it difficult to determine exactly which version of the play was screened in Montréal. For more on the Passion Play and early cinema, see Charles Musser, 'Passions and the Passion Play: theatre, film and religion in America, 1880–1900', *Film History*, vol. 5, no. 4 (1993), pp. 419–56.

34   Lacasse, *Histoires de scopes*, p. 27.
35   Michael Warner, 'The mass public and the mass subject', in Craig Calhoun (ed.), *Habermas and the Public Sphere* (Cambridge, MA: MIT Press, 1990), pp. 377–401.
36   Bélanger, *Les Ouimetoscopes*, pp. 110–13.
37   Lacasse, *Histoires de scopes*, p. 17.
38   Larente, 'The beginning of moving pictures', p. 4. Larente also claims Henri Bourassa intervened on behalf of the theatre owners in their negotiations with the Canadian government. See National Archives of Canada. Visual and Sound Archives. Oral History. Interview with Arthur Larente (on cassette). Interviewer: Bill Galloway. Accession no. 1972–0012.
39   Lacasse, *Histoires de scopes*, p. 29.
40   André Gaudreault and Germain Lacasse, 'La naissance de la censure au "pays des ennemis du cinéma"', in Gaudreault et al., *Au Pays des ennemis du cinéma*, p. 105.
41   The history of the politics behind *L'Action française* can be found in Susan Mann Trofimenkoff, *Action française: French Canadian Nationalism in the Twenties* (Toronto: Viking, 1992), pp. 78–97.
42   Father Lionel Groulx, cited in 'Mot d'ordre: contre cinéma', *L'Action française* 12 (July 1924), p. 3.
43   Harry Bernard, 'L'ennemi dans la place: théâtre et cinéma', *L'Action française* 12 (August 1924), p. 70.
44   Ibid., pp. 71–2.
45   Ibid., p. 73.
46   Ibid., p. 75.
47   Ibid., p. 76.
48   Ibid., p. 79.
49   Father Phillipe Perrier, 'Contre le cinéma, tous', *L'Action française* 17 (February 1927), p. 85.
50   Hermas Bastien, 'Le cinéma déformateur', *L'Action française* 17 (March 1927), p. 168.
51   Ibid., p. 169.
52   Esther Delisle, *The Traitor and the Jew: Anti-Semitism and Extreme Right-Wing Nationalism in French Canada from 1929 to 1939*, second edition (Toronto: Robert Davies Publishing, 1993), pp. 17–35; and Mordecai Richler, *Oh Canada! Oh Québec! Requiem for a Divided Country* (Toronto: Viking, 1992), pp. 78–97.
53   Pierre Anctil, *Le Devoir, les juifs et l'immigration: de Bourassa à Laurendeau* (Québec: Institut québécois de la recherche sur la culture, 1988); Anctil, *Les Juifs de Montréal face au Québec de l'entre deux guerres: le rendezvous manqué* (Québec: Institut québécois de la recherche sur la culture, 1988); and Jean-François Lisée, 'Interview with Pierre Anctil', in William Dodge (ed.), *Boundaries of Identity: a Québec Reader* (Toronto: Lester Publishing, 1992), pp. 151–6.
54   See David Levy, '50 years later: the Laurier Palace fire', *The Montréal Gazette*, 8 January 1977, p. D–1.
55   Perrier, 'Contre le cinéma, tous', p. 84.
56   Charles Taylor, 'Liberal politics and the public sphere', in *Philosophical Arguments* (Cambridge, MA: Harvard University Press, 1995), p. 259.
57   Michael Warner, *The Republic of Letters: Publication and the Public Sphere in Eighteenth-Century America* (Cambridge, MA: Harvard University Press, 1990).
58   Ibid., p. 9.
59   For the history of the development of Canada's film industry in the light of the effects of politics, globalization and capital, see Ted Magder, *Canada's Hollywood: the Canadian State and Feature Films* (Toronto: University of Toronto Press, 1993).

60 Discussion of Tessier's work can be found in René Bouchard, *Filmographie d'Albert Tessier* (Montréal: Boréal, 1973); Bouchard, 'Un précurseur du cinéma direct', *Cinéma Québec* vol. 6, no. 1 (1977), pp. 19–24, 27–33; and David Clandfield, 'From the picturesque to the familiar: films of the French Unit at the NFB', *Ciné-tracts*, no. 4 (1978), pp. 50–62.

5 If looks could kill: image wars in *María Candelaria*

Andrea Noble

In his wittily titled essay 'All the people came and did not fit onto the screen', Mexican cultural critic Carlos Monsiváis outlines the impact that the cinema had upon Mexican society. In particular, Monsiváis is concerned with cinema's role in the modernizing processes at work in the first half of the twentieth century, as the State sought to redefine national identity and make the transition from a predominantly rural to urban, Catholic to secular, and premodern to modern cultural/political entity. In the face of the uneven social, cultural and economic effects of these processes, the role of cinema was crucial: 'With hindsight, we can see the basic function of the electronic media at their first important moment of power: they mediate between the shock of industrialization and the rural and urban experience which has not been prepared in any way for this giant change, a process that from the 1940s modifies the idea of the nation'.[1] The suggestive title of Monsiváis's essay obliquely signals the importance of the cinema's role as cultural mediator: one that was, moreover, predicated on a screen–spectator relationship. 'All the people came and did not fit onto the screen' indicates a screen–spectator relationship that promoted spectatorial identification with a repertoire of new and traditional images associated with 'Mexicanness' (*lo mexicano*) that were played out onscreen. Given that spectatorship is clearly a key issue for an understanding of the intersection between the reconfiguration of Mexican national identity in the twentieth century and the parallel development of the Mexican cinematic industry, how might we offer an account of the specificities of Mexican spectatorship?

Over the last thirty years, spectatorship as a mode of analysis has gained currency in theoretical approaches to both film and the visual arts, particularly in Anglo-American scholarship. Here is not the place to offer a detailed account of the development of this field of study: it is already well documented.[2] In this essay, which aims to address issues of spectatorship within the context of Mexican cinematic experience, the following points will underpin the discussion: (1) the dynamic exchange of looks (the gaze) that takes place in the cinema; (2) the way in which the screen addresses the spectator and the spectator's active role in the production of meaning; (3) the way in which screen images are neither innocent nor neutral, but implicated in ideological configurations of power; (4) the way in which film texts promote spectatorial identifications and thereby produce ideological subject positions.

Classic approaches to spectatorship have, however, recently become the subject of scrutiny and revision in Anglo-American film studies. They have been critiqued on the grounds of certain totalizing tendencies: on the one hand, classic studies in spectatorship tended to convert the spectator into a passive victim of the processes at work in the viewing experience; and on the other, an emphasis on psychoanalytical paradigms resulted in a tendency to foreclose the possibility of offering a more culturally and historically inflected account of viewing relations. In the words of Linda Williams in her introduction to *Viewing Positions*:

> The singular, unitary spectator of what I will, for purposes of abbreviation, call gaze theory, has gradually been challenged by diverse viewing positions. Whereas 1970s and 1980s film theory tended to posit . . . a unitary way of seeing, contemporary discussions of spectatorship emphasize the plurality and paradoxes of many different historically distinct viewing positions. The issue that now faces the once influential subfield of spectatorship within cinema and indeed all visual studies is whether it is still possible to maintain a theoretical grasp of the relations between moving images and viewers without succumbing to an anything goes pluralism.[3]

Williams's notion of the plurality and paradoxes of historically distinct viewing positions and the issue of whether it is indeed possible to offer a theoretically informed account of the screen–spectator relationship are fundamental to this discussion of the viewing subject in Mexican cinema. If moviegoing was on the rise, particularly in the 1940s during the so-called 'golden age' of Mexican cinema, and if, as Monsiváis argues, cinema took on a crucial modernizing role, then I suggest that this period also saw the emergence and formation of a specifically Mexican cinematic gaze. However, this gaze did not simply emerge from a cultural vacuum. Rather, it will be my contention that the gaze has a history in Mexico, a history whose origins can be located in the matrix of looking relations that developed prior to the advent of cinema in the twentieth century, namely in the colonial period. Despite the ideological chasm that separates them, the gaze that is subject to the processes of modernization in the 1940s and the gaze constituted in the colonial period overlap in surprising and significant ways. In what follows, I explore *María Candelaria* (Emilio Fernández, 1944) as a film that furnishes a field upon which historical conflicts and transformations at the level of the gaze are registered and inscribed. There will be two interconnected strands to my argument. The first is concerned with the film's intradiegetic looking relations; the second with the convergence of intradiegetic with extradiegetic looking relations within the context of the cinematic experience in 1940s Mexico.

Set in 1909, *María Candelaria* is narrated in the form of a flashback triggered by a conversation that takes place between a woman journalist (Beatriz Ramos) and an unnamed painter (Alberto Galán), in which the latter explains to the former his motives for refusing to sell his famous nude painting of an Indian woman. (This frame narrative and particularly the famous painting will become central to my discussion below.) The indigenous woman in question is María Candelaria, ostracized by nearly all in her community (on the grounds that her mother was a prostitute), except Lorenzo Rafael (Pedro Armendáriz). The idealistic but impecunious couple plan to marry. María Candelaria, however, falls ill with malaria and, denied the state-provided quinine by the villainous don Damián (Miguel Inclán), Lorenzo Rafael breaks into don Damián's shop and steals the quinine along with a dress. Lorenzo Rafael is imprisoned and, in order to secure the money for his release, María Candelaria agrees to model for the painter, who early on in the film becomes enraptured by her 'indigenous beauty'. On discovering that the painter wishes her to model for a nude study, María Candelaria refuses, leaving the painter to complete his image based on the body of another Indian woman. The villagers see the painting and, assuming that María Candelaria has indeed modelled for it, burn her home and stone her to death.

What particularly interests me about *María Candelaria* is that at the centre of Fernández's film lies a contest between two clearly delineated gazes with origins in the colonial period. The loci of these gazes are embodied in the unnamed painter and Lorenzo Rafael, who represent white *criollo* versus indigenous Mexico respectively. These two characters engage in a struggle over the right to possess María Candelaria that is presented in both visual and economic terms. The spectator witnesses this conflict in the scene set, significantly, in a marketplace in which the painter first encounters María Candelaria. He offers to purchase all María Candelaria's flowers, a transaction that would resolve the couple's economic problems, in return for permission to paint her. Lorenzo Rafael angrily denies him consent and, muttering some unsubtitled words in Nahuatl, the indigenous language, hastily sends María Candelaria away. Later in the film, after Lorenzo Rafael's imprisonment, he stubbornly refuses the painter the right to represent María Candelaria, accepting the painter's 'sweetener' also to paint him; but is emphatic that 'as far as painting María Candelaria is concerned, I prefer you not to'. Such a substitution (him for her), however, is not a viable option. Within the painter's (and the film's) visual economy, María Candelaria's commodity value resides in what she represents, namely 'the very face of Mexico' ('el rostro mismo de México'). Or, as an object belonging to an enduring western painterly tradition, namely the female nude, María Candelaria might more aptly be described as 'the very body of Mexico'.[4] In other words, the contest that lies at the heart of the film revolves around the right to gaze not just upon a woman, but upon the (feminine) embodiment of the nation.

That the film semiotizes María Candelaria as 'Mexico' is made abundantly clear throughout. Moreover 'Mexico', as embodied (and en*visage*d?) by María Candelaria is an essentially syncretic, hybrid entity. In her detailed discussion of the film, Joanne Hershfield points out that the opening sequence establishes an association between the female indigenous subject, the pre-Columbian past and the post-Columbian present:

> A montage of pre-Columbian images illustrating this indigenous past ends with a shot of a young Indian woman standing next to the stone figure of an Aztec woman that has the same high cheekbones and proud facial expression as the live woman. . . . Fernández's shot specifically links that past to the present through his representation of Mexico's 'eternal' Indianness.[5]

This metonymic chain of associations, in which woman-as-cultural-artefact links past to present, is further extended to María Candelaria, whose parallel status in the frame narrative as artefact is manifest in the presence of the fateful painting and the curiosity that it arouses. She too is linked to the imagistic dialogue between pre-Columbian past and post-Columbian present established within the film's diegesis and made explicit in the painter's explanation of what the famous painting depicts: 'an Indian of pure Mexican race. As you can see, this Indian possessed the beauty of the ancient princesses whom the *conquistadores* came to subjugate'.

But even as María Candelaria is associated with pure indigenous 'essence', she is also an embodiment of the post-Columbian Mexican Virgin of Guadalupe.[6] There are two key moments in the film in which this association is dramatically crystallized. The most obvious occurs after Lorenzo Rafael is imprisoned, when María Candelaria visits the church to remonstrate with a statue of the Virgin: 'why don't you listen to me? . . . you are hard on us' ('¿y tú por qué no me oyes? . . . con nosotros eres dura'). At this point, the film cuts from María Candelaria, with her hands in a gesture of prayer and uplifted face framed by her shawl, to the statue of the Virgin in order to draw a clear visual analogy between the two figures. Less obviously but no less significantly, earlier in the film Lupe (Margarita Cortés), María Candelaria's jealous rival for Lorenzo Rafael's affections, casts a stone and shatters an image of the Virgin of Guadalupe in María Candelaria's humble home. This act of violent iconoclasm prefigures the circumstances of the latter's tragic demise, stoned to death by members of her own community. Given the Virgin of Guadalupe's status as a unifying national symbol in Mexico, the pure and virginal María Candelaria's own symbolic burden as 'the very face/body of Mexico' is further reinforced.

By foregrounding the conflict in the main body of the narrative between the white *criollo* painter and the indigenous Lorenzo Rafael over the right to possess María Candelaria as quintessential 'Mexican' artefact, the film invokes an originary moment in the history of looking relations in Mexico. Such a history has been plotted by ethnohistorian Serge Gruzinski in his fascinating study *La guerra de las imágenes/The War of Images* which, as the title signals, narrates the conquest of Mexico and the colonial society to which it gave rise in terms of a visual conflict. That is to say,

Gruzinski reads the conquest and colonization of Mexico as a struggle by one culture to impose a system of visual representation upon another in an analysis in which concepts of the gaze and power occupy charged and contested positions. A number of points emerge from the study that are extremely productive for the present discussion. The first is Gruzinski's notion of the conquest as a clash between two competing and radically different visual traditions in which he notes: 'a radical abyss separated the two worlds: the Indians did not share the Spanish concept of the image'.[7] The abyss separating the two revolves around the fact that while Christian iconography is predicated upon the notion of representation, such a concept cannot readily be transferred to comparable indigenous iconographic traditions. In other words, the Spaniards' relationship to their religious icons was founded upon an essential understanding of the distinction between the signifier and the signified: an icon of the Virgin Mary is *not* the Virgin Mary but an anthropomorphically fashioned object that stands in for a transcendentally located entity that is other to the icon itself. By contrast, the indigenous eye recognized no such radical split between signifier and signified in a belief system in which the 'divine' is not trans-cendental, but instead effective presence and immanence. Gruzinski elaborates upon the indigenous system of 'representation' by recourse to the Nahuatl term *Ixiptla*:

> The Nahuatl notion [*Ixiptla*] did not take for granted a similarity of form. . . . The *Ixiptla* was the receptacle of a power, the recognizable, epiphanic presence, the actualization of a force with which an object was imbued, a 'being-there', where indigenous thought was in no hurry to distinguish the divine essence and its material support. It was not an appearance or a visual illusion that referred to somewhere else, to a 'beyond'. In this sense, *Ixiptla* was located on the margins of the image: it underlined the immanence of the forces that surround us, whilst the Christian image, by way of an inverse displacement, one of ascension, gives rise to an elevation towards a personal god, it is a flight from the copy to the prototype guided by the similarity that unifies them.[8]

Given the radically different indigenous and Spanish visual systems, the colonization of Mexico not only involved the imposition of Catholic icons, but also the re-education of the indigenous gaze through a politics of the image which consisted of saturating the visual sphere with a new social and cultural imaginary. In this way, the image came to play a constitutive role in the construction of colonial society, whereby:

> the image revealed to the Indian his/her new body, the visible flesh of which covered an invisible soul. By means of perspective, it assigned him/her a spectator's point of view outside of the visual field, but privileged, a spectator whose look and whose body participated fully in the contemplation that the image established. A spectator endowed ideally with a 'moral eye' which,

thanks to free will and faith was supposed to master the real image in order to free him/herself from the deception of the devil and the traps of idolatry.[9]

It does not require much imagination to see that the immensity and complexity of the task of visual colonialism in hand was to produce uneven, contested effects, and that the carefully orchestrated politics of the image was to run out of the church's control. The resulting war of images, according to Gruzinski, gave rise to an essentially syncretic, hybrid cultural imaginary. Hybrid, it must be stressed, not only in the sense of physical objects that partook of both indigenous and Spanish systems of representation, but hybrid also precisely at the level of the gaze, in that two very different systems for visualizing the world converged in the colonized viewing subject.

As William Rowe and Vivian Shelling point out, Gruzinski's analysis of colonial relations is extremely valuable for 'the comprehensiveness with which it distinguishes between different levels and modes of interaction without reducing them to the binary of dominant versus subordinated'.[10] Having taken a brief detour via Gruzinski's exploration of colonial looking relations, I shall now consider how such a refusal of reduction might inflect an understanding of the visual struggle between the painter and Lorenzo Rafael over the right to possess María Candelaria. Reading Fernández's film through the prism of Gruzinski's analysis, I would suggest that the narrative syncretically encodes María Candelaria simultaneously as indigenous 'idol' and Catholic 'icon' precisely through her association with, and status as, a visual image. As such she becomes the locus of a visual conflict which echoes the encounter between the colonizing gaze of the *criollo* painter and the resistant gaze of the indigenous male subject, who hurries to hide away his 'effigy' (idol or icon?). In this way, Lorenzo Rafael's action can be seen to replicate that of the post-conquest Indians, who according to Gruzinski: 'Faced with Spanish iconoclasm, the Indians organized their response which was, above all, defensive. By any means possible they tried to hide their gods from the invader'.[11]

This visual conflict, nevertheless, raises not only colonial, but also gender issues. To the critical eye steeped in the traditions of feminist film and visual theory, the resonances of María Candelaria's positioning hardly require spelling out. As the film invokes an originary colonial scenario, it also reproduces a time-honoured trope whereby Woman (in this case Indigenous Woman) functions as object-of-the-gaze thereby providing the grounds for an exchange of looks. Elizabeth Grosz has the following to say about the implications for this kind of gendered positioning:

[W]hile women are the conditions of symbolic exchange and thus of culture, they function as objects of exchange. . . . This means that the social order and the exchange relations which guarantee it are hommosocial [*sic*] relations between men alone. Women are merely the 'excuses', the 'goods' and mediating objects, linking men to each other.[12]

As a mediating object with symbolic resonances, María Candelaria (both woman and painted image) bespeaks the different histories that fuse to make modern Mexico. But, more than this, her 'Mexican embodiment' points to the co-existence within the film of different loci of the gaze. Furthermore, if María Candelaria, visually codified as cultural artefact, represents the conceptual space for an exchange of competing looks with vestiges of colonial looking relations, then there is a third party in this visual conflict whose gaze has yet to come into focus within this discussion: the spectator of the film who is implicitly positioned within the over-lapping and contradictory discourses of 1940s modernization and these older colonial looking relations. This viewing subject of *María Candelaria* is structured into the film text in quite specific ways that require further elucidation and which revolve around the presence of the painting in which a series of meanings is condensed. This painting, I suggest, is moreover linked to the modernization of the spectator's gaze.

A particularly striking feature of the frame narrative of *María Candelaria* is the way in which it sets the spectator up in the expectation that he[13] is to see the image depicted upon the canvas. This expectation is, however, thoroughly thwarted. Anticipation is built up gradually across a number of shots that I will describe in detail. After the opening montage sequence featuring the pre-Columbian figures and model, the spectator is first presented with a long shot of an artist's studio establishing the positions of the painter seated at his easel, his model and the group of journalists behind him. There follows a medium shot focusing on the journalists and the painter at his easel which, while presented side on, is clearly a visually important element in the shot, another device to arouse curiosity and suspense. The assembled journalists conduct their interview as the painter continues his work. The film then cuts to a medium close-up, this time foregrounding the woman journalist and the painter, at which point the woman's questions turn to the painter's famous image which, she says, everyone is talking about, but no one has ever seen. That the painter is visibly disturbed by this line of questioning is figured by a series of shot/reverse-shots between painter and journalist. At this point the spectator catches the first glimpse of the canvas currently in progress, thereby establishing an auditory/visual connection between learning of, and seeing, that other painting.

The spectator's desire to see the painting is intensified by the painter's hyperbolic language when referring to the image: 'There are things that simply by being touched bleed – do you understand me? This is one of them. I painted this painting many years ago but I cannot think of it without horror because it was the cause of a tragedy'. Once the other journalists have left the studio, the painter reluctantly agrees to show the notorious painting to the woman journalist, whereupon the spectator sees the two mount the stairs before there is a cut to the upstairs room in which the painting is stored under wraps. A deep focus shot brings into view both the easel in close-up to the left hand of the frame, and the door in long-shot, through which the journalist and painter pass in order to reach the painting itself. It is significant to note that the deep shot means that the spectator 'reaches' the painting before the journalist or painter, once again intensifying the spectator's sense of anticipation. Now positioned in front of the easel, the painter lights a lamp and throws off the cloth to reveal the canvas to the journalist, whose surprise is registered in a medium close-up of her face whereby the camera occupies the place of the easel. At this point, filmic convention dictates a reverse shot from the journalist's point of view, which of course would afford the spectator a glimpse of the image. But no such shot occurs and the spectator is left as the only participant in the scene not to have caught sight of the image on the canvas. Although the painting does not make another appearance until towards the end of the film – when the spectator, unlike the villagers, is privy to its making and thereby witnesses María Candelaria's refusal to model naked – nevertheless, the image on the canvas is never manifest visually except through others' reaction to it.

Given that the spectator's heightened expectation of seeing the canvas is structured into the film through elements of mise-en-scene, dialogue and point-of-view conventions, why does the spectator never get to see the fatal image? To understand the spectator's frustrated gaze, I suggest that it is essential to contextualize the spectator in broad terms as a subject constituted by what Ella Shohat and Robert Stam term 'ambient discourses and ideologies', which in the case of 1940s Mexico revolve around cultural nationalism.[14]

The rise of cinema in the 1940s in Mexico coincided with the heightened cultural nationalism of the post-Revolutionary period, a project in which, as throughout the colonial period detailed by Gruzinski, the visual was to occupy a privileged position. John Mraz argues that 1940s cultural nationalism must be seen as a product of an 'authentic' search for identity and an ideological imposition. The first was a consequence of having lived through a Revolution (1910–20) that redefined Mexico, and the processes of urbanization and industrialization that were transforming the country. The second was an imposition of the political ideology of *Alemanismo* (a political ideology named after President Miguel Alemán, 1940–46), which utilised nationalism to cover up US domination and to obfuscate class struggle. As Mraz states:

> The period was marked by the development of the ideology of a form of 'Mexicanness' without contradictions. The divergences and differences that had characterized *Cardenismo* were replaced by an insistence on 'national unity'. Carlos Monsiváis defined the spirit of the epoch as 'Nothing to do with "plural country" or "diversity of cultures", *Mexico is one*.'[15]

The challenge that confronted cultural nationalism, then, was how to create a coherent notion of Mexican identity in the face of the fissures and discontinuities that were the product of a multi-ethnic body politic. As an integral dimension of cultural nationalism, *indigenista* discourses sought to retrieve a pristine notion of the myriad and diverse Indian communities and to incorporate it within the boundaries of the modern nation state. This retrieval took place across a range of cultural spheres, including the visual arts and film and, to put it crudely, involved a celebratory and yet deeply ambivalent representation of the 'Indian' as a national figure. The 'Indian' was at once revered as the receptacle of authentically Mexican values, yet whose resistance to the processes of modernization threatened to call them into question.

At the forefront of cinematic cultural nationalism, Emilio 'el Indio' Fernandez has passed into Mexican film lore as the originator of a specifically Mexican national cinema. Julia Tuñón states that his 'basic concern was to produce a Mexican cinema: "I dreamt and am still dreaming of a different cinema, of course, but Mexican, pure. Now I have this great desire to Mexicanize the Mexicans, for we are becoming Americanized"'.[16] To 'Mexicanize the Mexicans' involved, on the one hand, a new repertoire of stories and images; it also entailed, on the other, mobilizing the spectator, by drawing upon historically contingent looking relations. In other words, to pick up on the tantalisingly open title of Gruzinski's book – *La guerra de las imágenes: de Cristóbal Colón a Blade Runner / The War of Images: From Christopher Columbus to Blade Runner* – in the twentieth century the moving image takes up where the still, sacred image of previous epochs left off. However, if previously the Church had striven to Christianize the gaze, it fell to cinema in the twentieth century to modernize that same gaze.[17] Indeed, in his study, Gruzinski picks up on the modernizing role of the cinema in the 1940s, remarking:

> The images of Mexican cinema, during its Golden Age in particular, prepared the rural and urban masses for the traumas of industrialization of the forties; they expressed an imaginary which, in accord with the radio, successively undermined or brought tradition up to date, initiating the masses into the modern world through its mythic figures: Pedro Armendáriz, Dolores del Río, María Félix and many others.[18]

Gruzinski, furthermore, in a brief but suggestive footnote that focuses specifically on *María Candelaria*, proposes that the painting at the centre of the film is a 'symbol of modern Mexico' ('símbolo de México moderno').[19] If, as Gruzinski himself argues, cinema was involved in the process of modernization, why then was the very subject of this process (that is, the spectator) prevented from seeing this symbol of modern Mexico? How, moreover, can an absent painting symbolize a nation? I would like to suggest that these basic paradoxes lend themselves to a particular reading of the relationship between the 1940s viewing subject and the onscreen painting. Namely, the modernity of this symbol can only be apprehended by the modernized gaze, a gaze structured into the film text, and one that was being actively produced by and through the cinematic experience.

In *María Candelaria*, if the spectator constitutes a frustrated participant in the struggle to see the painting, his gaze is, nevertheless, confronted with a range of looking relations: these alternately promote identification with the characters on the screen and prevent such identification from taking place. Such identification with and distanciation from the painter and the indigenous denizens of Xochimilco, in particular, at once reverberate with the power dynamics of the colonial visual sphere, and, at the same time, are constitutive of the modernizing process. The painter himself may, as Gruzinski's footnote suggests, be the creator of a 'symbol of modern Mexico', but this does not imply that the film presents him as necessarily the locus of the modern gaze. Insofar as the painter's gaze is associated with elite cultural values with ties to colonial social relations, his character invites little or no spectatorial identification.[20] As Hershfield argues, the painter's intervention in the frame narrative can be read as an attempt to absolve himself of his guilt in the murder of María Candelaria.[21] No matter how much he may deny his agency in the frame narrative – 'there are times when life converts one into an instrument of other people's misfortunes' ('hay veces cuando la vida le convierte a uno en instrumento de la desgracia ajena') – as María Candelaria's story unfolds, the painter's fundamental misunderstanding of the culture into which he has intruded becomes clear to the spectator.[22] Drawing the indigenous Other into his own iconographic scheme, in a gesture that echoes an older colonizing gaze, leads to her death. Or, to put it another way, within the visual logic of *María Candelaria*, looks can, and indeed do, kill.

Significantly, however, the painter is not the sole locus of the deadly look; his gaze is conjoined with that of the Indian villagers who perform the actual murder, stoning María Candelaria to death. Moreover, just as the spectator (recognizes and) rejects participation in the painter's colonizing gaze, the film prevents identification with the Indian denizens of Xochimilco. The film seems to set up a clear distinction between María Candelaria and Lorenzo Rafael and what Emilio García Riera terms the *populacho*.[23] On the whole, the *populacho* is presented as a collective, as at the beginning of the film when the villagers prevent María Candelaria from selling her flowers; or again in the final scenes when she is stoned to death. Collective cinematic identity perforce functions here to prevent close spectatorial identification. Furthermore, those members of the *populacho* who are individuated are presented as violently jealous (Lupe), shrill (*La chismosa*, Lupe Inclán) or downright primitive (*La huesera*, Lupe del Castillo).

Identification and distanciation are not only promoted in terms of characterization, however, but also at the level of the gaze. For the gaze associated with the *populacho* is suffused with dissonant vestiges of both pre- and post-conquest looking relations and is presented, moreover, as decidedly premodern. The palimpsestic complexity of this gaze is manifest in two key iconoclastic moments in the film. First, there is the scene already mentioned, in which Lupe jealously casts the stone, shattering María Candelaria's icon of the Virgin of Guadalupe. As suggested earlier, this scene at once establishes a link between the Virgin and María Candelaria and also prefigures her violent murder at the end of film. Where in the earlier scene Lupe's iconoclastic impulse is directed towards an image, that is to say, towards the signifier, in the later scene the target of the *populacho*'s scandalized violence is instead the signified (María Candelaria) and not the signifier (the painting). Viewed in tandem, these two iconoclastic moments bespeak a profoundly ambivalent attitude towards the concept of visual representation. To the extent that there is a slippage between signifier and signified, I would suggest that these acts of iconoclasm reveal vestiges of a pre-conquest visual schemata that find echo in Gruzinski's explanation of *Ixiptla*. This slippage between signifier and signified within the terms of the film has disastrous consequences for the object of this gaze, María Candelaria.

If these iconoclastic acts resonate with pre-conquest looking relations, nevertheless, the same pre-conquest gaze is overwritten with what Gruzinski terms the post-conquest 'moral eye'. According to Gruzinski, during the colonial war of images, the Spaniards imposed their Christian concept of morality upon the indigenous masses. It is this imposed colonial 'moral eye' that is so scandalized by María Candelaria's 'immoral' act of posing nude. The film, however, associates the scandalized eye not with insight, but rather with metaphorical blindness. In this context it is interesting to note that Alexander S. Dawson, in his discussion of *Indigenismo* in the 1920–40 period, argues that influential *indigenistas* such as Carlos Basauri 'applauded the absence of Catholic domination in [some indigenous] communities by commenting that 'among some tribes the virginity of women is not held in the same high esteem as can be seen among Western cultures'. This fact showed that indigenous peoples were in some sense far more liberated than most Mexicans, and offered a future course for change.'[24] Clearly, the Xochimilcans depicted in Fernández's film do not belong to the 'enlightened' Indians celebrated by Basauri. However, the film does espouse the latter's view extradiegetically in the way in which it promotes spectatorial distanciation from the 'primitive' gaze of these Indian subjects.

This distanciation takes place on a number of levels. First, the opening intertitles describe the events about to be witnessed as 'a tragedy of love snatched from an indigenous corner of Mexico, Xochimilco in the year 1909' ('una tragedia de amor arrancada de un rincón indígena de México, Xochimilco en el año 1909'). In this way, the urban spectator viewing the film in the 1940s is distanced both temporally and geographically from the events on the screen. Second, in general terms and as suggested, given that the convention of cinematic identification is predicated upon individualization, the *populacho* as collective protagonist prevents identification. Third, the spectator has information – María Candelaria does not in fact pose nude – that the violent *populacho* does not possess. The spectator's superior knowledge ultimately confirms the *populacho*'s scandalized morality as hollow. And fourth, the spectator, whilst he does not see the final painting itself, nevertheless does witness the scene of its making and therefore catches sight of the naked model (Nieves) on whose body the final, composite image is based. This last point is crucially important to an understanding of the modernizing process at work in the viewing experience.

Even though the spectator knows that María Candelaria does not pose naked for the image, the distance and fundamental difference between the premodern gaze of the *populacho* and the spectator's 'gaze-being-modernized' is ultimately reinforced by the act of witnessing the scene of painting. What for the *populacho* is so scandalous that it is led to commit murder is perfectly acceptable for the spectator of the film in the 1940s. The naked model Nieves is introduced so unobtrusively as to pass as 'normal', and as such serves as an index of the modernity of the 'liberated' gaze.

All this is to say that the spectator of *María Candelaria* is presented with the spectacle of looking relations in which certain historically resonant gazes are intimately associated with violence and death. What, though, are the ideological implications of such an association for an understanding of the positioning of the spectator within the ongoing war of images in 1940s Mexican cinema? By way of conclusion, I want to suggest that the clue to understanding spectatorial positioning lies in the painting, whose presence, *Meninas*-like, haunts both the film and this discussion. In fact, Velázquez's seminal painting arguably holds the key to the final significance that I wish to attach to the painted image and attendant issues of spectatorship in *María Candelaria*. After Foucault, *Las Meninas* has become synonymous with self-reflexivity, where the painting-within-the-painting signals the work of (painterly) representation.[25] Furthermore, *Las Meninas* is widely considered the first painting within the canon of western art history to foreground the position of the spectator. To return to Fernández's film, the painting-within-the-film can be seen to share an analogous status to that of its art-historical counterpart.[26] In *María Candelaria*, however, if the painting foregrounds the work of representation, then this self-reflexive gesture points to the cinematic apparatus itself. And, in Fernandez's film the combination of the invisible painting and the painting as signifier of the work of cinematic representation is consistent with the fact that the spectator is not privileged with so much as a glimpse of the symbol of *México moderno*. Why might this be so? I would like to suggest that this is because *México moderno* does not exist as an object, but rather as a relationship: *México moderno* cannot be represented on the canvas, but instead resides in the relay of looks between the screen and the spectator. Moreover, as I have shown, this relay of looks is older than cinema itself, imbued as it is with the charged and contested remnants of nearly five hundred years of looking relations.

Given that the majority of work on spectatorship has developed within the context of Anglo-American film theory, is it then possible to offer a theoretically informed account of looking relations within the context of the Mexican cinema? If the response is simply to impose a ready-made body of theory onto this cinematic context, I would suggest that the answer is no. Such impositions amount to nothing more than colonizing gestures that cannot hope to offer an account of the specificities of Mexican looking relations, which are themselves the products of colonial encounters. If, however, the response is to take such theoretical insights as a starting point, rethinking them within the specific context of Mexican cultural history and the privileged position of the visual within that history, then, and only then, do the complexities and ambiguities of such looking relations come into focus.

Notes

1   Carlos Monsiváis, 'All the people came and did not fit onto the screen: notes on the cinema audience in Mexico', in Paulo Antonio Paranaguá (ed.), *Mexican Cinema* (London: British Film Institute, 1995), p. 151.

2   For an overview of spectatorship studies see Susan Hayward, *Key Concepts in Cinema Studies* (London: Routledge, 1996). For a more detailed discussion see Judith Mayne, *Cinema and Spectatorship* (London: Routledge, 1993).

3   Linda Williams (ed.), *Viewing Positions: Ways of Seeing Films* (New Brunswick, NJ: Rutgers University Press, 1994), p. 4.

4   See Lynda Nead, *The Female Nude: Art, Obscenity and Sexuality* (London: Routledge, 1992) for a detailed discussion of the status and significance of the female nude within the western iconographic tradition.

5   Joanne Hershfield, *Mexican Woman: Mexican Cinema* (Tucson, AZ: University of Arizona Press, 1996), p. 55.

6   See Jaques Lafaye, *Quetzalcoatl and Guadalupe: the Formation of Mexican National Consciousness, 1531–1813*, trans. Benjamin Keen (Chicago, IL: University of Chicago Press, 1974).

7   Serge Gruzinski, *La guerra de las imágenes: de Cristóbal Colón a 'Blade Runner'* (1492–2019), trans. Juan José Utrilla (Mexico City: Fondo de Cultura Económica, 1990), p. 60. All given translations from this book into English are the author's.

8   Ibid., p. 61.

9   Ibid., p. 100.

10   William Rowe and Vivian Schelling, *Memory and Modernity: Popular Culture in Latin America* (London: Verso, 1991), p. 45.

11   Gruzinski, *La guerra de las imágenes*, p. 62.

12   Elizabeth Grosz, *Sexual Subversions* (London: Allen and Unwin, 1989), p. 147.

13   Julianne Burton Carvajal asserts that up until the 1970s, moviegoing in Mexico was primarily a family experience: 'La ley del más padre: melodrama paternal, melodrama partriarcal, y la especificidad del ejemplo mexicano', *Archivos de la Filmoteca*, no. 16 (1994), p. 51. Given that the sexual politics of *María Candelaria* construct an implied male spectator, I have elected to use the masculine pronoun.

14   Here I am indebted to the work of Ella Shohat and Robert Stam in *Unthinking Eurocentrism: Multiculturalism and the Media* (London: Routledge, 1992). In the final chapter, 'Multiculturalism in the postmodern age', Shohat and Stam propose that a comprehensive ethnography of spectatorship 'must distinguish multiple registers' of which I have adopted three, namely 'the spectator as fashioned by the text itself'; 'the spectator fashioned by the institutional contexts of spectatorship'; and finally 'the spectator as constituted by ambient discourses and ideologies' (p. 350).

15   John Mraz, 'Lo gringo en el cine mexicano y la ideología alemanista', in Ignacio Durán, Iván Trujillo and Mónica Verea (eds), *México-Estados Unidos: encuentros y desencuentros en el cine* (Mexico City: Filmoteca UNAM/IMCINE/CISAN, 1996), p. 86. Author's translation.

16   Julia Tuñón, 'Emilio Fernández: a look behind the bars', in Paranaguá, *Mexican Cinema*, p. 184.

17 Alejandro Rozado makes a similar point in his fascinating study, *Cine y realidad social en México: una lectura de la obra de Emilio Fernández* (Guadalajara: Universidad de Guadalajara/Centro de Investigación y Enseñanza Cinematográficas, 1991), p. 19.

18 Gruzinski, *La guerra de las imágenes*, p. 211.

19 Ibid., p. 212.

20 The painter, however, offers a realistic social characterization of the Mexican muralists (especially Diego Rivera) who, in the post-revolutionary period, were busy establishing a celebratory iconography of the Indian within the space of the nation. As Laura Podalsky points out in her excellent discussion of the film that problematizes the emergent tradition of Indian representation, the model in *María Candelaria* is none other than the one used by Rivera. Laura Podalsky, 'Disjointed frames: melodrama, naturalism and representation in 1940s Mexico', *Studies in Latin American Popular Culture*, no. 15 (1993), pp. 57–73.

21 Hershfield, *Mexican Cinema/Mexican Woman*, p. 57.

22 In *Cine y realidad social en México*, Rozado argues that the painter is a well-intentioned lover of Indian beauty' (p. 84). Although Rozado's neglected study is extremely insightful and breaks the primarily historiographical mould of much Mexican film criticism, I find this reading of the painter difficult to sustain.

23 The word *populacho* means the masses but with a pejorative inflection. Emilio García Riera, *Historia documental del cine mexicano, Volume 3, 1943–1945* (Guadalajara: Universidad de Guadalajara, 1992), p. 67.

24 Alexander S. Dawson, 'From models for the nation to model citizens: *Indigenismo* and the "revindication" of the Mexican Indian, 1920–40', *Journal of Latin American Studies*, no. 30 (1998), p. 290.

25 Michel Foucault, *The Order of Things: an Archaeology of the Human Sciences*, (London: Tavistock, 1970).

26 In an analysis of another Fernández film, *Enamorada* (1946), also with an important narrative focus on a painting, Jean Franco suggests that the particular scene involving the painting 'points to the importance of representation as a way of mediating conflicts. Indeed, portraits were commonly used in Hollywood film when emphasis was being placed on the work of representation.' Jean Franco, *Plotting Women: Gender and Representation in Mexico* (London: Verso, 1989), p. 150.

6 Pictures of the past in the present: modernity, femininity and stardom in the postwar films of Ozu Yasujiro

Alastair Phillips

I have always been struck by the emotionally charged scene in Ozu Yasujiro's *Tokyo monogatari/Tokyo Story* (1953)[1] in which the visiting grandmother, played by Higashiyama Chieko, takes her young grandson for a walk outside his house. Her visit will probably be the last time that she will see the boy, for she has to return to the distant town of Onomichi by the sea. The grandson plays while the grandmother wonders aloud about her old age and what will become of the young boy. The scene might well embody all the sentimental appeal of the classical Zen notion of *mono no aware* (loosely translated as the notion of the fleeting transience of all things), but it also seems to me to present another issue, one that is more firmly located in the specific instance of the year of the film's release. It would have been well known to the audience of the time that the world the grandson was going to inherit would be vastly different from that known by his grandmother. The reconstruction of the Japanese nation following defeat at the end of World War II and the end of the US occupation meant that the traditions of the grandmother's generation were dissolving. If these traditions were perhaps not being replaced, they were certainly being renegotiated by a new interpretation of a nationally specific modernity. In other words, through a nuanced demonstration of feminine emotion, this scene articulates a sense of transition which must have had a bearing not just on the 1950s audience's feelings about themselves and their own mortality, but also on their broader feelings about their relationship to the nation as a whole.

In this essay, I shall turn away from the well trodden path of a number of western critics who have primarily seen the need to place Ozu in formalistic terms by arguing that his films look and feel significantly different from the western canon.[2] Instead, I want to highlight the fact that his work falls almost entirely within the genre of the Japanese *gendai geki* – the contemporary drama. By choosing not to focus on any distinctive employment of timeless Japanese aesthetic strategies, the director's postwar films, I shall propose, should be understood as an engagement with the depiction of contemporaneous social change and its specific effect on gendered cultural milieux and social relationships. I shall suggest that they vividly enact a particular contestation between tradition and progress in Japan's immediate postwar social order at a time when the concept of a new formulation of nationhood was intertwined with a concurrent and inevitable sense of loss due to change. By looking especially at questions of femininity and stardom, I shall argue that the central issues of modernity and national identity, which run as a continuous theme in these films, also need to be examined in relation to a number of gender-related social, cultural, political and economic contexts – such as new patterns of consumption and work practice, shifts in the family structure and different perceptions of womanhood in Japanese society. I shall be asking, therefore, whether these films were popular as much for the particular roles their female stars played and where these performances were placed, as for any intrinsic sense of aesthetic uniqueness. In other words, was it perhaps through the specific interaction of female stardom and the representation of female social space that the contestation between the seemingly irreconcilable elements of tradition and transition was actually articulated?

As a subset of the *gendai geki*, the *shomin geki* or home-life drama, films like *Banshun/Late Spring* (1949),[3] *Bakushu/Early Summer* (1951)[4] and *Tokyo Story* clearly deal with questions of continuity, tradition, timelessness, memory and change from a strong female perspective. Ozu's postwar work for the Shochiku studios at Ofuna, under the managing guidance of Kido Shiro, achieved a reputation among a popular, especially female, audience for humanistic, everyday fictions that evoked a carefully constructed mix of social criticism, comedy and melodrama. These films generally had a distinctive emotional timbre which would deal with a commonly recognizable social reality but imbue it with what was critically termed a 'positive warm-hearted'[5] approval. The themes of memory and tradition are given an extra dimension by being placed in a mode of representation which itself emphasizes a sort of filmic heritage. Ozu and his regular team of fellow filmmakers – which included the scriptwriter Noda Kogo, the set designer Hamada Tatsuo and the cinematographer Atsuta Yuharu – used the flavour of the Shochiku genre and the repertoire of Shochiku stars and character actors to produce a recognizable product that had its own particular currency for the national audience.[6] This currency would have circulated in the film magazines and among the expectations of the filmgoer prior to and during the viewing of a new release. Even today, for most Japanese people it is impossible to think of Ozu without also thinking of the intertextual qualities of Hara Setsuko's daughter figure and the mothers, aunts and sisters played by the likes of Sugimura Haruko, Tanaka Kinuyo and Miyake Kuniko.

This dynamic interrelationship between Japan's vibrant popular film culture and the mass female audience has a long tradition, dating from the early stages of the nation's industrialization at the turn of the century, when new patterns of urban production and consumption emerged in relation to working women. If it is true that there were still significant debates about the relevance and desirability of actually having female performers on screen well into the 1910s, as Joanne Bernardi has amply demonstrated in her pioneering research into early Japanese cinema,[7] one may nonetheless note the proliferation of new classes of Japanese female consumers and spectators in the burgeoning city economies of offices and department stores, coffee shops and textile factories. These women developed highly specific and sophisticated tastes with regard to performers and actors. It was no accident, then, that the place of women in Japanese culture was central to debates over the nature and the direction of Japan's modernity throughout the century, and that Ozu's contemporary dramas, especially those of the postwar years, spoke directly to these concerns. This is not to say that Ozu's dramas were the only examples of this phenomenon. A detailed archaeology of the multiple relationships between female stardom and popular feminine genre cinema of the period has yet to be undertaken, but one might mention, for instance such contemporaneous films and actresses as Takamine Hideko in Kinoshita Keisuke's *Nijuyon no hitomi / Twenty Four Eyes* (1954), Tanaka Kinuyo in Gosho Heinsuke's *Entotsu no mieru basho / Where Chimneys are Seen* (1953) and Hara Setsuko again in Naruse Mikio's *Meshi / Repast* (1951), the latter being based on a work by the popular women's writer Hayashi Fumiko.[8]

In order to address the question of what modernity in the Japanese instance might mean, I want to take Stuart Hall's definition of modernity as a multiplicity of processes which are realized in political, economic, social and cultural terms over time.[9] However, I shall qualify it on two accounts, especially in relation to the specific question of femininity, spatial representation and the work of Ozu. First, the social transformation did not run concurrently along some single streamlined continuum. It is important to discern different durations to the modulations of change and to acknowledge that modernity was never fixed or ideally located at some particular juncture. In Japan, as elsewhere, these streams clearly played on the consciousness of the nation according to different interrelated variables such as regional location, age and especially gender. Second, and very importantly, Japanese modernity was never the equivalent of western modernity, despite the fact that, for the most part, modernity has meant what Harry Harootunian has termed 'the West, its science, and the devastating effects it had inflicted on the face of traditional social life'.[10]

It is important to unpick the thinking behind this second point. When the Tokugawa shogunate, which had ruled Japan in isolation for over two centuries, was overthrown in 1868, much of the apparatus of western civilisation was adopted by the incoming oligarchy of the Meiji Restoration. This is not the same, though, as saying that with an enhanced material infrastructure of trains, machinery, communications media and so on, Japan modernised and thus 'westernised' at the same time. Indeed, if one examines Japan's recent past prior to World War II, during which Ozu had produced mass entertainments from the 1920s, one can see that what modernity meant to Japan was deeply contested. In the first instance, the process of modernisation meant catching up with the West and developing a contemporary infrastructure which could stand on a par with such countries as the UK and Germany. This not only had material significance; it also had geopolitical relevance in relation to Japan's wider imperial interests within the rest of the East

Asian region. Nonetheless, several contemporary Japanese thinkers were acutely aware of the problems that lay behind Japan's sense of itself in relation to the modern as constantly being mediated by a comparison with the West. This was expressed in terms of an anxiety about the loss of the intrinsic spirituality of the people – a dilution of the cultural essence of the Japanese folk (*minzoku*). What consequently developed was the transfer of a bureaucratic, state-based conception of the roots and branches of the traditional folk village (*mura*) onto a holistic model of the nation as a family overseen by the divine Emperor. According to this logic, as Naoki Sakai has observed, pre-World War II Japan actually had to 'modernise and adapt things from the West in order to resist it'.[11]

Japanese modernity in the postwar period therefore entailed an ostensible severance with this past. Under the orders of the commanders of the Occupation, which lasted until 1952, the feudalistic worship of the Emperor under the guise of state–military ideology had to be renounced. A new, more authentic, nation was to appear, constructed on the basis of a democratized version of subjectivity. Importantly, women were for the first time given suffrage, and the populace as a whole was encouraged to see itself as victim of an unjust and corrupt leadership that had led it to take the wrong path on the route to a modern conception of the state. But secondly, and in a way contradictorily, there also had to be a sense of continuation of the modern, in that there was no going back to tradition and the absence of the material benefits of progress. The Japanese writer Maruyama Masao has talked about the 'double image'[12] of the postwar period in relation to these two ideas. A 'new' nation had to be constructed which could reconcile what had gone on before with the need to recover prestige in the international arena. Economically, this reconstruction came to mean *kodo seicho* (high growth) and the appearance of the myth of a *shin chukan taishu shakai* (new middle-class society). Carol Gluck thus argues that 'the alleged break in 1945 in fact posited a continuity not between pre-war fascism and post-war democracy, but between modernisation in its first phase and the chance the second time to get the modern right'.[13]

Over the period in which Ozu made his cycle of postwar dramas, Japan witnessed an extraordinary surge of industrialization and productive capacity. This was accompanied by the drift of the populace to major urban centres such as Osaka and Tokyo, and an enhanced and much expanded material infrastructure. New patterns of consumption emerged during the 1950s. The upsurge in magazine publishing, the advent of television, the growth of rail and billboard advertising, all heralded an enhanced visual culture which was connected to a growth in disposable income and an awareness of new *seikatsu* (lifestyle or standard of living). All of these changes, and their distinctive social and emotional consequences, are vividly apparent in the dramatic narratives of Ozu's female-centred *gendai geki*. The pace of industrialization is observed, along with the development of commodification and the new consumer culture. The trains and stations incorporated into the narratives suggest new kinds of movement and relationships between spaces and citizens. The conflict between the national tradition of the family unit and individual female desire is played out in the feminized domestic space of the home drama. The new subjectivity posited by democracy is given emphasis by the reluctance of the younger, especially female, generation to follow prescribed norms. The city as a world of changing leisure and work patterns is observed. Many characters have actually moved from the city to the new industrial suburbs that proliferated after the war. These geographical spaces exist in the films alongside traditional sites of Japan's past, such as the 'touristed' temples and gardens in the old capitals of Kyoto and Kamakura, or the *furosato* (home town) which embodies the notion of a village-style consciousness being eroded by urbanism.

The conventional reading of the progression of Ozu's place in the development of the home drama is embodied in Tadao Sato's position that, following the liberation of the genre from wartime policy which required that the concerns of the family should be represented as subordinate to the interests of the state, the home drama under Ozu relinquished its relation to society. From *Late Spring* onwards, Sato says, 'there was no tension between the outside world and the home.'[14]. For me, though, Ozu's films of this period do not seem to embody a unitary and excluding discourse of the family. Rather, they present a series of somewhat contradictory ideas that can be explored by examining the specific issue of femininity and spatial representation. By looking at the place of the young female inside and outside the home, I want to argue that Ozu was actually dramatizing questions of belonging and change in ways that could speak to the national female audience about the very things Sato and others have claimed were ignored.

Central to the matter of femininity in the postwar films are two recurrent elements. First, there are the powerful and charismatic performances by Shochiku's rota of character actresses and top-billing stars, perhaps the most famous and celebrated being Hara Setsuko, who had come to prominence in the prewar era in films such as the Japanese/German coproduction *Atarashiki tsuchi/Die Tochter des Samurai* (Itami Mansaku and Arnold Fanck, 1937). She had also been a forces sweetheart during the war, and was known for leading roles in postwar films such as Kurosawa Akira's *Waga seishun ni kuinashi/No Regrets for our Youth* (1946). Indeed, so famous was her recurring role as Noriko in *Late Spring*, *Early Summer* and *Tokyo Story* that the name Noriko itself became one of the most popular female names of the early postwar generation. Second, there is particular prominence given to feminine space in the home and, with that, aspects of female friendship. In *Late Spring* and *Early Summer*, for example, Noriko's significant confidante and ally, especially when it comes to discussing the inadequacies of men, is Aya (played in both films with great comic vivacity and flippancy by Tsukioka Yumeji and Chikage Awajima respectively). Like Noriko, Aya is represented as a modern and independent woman, aware of the societal pressures on women to conform eventually to the standard pattern of dutiful wedlock and maternity. In *Late Spring*, for instance, the pair are literally separated from the mainstream by their taste for private, non-Japanese-style living spaces above the conventional paternal space below. In a reversal of the standard father–daughter procedure, it is Noriko's father who has to bring a tray with bread and tea upstairs to her *Anne of Green Gables*-style room; but because he is neither familiar nor comfortable with this modern feminized environment he forgets two of the key components of the occasion, sugar and spoons.

Hara Setsuko is also associated with markers of western modernity in other sequences of *Late Spring*. The freedom and spontaneity of a seaside bicycle ride is linked with the prominence of a Coca-Cola sign, and her character is also revealed in a conversation with the uncle to have had a bobbed haircut, which would have placed her before the war as a stylish *moga* (modern girl).[15] Both Aya and Noriko have working lives outside the home and are pictured with a certain amount of mobility on trains, in street scenes and in coffee shops. Aya, however, is given a more humorous function, partly as a consequence of her somewhat driven efforts to be up to date and 'westernized'. In *Late Spring*, her apartment is also decorated in an over-folksy style of Americana and she has zealously spent the afternoon making shortbread, which unfortunately burns. Aya's taste for irreverent gossip is part of the reason she is not taken as seriously as Noriko; but the main reason for the centrality of Hara Setsuko's place in the film is that she crucially occupies several almost contradictory spaces, whereas Chikage Awajima remains simply the figure of the modern.

The figure of Noriko, as played by Hara Setsuko, seems to occupy more than one space in these films because of the films' narrative emphasis on transition and change. Her sensitivities to the continuities of the past, and especially her reconciliation with older forms of femininity, position her as a pivotal, if ultimately consensual, figure in Ozu's representations of the world of postwar Japan. Kathe Geist has noted Ozu's extensive reliance on symbolic 'allusions to passing time',[16] such as clocks, smoke-stacks and steam, and weddings and funerals. Time and again these appear as central components of the way the life cycle is venerated in Japanese ritual culture. In this context, the figure of Noriko takes on added dramatic significance: through marriage in *Late Spring* and *Early Summer* and through the death of her mother-in-law in *Tokyo Story*, she literally embodies the important link between one generation and the other. In the funeral sequence in *Tokyo Story*, for instance, the figure of Noriko is positioned centre frame. That she has bridged past and present is indicated by her father-in-law Shukichi's (Ryu Chishu) passing on to her his dead wife's watch. In an exquisitely moving sequence, Ozu links the continuity of female sympathy and the awareness of the passage of generations by soon afterwards showing Kyoko (Kagawa Kyoko), the youngest daughter and newly placed friend of Noriko, looking out of her school classroom. She glances at *her* watch as she gazes on the as yet unseen space. This cuts to a shot of Noriko aboard the Tokyo-bound train as she looks down at the watch given her by Shukichi. The women are linked by apprehension of the continuity of time.

It is perhaps the strength of the impression given by western critics, such as Robin

Wood, who view the Japanese *o-miai* (arranged marriage) as 'a tragic fate'[17] that accounts for the lack of critical attention hitherto given to the relationship between the slightly altered Noriko in *Early Summer* and her sister-in-law Fumiko, played according to the conventions of *ryosei kenbo* (good wife, wise mother) by Miyake Kuniko. *Ryosei kenbo* was part of an historically shifting ideology concerning women's role in Japanese society that had been initiated in the later years of the nineteenth century in order to fortify the country in relation to the perceived cultural hegemony of the West. As Kathleen S. Uno explains, the Japanese 'good wife' 'carefully managed the affairs of the household and advanced the well-being of its adult members, while the "wise mother" devoted herself to rearing children to become loyal and obedient imperial subjects'.[18] Miyake Kuniko's depiction of this figure is far from being an unremarkable component of the film. She is, in fact, another key factor in the film's consensual depiction of social change through the prism of the representation of femininity. Miyake Kuniko was herself a well known actress of the time in Japan, having worked for the Toho and Shochiku studios since the 1930s, and next to the somewhat indecipherable, even foreign, features of Hara Setsuko she represented the less westernized, and perhaps ultimately more reassuring, face of contemporary Japanese female stardom.[19] The unassuming aspect of Miyake Kuniko's performance serves as a contrast to the way Noriko is here explicitly linked to the wilful and dynamic star persona of Katherine Hepburn through her collection of photos of the star.[20] In terms of the film's conceptualization of domestic space, Fumiko is constantly pictured interacting with conventional domestic Japanese design elements, Aya, however, imagines Noriko 'to live western style with sweet music, a flower garden and Coca-Cola lined up'.

The *ryosai kenbo* ideology in the immediate prewar period in Japan had been explicitly linked to the identity of the nation, in that the figure of the mother was central to the notion of the *national* family, After the war, as Uno has pointed out, despite the new wide-ranging civil and political rights accorded to women, the figure of the mother still remained central in the culture and 'rather than wifehood, [motherhood] became the dominant image of Japanese womanhood'.[21] It is thus reasonable to assume that the figure of Fumiko represented the norm for the audience of *Early Summer* in 1951, and that Noriko represented a hitherto unassimilated identity. Noriko is certainly represented as the potential voice of radicalism in one of the film's opening scenes, in which as the stiff and humourless Koichi (Ryu Chishu) she and Fumiko are discussing 'the increasing impudence of women'. The film places the group in three-shots, and cuts between these and one-shots of the husband and wife, so that the spectator does not see Hara Setsuko's features until a vital reaction shot, when she says 'No, we're normal now. Men were over-important.' The 180-degree line is also breached, emphasising through matching eyelines the camaraderie that exists between the two women. This camaraderie is a constant throughout the film, with Noriko having both more mobility within the frame and also the mobility to come and go from the family home. The ways in which Hara's performance is represented by the mise-en-scene and editing at other significant moments in the film may still work to limit, rather than fully to delineate, a complete and transparently progressive female subjectivity; but one cannot ignore these sensitively articulated seams of feeling and meaning.

The most important exchange between the two women occurs in one of the key scenes towards the end of the film: these, significantly, are shot on location outside the house. Noriko has announced that she intends to marry Yabe Kenkichi (Nimoto Ryukan), to the dismay of her family. In the previous shot she has been depicted eating alone, in a darkened deep-focus image and isolated in the frame. There follows a cut to an abstracted empty shot of the sand and sea grass, and then a further cut to a highly unusual crane shot of the figures of Miyake Kuniko and Hara Setsuko moving over a dune. As the camera rises, a further layer of dune is revealed and then, finally, the distant haze of the ocean beyond. The figures are pictured in an evocative landscape shorn of all social trappings, and the conversation that ensues between the two women consequently has an openness and intimacy rare in the more ritualized spaces of the family household. What is so moving and even astonishing in this sequence is the way Noriko's previously perceived act of recalcitrance is dealt with as a kind of sympathetic model of independence, which can be grasped – and even apparently envied – by the hitherto more conservative Fumiko. There follows a fuller two-shot from behind the couple, as they gaze out at the water from the ridge. Noriko sits down and Fumiko follows. In a frontal reverse-shot, a dialogue then begins about Fumiko's apprehensiveness over Noriko marrying an older man with a young child. The women both seem to be wearing identical white short-sleeved shirts; but Noriko's proximity to the artificial side-fill lighting gives her an extra luminescence that adds to the tone of ease and confidence that she strikes. They talk about motherhood and housekeeping, but in a way that resolves the fears Fumiko has for the future. Noriko has decided to reject her other suitor, a business colleague of her boss: 'Frankly, I don't trust a man who is still single at forty. I trust a man who has a child', she says, looking out at the horizon. Fumiko turns and looks at Noriko. 'You're wonderful Noriko', she says. 'I knew nothing when I got married'. It is an emotional recognition of the entrapment that the film has hitherto, in muted reaction shots, only hinted at. Soon afterwards, Noriko rises and runs down from the ridge and out of sight. Fumiko stands and watches, her hands composedly clasped. There then follows one of the most liberating images of Ozu's career – Setsuko Hara running with joyful open-air freedom across the beach towards the shoreline. She waves to Fumiko as if to encourage her to share her spirit of release. Fumiko decides at last to let go and run after Noriko, tracing her sister-in-law's steps. The film's final closer tracking shot shows the two women walking by the shore, together and reconciled.

So far in this essay, I have followed Thomas Elsaesser's dictum that 'nationhood and national identity are not given, but gained'.[22] I have argued that 'Japaneseness' is a mobile concept that must be understood according to historically specific terms and gendered differentials. To caution against any notion of an embedded fixity to the concept of a 'national culture' means instead to be aware of how the concept has been appropriated and, in turn, reformulated according to shifting social circumstances. We have seen that the postwar period in Japan was one of rapid and ongoing change, and it is tempting to say that Ozu's filmic representations suggest a clearly separable set of differences between the old and the new. But this is not the case. Rather, the national is achieved as the result of an active contestation between past and present, so that a more appealing consensual version of continuity, a sense of the past within the present, is formulated for the national audience. As I shall now argue, this can also be seen in Ozu's appropriation of discourses of the past and national tradition for his representations of place and femininity outside the sphere of the domestic.

Since they are organized along the principle of linear progression, most national narratives evoke the idea of a journey. The developmental journey from premodern society to the modern is always seen as unfinished, in that there is always more to be achieved in the name of progress. This is necessary so that the contemporary citizen is allowed a part in organizing the way the future is going to be. It can be argued that in order for this narrative, this biography of nationhood, to make sense, a parallel journey must be conceived of, one that takes account of the past. In the face of the contradictions of Japan's postwar modernity, contradictions that existed partly because of the unresolved definition of the legacy of the war and partly because of Japan's unfinished engagement with the West, Ozu's female-centred dramas specifically enact this process of two-way looking. Part of the reason the director has been celebrated as the standard-bearer of Japaneseness is that he appears to have undertaken this process of remembering, recording and inscribing what it means to be a citizen of Japan.

His films worked as a form of census, in that over time they captured the full range and vitality of the ordinary female and male members of the national community. The variety of social types and the attention given to modes and norms of everydayness constituted a kind of record. His films can even be seen as social and visual maps, in that they describe with infinite precision the contours and details of places which, once again, seem chosen for their typicality. This much is glimpsed in his representations of domestic space, but it can also be argued that the same is true for his other locations. Thus, for example, the railway, that all-pervading element of Ozu's cinema, can now be seen in its fullest context. The train not only makes the mapping of the nation visible to the audience by literally picturing transition from one place to another – be it from Onomichi to Tokyo in *Tokyo Story*, or Tokyo to Okayama in *Soshun/Early Spring* (1956); it also suggests, through the duality of departure and arrival, the two-way nature of modernity. To get somewhere, you have to leave something behind.

The journey is used as a significant element in the narrative of *Late Spring*. Although there are a number of representations of travel between Kamakura and the modern capital in the film, the most significant journey, from Tokyo to the ancient capital of Kyoto, occurs towards the end of the story. It is a moment resonant with endings and beginnings, for this is the last occasion on which Noriko will spend time alone with her father before embarking on the further journey of marriage. Although we do not see the train itself, the process of journeying is vividly evoked in the everyday intimacy of the conversation between Noriko and Somiya (Ryu Chishu) in the *ryokan* (inn). As their recounting of the key locations en route suggests, the journey between Tokyo and Kyoto is already mapped in the consciousness of the Japanese citizen. In feudal times the lords and their vassals had to make an annual pilgrimage to pay respect to the *shogun* in Tokyo (or Edo as it was then called). This route was called the *Tokkaido*. For most modern Japanese the *Tokkaido* is now traced in reverse to facilitate another pilgrimage of sorts – that of the rediscovery of traditional values and heritage connected to Japaneseness. Kyoto is represented in the film both as a kind of museum, a place of shared belonging to a common past, and as a tourist destination.

In a key scene set on the ancient verandahs of the Kiyomizu temple, *Late Spring* poses an interrelationship between a citizen's apprehension of a communal history and a citizen's private, individual narrative. The sequence begins with a deep-focus shot looking out from an angle of forty-five degrees from the first verandah to a second, which is more or less parallel to the picture plane in the middle distance of the image. Between the two verandahs lies an expanse of space in which the odd tree or bush protrudes. The appearance of a group of sailor-suited schoolgirls, evidently on an organized excursion, suggests the status of the temple as a national monument and evokes the intermingling of the contemporary with the timelessness of tradition. This dualism is replicated on the soundtrack with the merging of the chanting of monks and the laughter of the pupils. As the girls leave the frame, Somiya and Misako, Noriko's uncle's new wife, enter and move to the foregrounded verandah. There is a cut to a medium closeup two-shot. Somiya remarks that Kyoto is so relaxing compared to Tokyo where there is 'only dust'.[23] This obvious reference to the results of the firebombing of the capital reminds one that Kyoto was spared the onslaught of the Allies and thus, in the postwar period, was able significantly to strengthen its image as the repository of Japanese heritage. Kyoto is a place to get away from the processes of modern national reconstruction and retrieve a sense of national continuity. This feeling is translated into personal terms when Somiya remarks nostalgically that this is the first time that he has visited the city since the war. There is a cry of 'Uncle' from the opposite verandah and a wave from one of three distant figures. This is followed by a cut to the establishing long shot, and Somiya returns the wave. The next shot reverses the field of vision across the empty space between the verandahs, with the three previously indistinguishable figures shot now from behind and pictured in medium closeup gazing across to Somiya and

Mitsuko. They are revealed to be Noriko, her uncle and her niece. With this shift in spatial location comes a move to a more private register, as Noriko and her uncle banter about his decision to remarry. That she finds this 'distasteful' is of significance, as Noriko's father, in order to persuade his daughter to find a husband, has pretended to find a prospective second wife. There follows a cut back to a virtually repeated long shot of the three figures, but this time deprived of any foreground element. The camera observes them engaging in a highly staged sequence of gestural play, as if the temple grounds have assumed the dimensions of a theatrical arena. We return to Somiya and Mitsuko, who walk offscreen as a new group of schoolgirls enters from screen right. Then comes the final, and most serene, shot of the sequence, in which the passing of both national and private time are simultaneously evoked. We see the image divided into three zones. On the left and the right are the solid architectural features of the wooden temple; in the centre is a gap. A traditional bamboo chute, associated with the purification of the soul in Buddhist ritual, is seen dripping water on the left. The water is an allusion to Noriko's ongoing comments to her uncle that she finds his decision to change his life 'unclean'; but it also evokes a sense of national ritual across time, for that water could have dripped for centuries. As if to underline this mention of renewal and continuity across the generations, more schoolgirls pass across the gap between the two zones, to the accompaniment of a reprise of the film's theme music. Because – unusually for Ozu, who tended to use boys in his casts – they are young girls, they also suggest a link to Noriko; and, because they are also in the national school uniform, they evoke the nation's future, the Japanese world to come.

In this essay I have challenged the view that Ozu's postwar cinema was an inward looking and fully conservative body of work. I have begun to move beyond the standard analysis of his distinctive style of filmmaking as a means of radical alterity to the western canon and started to consider the complex ways in which his films can be seen as representations that deal with the intertwined matters of Japanese modernity and a national gendered identity. Ozu's films of this period were home dramas, coinciding with a prevailing discourse which positioned women as facilitators of 'a transition from a patrilineal household system . . . to a woman-centred nuclear family in which . . . men's dominance in the public sphere was neatly complemented by women's power at home'.[24] But this evidently did not mean a wholescale regressive tendency. Through careful articulation of performance and spatial organization, the films suggest a set of negotiated tensions about the places women could occupy in a nation in which the values of tradition and modernity were in flux. The values and conflicts of contemporary urban life in the postwar period are dramatized by suggesting a prevailing sense of typicality and ordinariness. Ozu was minutely interested in the detail of national life and his visual style bears significant resemblance to the work of contemporaneous photographic social documentarists such as Kuwabara Kineo, Kimura Ihee and Hayashi Tadahiko. This attentiveness to the materiality of Japaneseness is also, it should be acknowledged, a result of the contributions of Tatsuo Hamada, his regular art director. But it is particularly because of the sophisticated range of the Shochiku female stars that prominence is so clearly given to the way feminine space became *the* field in which the contemporary and the traditional were fought over. Today these films appear to be historical artefacts – exquisitely composed images of a world already largely gone. But in their day, when cinema was still the way in which a nation saw moving images of itself, these films spoke to what was probably a largely female mass entertainment audience, ready to see a visualization of the necessarily two-way perspective it had on its own relationship to the national past and present.

Acknowledgements

I would like to acknowledge the kind assistance of V.F. Perkins and Mori Toshie during the course of the preparation for this essay.

Notes

1 Plot synopsis: Elderly parents Shukichi and Tomi leave their youngest daughter at home in the coastal town of Onomichi to visit their son Koichi and daughter Shige in Tokyo. They find their children preoccupied and too busy to take much of an interest in the visitors. It is Noriko, the widow of their dead son Shoji, who offers the couple genuine hospitality. After returning early from a hastily arranged visit to a noisy spa resort, the parents find themselves with no place to stay in the big city. Tomi stays with Noriko and Shukichi goes out drinking with old friends. Eventually, they return to Onomichi but shortly afterwards Tomi dies. The children rush to the parental home, but all except Noriko soon hurry back to Tokyo. Before Noriko leaves, Shukichi thanks her and urges her to remarry. He gives her his dead wife's watch.

2 Kristin Thompson and David Bordwell, 'Space and narrative in the films of Ozu', *Screen*, vol. 17, no. 2 (1976), pp. 41–75; Edward Branigan, 'The space of *Equinox Flower*', *Screen*, vol. 17, no. 2 (1976), pp. 74–105; Noel Burch, *To the Distant Observer* (London: Scolar Press, 1979); significant sections of David Bordwell's groundbreaking *Ozu and the Poetics of Cinema* (London: British Film Institute, 1988). For subsequent useful revisionary discussion of Ozu's aesthetics and their distinctive relation to Japanese cinematic practice, see, for example, Scott Nygren, 'Reconsidering modernism: Japanese film and the postmodern context', *Wide Angle*, vol. 11, no. 3 (1989), pp. 6–15; Mitsuhiro Yoshimoto, 'Melodrama, postmodernism, and Japanese cinema', in Wimal Dissanayake (ed.), *Melodrama and Asian Cinema* (Cambridge: Cambridge University Press, 1993), pp. 101–26.

3 Plot synopsis: Noriko lives with her father in Kamakura, the coastal ex-capital about 90 minutes from Tokyo. She appears content to remain single and care for her much-loved father, despite encouragement from some of her female ex-classmates to find a suitable husband. Only Aya, a modern city girl, sympathizes with her choice. Worried that Noriko will find herself alone in later years, her father and aunt concoct a scheme to persuade her to marry. Noriko's father himself pretends to be planning to remarry and tells his daughter that in time she will find happiness with her chosen suitor. They go

on a final trip together to Kyoto prior to the wedding. After the ceremony, the father confesses his duplicity to Aya and returns home to an empty house.

4 Plot synopsis: The Mamiya family is visited by the elderly brother of the grandfather. Noriko, a still unmarried daughter, works for Satake, who suggests the family investigate the marital prospects of a successful middle-aged businessman he knows. In the meantime Noriko's elder brother Koichi assigns their neighbour Yabe, a friend of Noriko, to a hospital post in distant Akita. One evening, Yabe's mother blurts out that she had always hoped that Yabe would marry Noriko. Abruptly, Noriko agrees to do so. The Mamiyas object and pressure Noriko to change her mind but she remains steadfast. Without her vital contribution to the household income, the family dissolves and the film ends with the grandparents living in the country with the elderly uncle who had visited them previously.

5 Kido Shiro, quoted in Bordwell, *Ozu and the Poetics of Cinema*, p. 20.

6 There are two further points to be briefly made about Shochiku and national identity. First, all Shochiku films bear the house logo of Mount Fuji, the sacred symbol of the Japanese nation. Second, as Darrell William Davies has demonstrated, Kido Shiro actively collaborated with the military authorities in the prewar period, especially in relation to the 1939 Film law which 'mobilized' the film industry 'as a cog in the vast government propaganda machine'. Apparently it was Kido Shiro's idea to adapt the *Kulturfilm* from Nazi Germany. Cinemas were compelled to show *Bunka eiga* (culture films) under the Film Law. See Darrell William Davis, *Picturing Japaneseness* (New York, NY: Columbia University Press, 1996), pp. 64–8.

7 Joanne Bernardi, *Writing in Light: The Silent Scenario and the Japanese Pure Film Movement* (Detroit, IL: Wayne State University Press, 2001), pp. 52–66.

8 See Donald Richie, *A Hundred Years of Japanese Film* (Tokyo: Kodansha, 2001), pp. 117–45. For more on the important work of Naruse Mikio from a feminist perspective, see Freda Freiburg, 'The materialist ethic of Mikio Naruse', *http://www. sensesofcinema.com/contents/02/20/naruse.html* [30 August 2005]; Catherine Russell, 'Mikio Naruse and the Japanese women's film', *Asian Cinema*, vol. 10, no. 1 (1998), pp. 120–25; Catherine Russell, 'From women's writing to women's films in 1950s Japan: Hayashi Fumiko and Naruse Mikio', *Asian Journal of Communication*, vol. 11, no. 2 (2001), pp. 101–20. For an innovative study of the interrelationship between Tanaka Kinuyo and Mizoguchi Kenji, see Chika Kinoshita, 'Choreography of desire: analysing Kinuyo Tanaka's acting in Mizoguchi's films', *http://www.latrobe.edu.au/ screeningthepast/firstrelease/fr1201/ckfr13a.htm* [30 August 2005].

9 Stuart Hall, 'Introduction', in Stuart Hall and Bram Gieben (eds), *The Formations of Modernity* (Cambridge: Polity, 1992), pp. 1–16.

10 H.D. Harootunian, 'Visible discourses/invisible ideologies' in Miyoshi and Harootunian (eds), *Postmodernism and Japan* (Durham, NC: Duke University Press), p. 68.

11 Naoki Sakai, 'Modernity and its critique', in ibid, p. 116.

12 Masao Muruyama, quoted in Carol Gluck, 'The past in the present', in Andrew Gordon (ed.), *Postwar Japan as History* (Berkeley, CA: University of California Press, 1993), p. 79.

13 Gluck, 'The past in the present', p. 79.

14 Sato Tadao, *Currents in Japanese Cinema*, trans. Gregory Barrett (Tokyo: Kodansha, 1982), p. 142.

15 For more on the genealogy of the *moga*, see Miriam Silverberg 'The modern girl as militant', in Gail Lee Bernstein (ed.), *Recreating Japanese Women, 1600–1945* (Berkeley, CA: University of California Press, 1991), pp. 239–67.

16 Kathe Geist, 'The role of marriage in the films of Yasujiro Ozu', *East–West Film Journal*, vol. 4, no. 1 (1989), p. 46.

17 Robin Wood, 'The Noriko Trilogy', *Cinéaction*, nos. 26/27 (Winter 1992), p. 73.

18 Kathleen S. Uno, 'The death of "good wife, wise mother"?', in Gordon (ed.), *Postwar Japan as History*, pp. 293–322. The quotation is from p. 297.

19 Setsuko Hara's grandfather was reputedly German, though this may have been a deliberate myth promulgated to publicize her leading role in *Atarashiki tsuchi/Die Tochter des Samurai* (1937). See Dan Harper, 'Setsuko Hara – the enigma of the 'eternal virgin'', *http://www.sensesofcinema.com/contents/02/23/symposium1.html#hara* [30 August 2005].

20 However, Catherine Russell argues differently that Hara is clearly unlike her supposed US counterpart Katherine Hepburn, in that rather than being seen as an active agent, she in fact has 'such independence thrust upon her'. See '"Overcoming modernity": gender and the pathos of history in Japanese film melodrama', *Camera Obscura*, no. 35 (1995), p. 157.

21 Uno, 'The death of "good wife, wise mother"?', p. 303. Uno offers three reasons for this. 'First, mothers became more visible in postwar households, for long-term demographic changes and postwar democratic ideologies made it less likely that a young bride, the mother of a household's young children, would share the hearth with another adult woman (generally her husband's mother) as she did before World War II. Second, the diffusion of vacuum cleaners, washers, refrigerators, gas ranges, indoor plumbing, and prepackaged foods eased somewhat a wife's burden of household chores, allowing her more time for childrearing. Third, the rise of employment for wages decreased the proportion of housewives working in family enterprises' (p. 304).

22 Thomas Elsaesser, 'The idea of a national cinema', BFI/UCLA seminar paper (unpublished), September 1993, p. 1.

23 According to Kyoko Hirano, because of the extreme sensitivity shown by the Occupation authorities towards mention or depiction of the Allied devastation, the word 'dust' was preferred to 'burned sites'. See Kyoko Hirano, *Mr Smith Goes to Tokyo* (Washington, DC: Smithsonian Institution Press, 1992), p. 56.

24 Lisa Skov and Brian Moeran, 'Introduction: hiding in the light: from Oshin to Yoshimoto Banana', in Skov and Moeran (eds), *Women, Media and Consumption in Japan* (Richmond, Surrey: Curzon Press, 1995), pp. 23–4.

Part III

Melodrama as a national and transnational mode

7 The melodramatic mode and the commercial Hindi cinema

Ravi Vasudevan

Indian film's dominant position in South Asia and popularity in the Middle East, parts of Africa, South East Asia and East Europe has been longstanding.[1] Its ascendancy in the home market emerged within a few years of the inauguration of the talkies[2] and has held resilient against the competition of the Hollywood cinema and other foreign films.[3]

Within this economy, Hindi feature film production has played a major role, catering to the largest linguistic market in the country. From the mid 1930s to the mid 1940s, the three major studios, Prabhat (in Pune, western India), Bombay Talkies (Bombay city) and New Theatres (Calcutta) produced both regional language and Hindi films; from the 1940s the Madras studios also started producing for the Hindi market. As a result, the Hindi feature has been the main component in national production.[4] This has changed recently, with large increases in southern language production,[5] but the Hindi film continues to have the largest domestic market.

Production units in the Indian industry were thrown into some chaos in the years immediately after the World War II, with the entry of a large number of financiers, bloated with wartime profits, into the market. Fierce competition led to the demise of the major studios. A large number of production companies, mostly shortlived, emerged. These were based in Bombay, which has remained the major Hindi film producing centre.[6] Such characteristics have tended to persist in the post-Independence period. The structure of the industry and its products has been heavily influenced by the power that exhibitors have exercised in conditions of limited cinema outlets.[7] This domination has created a strong emphasis on products conforming to a proven formula of commercial success, mainly relating to star combinations and famous musical directors.

This has not meant a lack of generic differentiation of the product, however. The Hindi film has produced the following narrative types: the mythological, drawing mainly upon the great Hindu myths; the devotional, about the relationship between devotee and deity; the stunt film, oriented to the spectacle of action; the historical drama, with an emphasis on period costume and setting; the social problem film, dealing with issues of social reform; and, much more broadly, the social film.

Though overlapping with the social reform film, this latter genre is not always so precise about the social ills it addresses. Set in modern times, the social film generates images that delineate ethical precepts raising questions of dignity, equality, honesty. The social referent is generally the plebeian or the *déclassé*. It has become the characteristic genre of the post-Independence cinema.

This essay analyses films from the social genre of the Bombay Hindi cinema, both because of their dominance and because the better known directors of the post-Independence period (Raj Kapoor, Guru Dutt, Mehboob Khan) were associated with this genre. The focus is on certain general textual features of the Hindi film, its modes of narration, subject construction and performative indices.

Characteristics present in European and American melodrama – non-psychological motivation, prevalence of contrived plotting (coincidence), a heavily musical component to dramatic construction, the employment of a Manichean moral universe[8] – are observable also in the Hindi film. I will therefore be using, heuristically, a framework evolved in relation to the melodrama. However, following Rosie Thomas's important work on the Hindi cinema,[9] I will be emphasising, within this general framework, the specificity of its textual operations.

The question of specificity is a complicated one. Thomas and other commentators have made the significant point that traditions of aesthetic theory in India differ markedly from Aristotelian poetics.[10] Rather than linear dramatic construction, a shifting discursive field – incorporating philosophical and ethical expression, emotional excess, comedy, song and dance – was theorised. This evidently poses problems for methods of analysis developed to deal with linear dramatic narrative.

Though such discursive shifts also characterise the Hindi film, an important background to film history is the articulation of other modes with 'traditional' form. This interaction emerged in the Indian urban theatre of the nineteenth and twentieth centuries.[11] The main agency here was the Parsi theatre, which travelled widely in the country, used a simple language or communication, and was very eclectic in the sources it drew on for its drama, sources which included western narrative. Apart from this anticipation of the geographical reach of the Hindi cinema and its hybrid structure, the Parsi theatre also employed the omnibus 'musical tragi-comedy' form, as it was termed. Further, these companies had a repertory of stock characters, of whom the comic character is particularly interesting for analogies with the Hindi cinema, because of the narratively unintegrated way his performance functioned: 'He enjoys extraordinary liberty, for his sole object is to create unbounded merriment in the theatre.'[12]

Such a form cannot be regarded solely in terms of the way it conforms to traditional aesthetics. The Parsi community of India's west coast was involved in modern forms of business and enterprise, and was familiar with European culture from an early period. The theatrical companies were strongly influenced by English melodrama of the period, imported stage machinery from England and advertised performances in terms of the novel attractions of 'transformation scenes' and 'dissolving views'. So they were also participant in that expanding 'culture of the visible' that has been seen as the nineteenth-century prelude to the cinema.[13]

I do not want to labour the connections between these theatrical forms and the Hindi cinema; as I will suggest later, other, more 'traditional', theatrical influences are also observable. I merely cite this as an instance of the difficulty of defining cultural specificity. When there is this kind of interaction in a colonial and post-colonial context, the positing of essences is always suspect, and in this case is likely to produce orientalising results.[14] Nowhere is this problem more emphatic than in analysing the relationship between the Hollywood and the Hindi industries. While marginal in terms of exhibition and the social depth of their popularity, large numbers of US films flowed into the metropolitan areas in which Indian films were being made. Certain plot similarities have often prompted the conclusion that the relationship has been one of imitation.[15] However, this view fails to see that such borrowings are subject to drastic revision in line with specific conceptions of narrative construction and performance.

As this issue is not the object of this essay, I will simply suggest that certain operations in the Hindi film narrative, around the articulation of male narrational authority and its subsequent disavowal, have a lot to do with the relationship between Hindi and US films being one of both attraction and denial. The capable, goal-centred hero of mainstream US cinema (leaving aside certain melodramatic revisions of this character) is often stated in the Hindi film – with local inflections – but is then displaced at a later point in the narrative. Also crucial is a narrative bipolarity in which the problem of cultural self-identification is central. The opposition between East and West is used to recover, in an often duplicitous, contradictory way, an 'authentic' Indian identity.

I will elaborate on this in the course of my analysis, which will focus on the peculiarities of narrative structure and narrational procedure and the gendering of narrative voice in the Hindi commercial cinema. I will also consider the ways in which the paranarrative units (song, dance and comic sequences) work to create parallel pleasures and perhaps to problematise the work of the narrative.

In looking at narrative structure and narration, I shall make the following standard entry points into the films considered here:

(a) The problem of the male subject as it is articulated in narrative structure: for whom is the story being told?

(b) The problem of the subject as it is articulated by narration: who is telling the story and/or who is determining its eventuation? I shall consider here the implications of narrational strategies for the female subject position.

(c) The mechanisms whereby the narrative moves along; the codes it employs to bind spectatorial interest.

To explore these questions, and those on the functions of the paranarrative, I shall refer to two important 'social' films of the studio period, *Devdas* (P.C. Barua, 1935)[16] and *Kismet/Fate* (Gyan Mukherji, 1943). The remaining references will mostly be to films of the 1950s, with a few instances from the 1940s, the 1970s and the 1980s: *Aag/Fire* (Raj Kapoor, 1948), *Andaz/A Sense of Proportion* (Mehboob Khan, 1949), *Deedar/Vision* (Nitin Bose, 1951), *Awara/Vagabond* (Raj Kapoor, 1951), *Baazi/The Wager* (Guru Dutt, 1951), *Shree 420/Mr 420* (Raj Kapoor, 1955), *Pyaasa/Craving* (Guru Dutt, 1957), *Mother India* (Mehboob Khan, 1957), *Saheb, Bibi aur Gulam/King, Queen Slave* (Akbar Alvi, 1962), *Pakeezah/the Pure One* (Kamal Amrohi, 1971), *Zanjeer/The Chain* (Prakash Mehra, 1973), *Deewar/The Wall* (Yash Chopra, 1975), *Sholay/Flames* (Ramesh Sippy, 1975), *Muqaddar ka Sikandar/Conqueror of Destiny* (Prakash Mehra, 1978), *Shakti/Power* (Ramesh Sippy, 1982).

In discussing narrative structure, I shall not present the plots of these films in detail, but rather indicate major patterns. Peter Brooks's contention that characters in melodrama take on essential psychic features of father, mother, child is applicable also to these plot structures.[17] What is played out again and again is the characteristic drama of the family triad: a fearsome father (standing in for the various articulations of Law in its opposition to desire), the nurturing mother and the traumatized son.[18] (Figure 7.1)

Within this Oedipal drama, the male subject oscillates between renunciation[19] and conflict. In *Devdas*, the hero, unable to realise his desire in the face of the strictures of class laid down by his father, takes to a life of dissolution. In *Deedar*, a

Figure 7.1 'The characteristic drama of the family triad': *Aag/Fire* (Raj Kapoor, 1948). Prod: R.K. Productions.

poor youth who has lost his sight recovers it only to blind himself again when he realises that the rich woman he desires cannot be his. In *Aag*, the hero refuses to follow the career of his lawyer father, turns to theatre and wins success. However, he discovers that the woman his close friend loves is fixated on him instead; he disfigures his face in order to end the girl's fascination. In the process he burns down the theatre, the very site of the contestation of his father's authority. In *Pyaasa*, the hero, a poet, is subject to a symbolic assault by a series of oppressive father figures. An oppositional aspect is lent to the act of renunciation, for it is done at the point when the hero, by the manoeuvring of the very father figures and others who had traumatized him, is given a place in the symbolic order. In another dominant scenario the male subject is implicated in a conflict with the father. This may be done unconsciously, for instance in the stories in which, as a result of a violent primal act on the part of the father, the son has been evicted from the house as a child (*Kismet, Awara*), and so does not recognise the father when engaged in conflict with him. The aggression may, however, be conscious, directed against a symbolic father (*Shree 420, Mother India*, and a number of 1970s films featuring Amitabh Bachchan). In certain instances, a combination of the renunciatory and aggressive features is posed, as with certain of the roles performed by Amitabh Bachchan in the 1970s (*Deewar, Muqaddar ka Sikandar, Sholay, Shakti*). In these stories restitution is never possible for the hero. Fated to live out a drama of 'lack' (of the mother, of the true, as opposed to the bad, father, of social position), the hero presents the illusion of control, but in a way which reasserts lack – in all the above-mentioned films he has to die – and achieves resolution at best for another couple.

In considering narrational authority and problems of sexual difference, I shall divide the narratives schematically into renunciation and identification plots. In the renunciation plot the hero is incapable of establishing his authority on the symbolic terrain. Within these limits, however, he has the capacity to generate female figures who will look after him. These are presented either as simple nurturing figures or, if more active (like the prostitutes Chandra in *Devdas* and Gulab in *Pyaasa*), their activity is motivated by the transformations wrought by the hero. The influence of the hero's presence (*Devdas*) and creative expression (in *Pyaasa*, Vijay's poetry) transforms the impure woman into a pure one, eligible to look after the hero. His authority, though circumscribed by the father, produces a protective field within which the drama of 'lack' is nonetheless enacted. In the identification plot, on the other hand, a real shift in authority often takes place. It is as if the authorisation of conflict and resolution by the male subject position is inadmissible; or as if the conflict between father and son is not capable of stabilisation without the arbitration of another figure.

The narrative may produce a mother figure to achieve identity for the male subject (*Kismet, Awara, Mother India*); however, the figure who would appear eligible to take this position may be rendered unsuitable by various inimical discourses (for example in *Baazi*, wealth; in *Zanjeer*, an excessive femininity). In such instances another (good) father may be produced. This latter figure may correspond to the insertion of the law (as an entity separate from the power of the father) into the narrative (for example, in *Baazi*), or, if the law itself appears ineffectual (as in certain early 1970s work such as *Zanjeer*), in the figure of another male who understands the logic of the reigning criminal order and can exercise his authority over this (excessively masculine) sphere.[20] More generally, a figure quite outside the dominant frame of narrative relations, the comic, may fulfil such functions. This point is taken up later in relation to questions of performance and narrative integration.

The female subject may be significant in narration simply as a nurturing figure, or as the one who takes over narrational authority to achieve identification for the hero. In either case, the male subject is caught within a regressive fantasy. This implies that the underlying objective of the narrative is the achievement of the classical couple as a dyadic fusion of mother and male child.[21]

This is indicated repeatedly. In *Devdas*, the hero conceives of his desire for his beloved, Paro, as that of a child for his mother. In *Kismet*, the hero's actions are motivated by the loss of his mother and the depredations of his grasping father. His beloved is the one who can finally correct the various imbalances caused by the father, thereby fulfilling the hero's search for a mother. In *Aag*, after the hero disfigures himself, he agrees to a marriage arranged by his parents, only to discover on his wedding night that he has married the woman he has been in pursuit of since his childhood. She loves him in spite of his hideous scar. Thus he recovers in the same figure both the innocent society of childhood and the absolute love of a mother. In *Andaz*, the focus on the improper conduct of the heroine brings into question her eligibility not only to be a wife but crucially also to be a mother. In *Awara*, the heroine clearly fulfils the functions of the absent wife for the hero's father; and she takes over a knowledge and fulfils ambitions that were originally located with his mother. In *Pyaasa*, the hero Vijay's poetry is unacknowledged by the world and yet admired by a prostitute, Gulab, who offers him the ministering functions his mother can no longer perform. It is she to whom Vijay looks when he renounces the plaudits of a corrupt society. In *Pyaasa*, the centrality of the mother to the fiction, as a source of virtue and as emblematic of that which is most threatened by evil, is horrifyingly rendered: in the stampede which climaxes the confrontation of good and evil in the film, Gulab's body is brutally trampled. (Figures 7.2 and 7.3) This relationship between the hero and the nurturing heroine often carries with it a certain emblematic moment of looking: the woman looking at the man who is unaware of her look, is indifferent to it, or is unable to return it, is representative of a protective field for the male subject. (Figures 7.4 to 7.6) This may be observed in both plot types.

This structure of looking presents the possibility of a series of allied functions. Fixing the mother function, its active denial may signify the denial of legitimacy to the woman. For example, a wife is debarred from her husband's presence/sight at the beginning of *Awara*, and dies because she catches his prohibited sight later. In

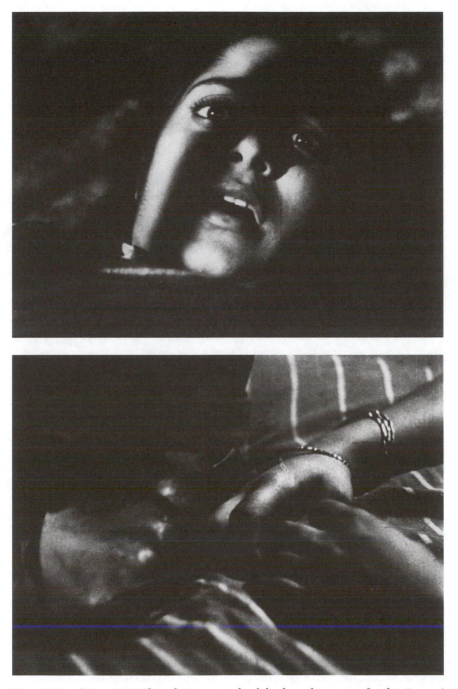

Figure 7.2 and Figure 7.3 The substitute mother's body as the target of evil in *Pyaasa/ Craving* (Guru Dutt, 1957). Gulab (Waheed Rehman), cast to the ground, looks up in horror as a man's boot crushes her. Prod: Guru Dutt Films.

Figure 7.4 Devdas (P.C. Barua, 1935): Paro (Jamuna) has just fainted, as her beloved, Devdas, enters his death throes many miles away. Surrounded by husband and son, her look, directed to a point outside the frame, cannot be returned. Prod: New Theatres.

Pyaasa, Vijay's ex-lover, Meena, castigated for her desire for wealth over her love for Vijay, is looking at Vijay when a train passes, blocking her view of him. Conversely, the male subject who does not conform to the position of the son may be denied the mother's look or may even, extending the logic of this structure, be subject to castration (the destiny of the transgressive sons of *Mother India* and *Deewar*).

In the identification plot, when desire is 'legitimate', the woman's look at the unaware protagonist is purely emblematic: it is otherwise returned, though within a narrational strategy which still projects the mother's functions onto her. However, in the renunciation plot the desire expressed by the woman is denied or transformed by the imperatives of this particular variant of male subject construction. Gulab's unreciprocated look at Vijay in *Pyaasa*, played against a song invoking the sensual longing and devotion of Radha for Krishna (mythical lovers), is representative of a larger strategy of denial and transformation. In *Devdas*, the hero often looks away in the face of the prostitute Chandra's desire for him, and yet this very unattainability exercises a power over her, transforming her into a figure who shelters and cares for him. In *Aag*, the hero Kewal disfigures himself to arrest the fascination of the actress who loves him; as I have noted, he longs instead for the simpler relationship of a childhood companion. In *Deedar*, the Dilip Kumar figure's self-blinding results

Figure 7.5 The blind hero (Dilip Kumar) and the doting country girl (Nimmi) in *Deedar/Vision* (Nitin Bose, 1951). Prod: Filmkar.

Figure 7.6 Vijay (Guru Dutt) and Gulab (Waheeda Rehman) in *Pyaasa/Craving*. Prod: Guru Dutt Films.

from the social gulf which makes it impossible to attain the woman he desires. But when he first recovers his sight, and looks at the woman he has so long desired, it is the presexual friend of childhood he sees (Figures 7.7 and 7.8): the woman is subordinated to the memory of an imaginary, pre-Oedipal relationship. The blinding also functions to maintain a relationship with a doting country girl who looks after him, a girl whose love he does not reciprocate. In effect the renunciation plot, dealing with the male subject's failure/withdrawal in his contest with the father, inscribes the woman as a figure subordinated to a narcissistic male structure of desire: one in which the male struggles to retain an undifferentiated relation with the mother.

In terms of narrative mechanisms, the pattern of the identification plot, in which authority may be shifted onto figures other than the male subject, in a sense constitutes the macronarrational movement, a movement which does the work of eliding the authority of the male otherwise displayed. The text undertakes a narrative and performative operation which allows for forbidden, transgressive, spaces to be opened up – spaces of familial conflict and aggression, of sexuality – and then closes them, reinstituting a moral order.

Often very important to this operation of transgression and denial in the identification plot is the manipulation of knowledge within the narrative. The narration tends to be highly communicative, providing the spectator with information which is denied to the fictional characters.[22] These gaps in knowledge in the fiction (misrecognition, misunderstanding in the relation between characters) effect vertiginous displacements in the narrative. Spaces are created – of misrecognition, of displacement of that which would be if knowledge were full. It is these spaces that characters enter in order to work out transgressive functions, revenge fantasies, restitutive deeds, in a kind of playing out of the dreamwork.

This blocking of knowledge is rarely informed by the spectatorial compulsion to see recognition take place in the fiction that is characteristic of western melodrama.[23] Rather it allows for a play of fantasy which would otherwise not be possible. However, this does not mean that the communication of significant knowledge is not important. It is morally necessary that it take place, and (generically) understood that it will do so. There must be a restoration of identities, a normalising, especially of family relations. As I have suggested, the woman's function – or that of other substitute figures – is to bring about this normalisation.

The necessity of this denial of conflict often has the aspect of a normative conclusion: as a result the blocked knowledge tends to be relayed in a peculiarly unsuspenseful way. For example, in *Awaara* and *Baazi*, the identity and virtue of the hero are at stake: the resolution hinges on the acquiring of concealed knowledge by a woman-lawyer and an inspector of police respectively. In neither instance is the method of acquiring the crucial information explained. In *Baazi*, there is a complete indifference to the deductive attributes of the policeman: 'detection' follows upon

Figure 7.7 and Figure 7.8 Deedar / Vision (Nitin Bose, 1951): on the hero's recovering his sight, he sees the woman he desires as the (presexual) childhood friend of his memory. Prod: Filmkar.

his instinctive targeting of the real culprit. In *Awara*, it is possible to infer that the woman-lawyer gets the relevant information about the identity of the hero through the hero, who in turn receives it from his mother. However, this is not shown taking place. So suspense as to whether this transmission of information will take place is not built up: it is merely assumed that it will. What is indicated is a moral universe of definite rules whose authority will be restored, irrespective of contradictions posed in its frame. Enigma is thereby underprivileged as a mode of binding spectatorial interest.[24]

What are generally privileged are other, culturally intelligible, forms of knowledge. For example, codings of dress – especially for women – are heavily marked in terms of fixing the function of characters, as are certain characteristic oppositions: good and evil, country and city, Indian and western, purity and sexuality, duty and desire. It is the manipulation of these moral terms that inaugurates the disturbance which it is the narrative's business to neutralise.[25] This disturbance does not have to be immediately conveyed in terms of a statement of lack. The codes used guide the spectator, and so a disturbance may be quite economically signalled. For example, at the beginning of *Andaz*, the heroine is shown wearing riding clothes (western culture) and riding a horse which goes out of control (sexual excess). We are automatically knowledgeable about the disturbances which are going to rock this particular fictional universe.

In this sense the voice of truth does not have to be revealed to the spectator: it is presented at the start, and the narration's work is to fix it in the fictional world. However, this does not mean that there is an absolute predictability to the narrative. Virtue, truth, clearly registered at the narrative's inception, are embattled, put in danger and subjected to a plethora of perils and humiliations. If the source is not in doubt (more likely than not, it is the mother), the strategy the narrative will use to endanger and then recover the virtuous subject is more flexible. As I will show, the oppositions which set up the terms of the subject's oppression are open to ambivalence and require a moral repositioning. In these micronarrational processes, spaces for transgression and conflict are opened up, and with them opportunities for spectatorial pleasure and identification that will ultimately be disavowed in a cleansing, reaffirming moral conclusion.

Such intermediate confusions in representation are illustrated in *Awara*. Judge Raghunath marries a widow, Leela, against social convention. Leela is kidnapped by the bandit Jagga who has sworn revenge against Raghunath. The bandit discovers that Leela is already pregnant and decides to restore her to her husband, knowing that the fact of her captivity will cast doubt on the child's paternity. Raghunath succumbs to this suspicion and casts the pregnant Leela out. Through all this it is possible to see Jagga acting as Raghunath's double. The doubt he sows about Leela's purity may be interpreted as a return of that which Raghunath repressed when he married – social codes which see the widow as inauspicious.[26] Raghunath's expulsion of Leela problematises the good–evil polarity and allows for the attribution of oppressive features to the father. This characterisation is reinforced by the way in which the narrative insistently brings the child, Raj, into contact with his unknown, and aggressively figured, father – a collision course which ultimately leads to the son's murderous attack on him. In a deviation from the patterns of knowledge circulation I have outlined, the attack is performed after Raj discovers that the Judge is his father; he deliberately sets out to kill him to revenge the injustice done to his mother. The attack is undermined by the invocation of the image of Rita, a figure associated with the mother's hopes of recovering for Raj his rightful position in respectable society. Rita's achievement of this task not only redeems Raj; by making the father acknowledge his son, she also enables the Judge to reenter the realm of the good.

Rita herself is the ambivalent focus of the opposition between sexuality and purity. While she needs to take over the mother's functions, she cannot remain bound within the attributes of purity associated with the mother figure. The function of sexuality is needed so that she can be a source of Oedipal contention between the Judge (her foster father) and his (unknown) son, Raj. In terms of representation, however, she has to conform to the culturally 'regressive' codings of western dress (skirts, ballroom gowns, a bathing suit); and so, although the character attributes that come under this representation are crucial to the narrative's recovery of the disinherited son, they must at the same time be punished (Raj hits the swimsuit-clad Rita when she playfully mocks him). From the moment she undertakes the role of restoring Raj to his position, she is clad in the traditional sari.

These two examples of contradiction make the point that within the apparently clear moral universe of the Hindi melodrama there is an ambivalence which addresses the forbidden fears, anxieties and pleasures afforded by the narrative – the fear of the father, the attractions of sexuality; the anxiety attached, in the polarity West–East, to the question of identity.

Nowhere is this instability in the process of meaning-making more pronounced than when female desire becomes the focus of narrative attention. In my general formulations about narrative resolution, I have suggested that the mother function is often projected onto the female, but that her position is simultaneously marked by a desire subordinated to the narrative requirements of the male subject. I will now look in some detail at *Andaz*, the second half of which is dominantly organised around a female viewpoint. The work is doubly significant because it employs a more typically western melodramatic organisation of knowledge.

In the first part of *Andaz*, the heroine, Nina, becomes friendly with an attractive young man, Dilip. Dilip assumes she has come to love him, and is then shocked to discover that she is engaged to be married to Raj, who was earlier out of the country. The day after her marriage, Nina, observing Dilip's gloom, tries to draw him out, and, to her dismay, is met by a declaration of love. She emphatically declares her devotion to her husband Raj, but also fears his discovery of Dilip's passion for her. There are moments at which she is on the verge of telling Raj, but cannot. One day, during a power failure, she goes over to a figure she thinks is Dilip and urges him to go away as his presence threatens her relationship with Raj; but it is Raj she has spoken to. Her assertions of innocence and devotion cannot check Raj's estrangement. When Dilip tries to convince him of the truth, Raj is furious and assaults him. On recovering, Dilip is unhinged and tries to force himself on Nina, wanting to believe that she loves only him. To defend herself, Nina shoots him. At the trial, Raj denounces Nina as wanton, corrupted by western ways; he claims that she killed Dilip to re-establish her virtue. Hearing this, Nina declares she will not defend herself and accepts that she is guilty. On finding a letter from Dilip which makes it clear she was innocent, Raj rushes back to court, but only in time to hear her being sentenced to life imprisonment. From behind bars Nina tells him not to reproach himself, she was guilty of having adopted customs alien to their land; she urges Raj to protect their little daughter from the contamination of foreign culture.

The first part of the film puts the spectator close to Dilip's position of knowledge. Although there are hints of Nina's being involved in another relationship, these tend to be elliptical. The second part, after Dilip's declaration of love, is clearly organised around Nina's fears of exposure. The difficult question, however, is: what can be exposed? The true range of the woman's fears are indicated in a displaced, 'hysterical'[27] way, through another's voice and through a dream sequence. Nina looks into a mirror; an image of Dilip materialises, declaring his love for her in terms more emphatic and extensive than before. The displacement of the woman's mute – and in fact strenuously denied – desires are projected onto another. Later, and less ambiguously, Nina dreams that she runs, joyously, down the garden steps to Dilip, and is followed by Raj, gun in hand. The two men prepare to fight a duel; Nina is a fearful spectator, but the outcome is concealed as a gunshot awakens her.

In my formulation, the blocking of knowledge leads to the institution of transgressive spaces in the narratives: in this instance it leads to a familiarity between Dilip and Nina when Nina is already betrothed. That this is a transgression is only known retrospectively, by the woman, when the man declares his love for her. However, from the sequences indicating the ambivalence of Nina's desire, it is clear that her strenuous assertions of duty and constancy to Raj are addressed not only to Dilip but also to herself. The displaced nature of these sequences will suggest how fraught with peril is the space of this transgression, conceived as it is through a female subjectivity. The play of fantasy is attenuated, literally unspeakable. As it is the woman's social ease which has led to this state – an ease associated with 'Western' norms – this must call forth an excessive denial of such norms and of any such ambivalence. The other male figure must be stripped of his attractiveness, he must be unhinged, desire must be unhinged; a transformation effected, brutally, by the aggression of the true husband. And the ambivalence of Nina must be fully excised by her killing of Dilip, thus violently aligning her with the correct position for the female. However, this action is still not enough; it can still be misread by the husband. Knowledge of her virtue comes too late. The woman's acceptance of her guilt is significantly articulated with her reference to the maternal position she has inadequately fulfilled: for she urges the husband to protect the daughter from the errors she herself has fallen into.

The double articulation of pleasure I have noted as prevalent – a transgression opening up a terrain of inadmissable conflict and desire which has to be ultimately neutralised – is in a sense reproduced in the female point-of-view narrative. We may see the first part of the film as blocking knowledge in order that the woman may indulge a repressed desire for a man other than her fiancé. However, the risks involved are evidently much more intolerable – to the woman herself – and so there is harnessed the drive to see recognition take place, for normalisation to be achieved. Significantly, virtue can only be recognised after the woman is irrevocably punished.

How does this broad structure of narration affect the codes of action, the relay belt, as it were, of narrative construction? The underprivileging of the hermenuetic code tends to suspend motivational mechanisms of a psychological-realist nature. Decisive developments in the narrative are not predicated on the providing, with-holding or distorting of information, or on the impact this has on character psychology. As an overt rationale is missing, cause–effect relations have to be looked for in terms of a melodramatic structuring of sequences. The order and succession of sequences reveal the underlying motivations at work. (In American melodrama, such latent cause–effect relations are present as well, but are displaced by an overlay of realist motivation).[28]

For example, in *Kismet*, the widowed father of Shekhar, the hero, remarries; the child is beaten by his father for denying his new mother, and he runs away from home. Many years later, Shekhar, now a thief, by a chain of exchanges (thefts), encounters an old man who leads him to the theatre owned by his father. Shekhar does not recognise his parents any longer but fixes on the expensive necklace his stepmother is wearing, and steals it. The necklace is ultimately handed over to Rani, daughter of the theatre owner whom Shekhar's father had supplanted. The ordering of these sequences emphasises the act of stealing. Its function in narrative (as distinct from performative) terms is as a metonymic chain that enables the linking of characters. Thieving is a displaced operation, relating both to a recovery of position lost by the hero (his self-disinheritance), and a relocation of that position with those whom we shall discover are its true heirs.

The pejoratively-regarded melodramatic mechanism of coincidence may thus be seen as a structural necessity pared down to certain motivating essences. One of its important functions is in relation to narrative temporality. For example, the apparently arbitrary separation and coincidental reunion of characters is actually motivated by the narrative requiring a certain time to lapse. These durations are related to the evolution of a set of substitutable functions (whether between characters, or within a character) in which the timing of substitution depends on the exhaustion of one figure, the maturation and acquisition of lacking functions in another.

This essentialism of character function and action indicates a narrational field in which mechanisms of surprise and suspense are of negligible significance. I will conclude this section by emphasising again that central to narration are culturally intelligible codes that are used in a shifting, contradictory way. They are attached to various figures and then shifted to others,[29] the imperative being to find means to get out of the moral mess that accompanies transgressive operations (of sexuality, revenge against the father, and so on). The blockage and unravelling of knowledge are merely the points of departure and arrival for the narrative. A great deal by way of cultural transaction and disavowal has to take place in the body of the text.

My analysis of the narrative structures of the Hindi commercial cinema may suggest a greater coherence than actually exists, for the song-and-dance sequences and comic insertions are not merely part of a narrative continuum. I would like to examine now how this apparent incoherence refers to a series of narrational positions and terms other than those specific to the narrative proper. I shall also indicate the ways in which the paranarrative is both integrated into the narrative and also operates a process of identification and pleasure that often literally parallels the work of the narrative.

There is a grid of performance whose reference points lie both inside and outside the film. This is related to the circulation between radio, record and film not only of songs but of dialogue as well. As a result, a dramatic exchange between hero and villain, or an emotional line of dialogue, is often well known. A more complex knowledge is conveyed around the musical performance. Spectators are aware that the voice singing the song is not that of the filmic performer, but that of a well-known playback singer. Within the spectator–film relationship, this presents the possibility of an investment in the performer–singer behind the filmic performance, who can be named and whose work is familiar through the radio, as well as through countless earlier films.

In narrational terms, this play of a knowledge generated outside the film may in a sense set up another point from which the authority behind the narrative is articulated. The singer is one of a set of extratextual indices emerging from the cinematic institution. The institution makes a series of nonfilmic investments that are integral to its popularity and reception, the multiple positions from which its performance is conducted. Therefore, even in songs with straightforward narrative functions – as for example those romantic songs marking the division and union of lovers – there is this extra layer of narrational authority: this 'other' voice telling/singing the story, standing both inside and outside the filmic text. Film of course adds its own medium-specific layer of authority, that of the simulation of live performance. The particular pleasure created here is indicated by the designation of the song as performance: by the tendency to have the simulation of singing accompanied by the simulation of instrumental performance by the star, sometimes for a diegetic audience.

There may be a complex layering of these intertextually defined positions from which the story is enacted. This is particularly true of the narrational song, the point in the narrative when music is used to interpret the significance of a sequence. Very often in these cases traditional form – perhaps 'vulgarised' in later cinema by integrating it with pop rhythms (in a kind of bricolage effect) – is employed. For example, in *Devdas*, the tradition of the singing mendicant is used to express the significance of Devdas's departure for the city. In *Awara*, the mother's expulsion from the father's house is accompanied by the singing of a song that compares her situation to that of the mythical Sita.[30] In *Shree 420*, one of the central song sequences has Raj singing of his experiences as a socially ignominious figure subject to the arbitrary oppression of the police. The structure of the performance has the diegetic audience (of pavement dwellers) surrounding him as in traditional (and indeed contemporary) folk-theatrical performance.[31] Raj's address circulates, through reaction shots, in the audience and culminates in a direct address to the camera which sets up a relation of correspondence and substitution between internal and external audiences. These various instances suggest that cinema not only has a strategy of taking over and implanting itself in other performative media, but also constitutes them as narrational instances of its own authority. So, in a sense, instead of introducing discordance or incoherence into reception, the paranarrative inserts the film and the spectator into a larger field of coherence, one that stretches beyond the immediate experience of viewing films.

It is possible to separate out, within these general arguments about the functions of music and performance within narration, those performances which are specifically marked as spectacular and non-narrative in the basic structure of their address. The cabaret and the comic sequences are the key ones here.

The cabaret sequence is related to functions of male fetishism of the female body. However, these sequences are often narrativised, for such a fashioning of the female image may be counterposed to the position of the mother. Indicated here is another point for the male subject's articulation in relation to the female, one likely to be stated and disavowed. For example, in *Devdas*, the hero has to leave the countryside and his beloved for the city, where he falls into the company of a courtesan. He denounces her impurity, but relies on her; and she turns from her despised profession and becomes a protective figure for him. More generally, the cabaret performer is often placed within a structure of oppositions with the chaste heroine. But in certain instances there may be an overlap of functions, with the heroine indulging in a spectacular demonstration of her sexuality (for which she is likely to be punished) and the vamp redeeming herself by sacrificing her life for the hero.

Such fetishisation may be used subversively. In *Saheb, Bibi aur Gulam*, Chhoti Bahu (Meena Kumari), wife of a landed scion, determines to acquire a sensual image in order to attract the attention of a husband who spurns her and seeks the company of courtesans. This self-fetishisation is used to fix the look of the husband. This draws out the power that such a fetishism potentially holds: the woman's authority in the construction of her image is excessive, beyond the narrative's powers of control. The image tends to float free into a register of sensual, autoerotic presentation. (Figure 7.9) The power is however both limited and reversible. The ambivalence is played upon and then punished, with the woman's death. In a later film with the same actress, *Pakeezah*, the first part is dominated by a courtesan's performance, a demonstration of the control exercised by the image over the gaze. This arrangement is disrupted by the subsequent placing of the woman in respectable society, by the triumphant reinstatement of narrative and, indeed, of her hitherto unknown father.

Both cabaret and comic sequences often employ direct address in their performance of songs (Figures 7.10 and 7.11), and their content expresses the pleasures – of entertainment and sexual fantasy – that they have been employed to purvey. Take, for instance, the song of Abdus Sattar (Johnny Walker), the wandering masseur of *Pyaasa*, which suggests a strong likeness between the pleasures afforded by head massages and by cinema:

> Massages, oil massages, head massages!
> If your head's swimming, or your heart's sinking,
> don't worry my darling, come to me! . . .
> Whoever has his head massaged by me
> will have a shining destiny . . .
> Listen listen listen, son, listen
> a myriad sorrows have a single cure, why not try it. . . .

Figure 7.9 The female image floating free into a register of sensual, erotic presentation: Meena Kumari in *Saheb, Bibi aur Gulam/King, Queen, Slave* (Akbar Alvi, 1955). Prod: Guru Dutt Films.

Figure 7.10 Raj Kapoor in *Shree 420 / Mr 420* (Raj Kapoor, 1955). Prod: Raj Kapoor Films.

Figure 7.11 Waheeda Rehman in *Pyaasa*. Prod: Guru Dutt Films.

However, despite these straightforward performative functions, the comic too may be articulated with the narrative. He is related to the hero as his distorted mirror image, he who has no heroic propensities, whose romantic forays tend to be spurned or farcical. Further, his positioning in a reassuring parallelism to the narrative proper, enshrining as it were the feature of a purely performative entertainment, may also be reinstated in the narrative precisely to serve the ends of narrative gratification. He may be used to correct the imbalances wrought in the narrative and to bring the hero out of his travails and back on course to accomplish his objectives. For example, in *Pyaasa*, Johnny Walker performs two important deeds. The heroine, Gulab, to be worthy of the hero, Vijay, must cease to work as a prostitute. The comic ensures this by fending off her threatening pimp. Later, Vijay is consigned to a lunatic asylum, and it is Johnny Walker who rescues him.

These comic functions may sometimes work in fact to redeem the narrative from its conclusions. This is especially apparent when the hero in *Awara* fulfils the comic role himself. In our first introduction to the ill-fated Raj, whom we will discover is socially ignominious, he is under the control of the bandit Jagga. He has to lie to his mother about his work, and sings the following song:

> I'm a vagabond, a good-for-nothing
> or am I a star in the firmament above?

The duality of the representation here confirms that it is not simply a narrative description of his state, but a star performance that invites a vicarious immersion in the star personality and the pleasure of transgression. This is indicated by the surrogate audience set up in the film in the figure of an old man who fascinatedly watches Raj's pickpocketing activities but scoots when Raj's attention turns to him. And throughout the film, Raj's abilities as a crook are coded as both remarkable and glamorous. This culminates in a splitting of response at the conclusion. In spite of the court's sympathy for the social difficulties he has faced, Raj still has to serve a three-year sentence as punishment for his criminal actions. The conclusion is thus set up for pathos, with the lovers separated by the jail bars, pledging constancy, and so on. If the pleasure of the uniting of the couple is thus deferred, there is nevertheless another, parallel, pleasure presented; Raj, who had earlier given Rita a stolen necklace, now presents her with another one, thus reasserting, within the pathos of their separation, the maintenance of the pleasurable transgressions which have led to his incarceration.

There is nothing ironic in this parallel presentation: it attests to a different ordering of pleasure, one in which it is not contradictory to move the audience, sometimes within the same sequence, along different trajectories, without the one compromising the other.

In a sense, what may be discerned is a displacement of authorities lost or abdicated in the narrative to these 'other' positions or negotiations of spectatorial involvement.

By foregrounding the performative and star elements, the major focuses of attraction, these paranarrative units mark out a realm of fantasy, of vicarious identification and reassurance that allows, alongside the pleasures of lack presented in the narrative, those of coherence and mastery at the level of performance.

It will be clear from the preceding account that the Hindi film melodrama is constructed through rather different narrational mechanisms than those observed for western cinema. The latter privileges spectatorial knowledge in relation to divisions in character point of view in order to generate the desire to see these divisions bridged in the fiction. Pathos arises out of the denial of this fulfilment. It may even arise out of its fulfilment, if articulated with adequate notations of deferral, difficulty and fantasy. In the Hindi melodrama it is not divisions of knowledge which tend to order spectatorial desire. More often than not, such divisions mask family relations and enable transgressive fantasies, the primary one being conflict with the father. However, the recovery of these relations is important in the establishment of the romantic couple, underlying which is sometimes the regressive fantasy of mother and male child.[32] It is in this sense that knowledge must be achieved as the necessary stepping stone to fulfilment.

Pleasure tends to have a double articulation. There is the pleasure of the ending, of the narrative closure achieved in the restoration of identities; a pleasure which tends to be of a predictable nature, but is none the less fulfilling for that. More profoundly, there is the pleasure afforded by the blocking of knowledge in the fiction. For it is precisely through such gaps in knowledge that the pleasures of transgression are enabled.

Without the pleasure of moral disturbance and of the displacing of identities there would be no cause for narrative; but the pleasure gained from this indicates that closure in the Hindi commercial cinema is a profoundly disavowing operation. The restitution of the bipolarities that define the moral universe of the narrative, effected by deeply contradictory operations, affords a moral confirmation after forbidden pleasures and anxieties have been experienced. In this arrangement, pathos is not based on the failure to know and to communicate. It arises from the narrative's registering of the moral occult,[33] an organisation of perception which articulates primal notations of fear and guilt otherwise repressed by moral censorship. In the Hindi film narrative, this field is also one of transgressive pleasure. The blocking of the knowledge of identities allows for a fantasy terrain on which battle takes place and the positions of oppressor (father) and victim (son) are outlined. This is at once a fantasy of revenge and power and one of lack, of helplessness, and therefore of pathos. The conclusion tries to put things back in order. Sometimes there are casualties – bad sons who desire their mothers, sons who never get the mothers they want. Pathos is then maintained. But, quite commonly, the narrative restores positions, achieves recognition, and integrates the work it has performed in reassuring ways.

As I have pointed out, a different inflection of the narration is observable when the story is organised around the problem of female desire. The transgression opened up is intolerable, and the pressure to see incommunication resolved and normalcy restored is given priority. However, the more common female function is to fulfil the various needs of the male subject, ranging from offering him the pleasures of sexuality to enabling the restoration of the moral order.

The need for such a closure would indicate the place of the various slips that occur in the narration: the renegotiation of character attributes through a kind of juggling of moral bipolarities; the acquisition and subsequent dislodging of contaminating 'western' characteristics; the statement and then denial of the male subject's narrational powers. The para-narrative units, especially those involved in fetishistic operations, may in a sense represent the end term in these processes, a term which threatens to float free of the business of narrative but then tends to be integrated so that the moral wellbeing of the spectator may be preserved. However, as I have suggested, the retention of a certain parallelism of pleasures ensures that this disavowal is problematic: the cinema's performance of transgression lurks within its resurrection of the moral order.

Acknowledgements

I would like to thank Behroze Gandhy, Richard Dyer, Thomas Elsaesser, Ginette Vincendeau, Radhika Singha and Ulrike Sieglohr for commenting on earlier drafts of this article.

Notes

1 In 1956, M. B. Billimoria noted that Pakistan and Ceylon were considered part of the home market. Parts of Africa, Mauritius, Fiji, Malaya, Singapore, Trinidad (i.e. wherever there were significant Indian communities), the Middle East and South East Asia were singled out as major foreign markets. He estimated that 15–17% of film revenue came from these sources. 'Foreign markets for Indian Films', *Indian Talkie, 1931–56* (Bombay: Film Federation of India, 1956), pp. 54–5 the popularity of Hindi films in Eastern Europe started in the 1950s.

2 During the silent era, US films dominated the Indian market, but this situation changed in the 1930s with the coming of Indian talkies. For details of this earlier influence see Kristin Thompson, *Exporting Entertainment: America in the World Film Market, 1907–34* (London: British Film Institute, 1985), pp. 144–5.

3 Imports were high at the time of Independence. In 1948, 250 US films were imported (85.9% of foreign film imports): *Handbook of the Indian Film Industry* (Bombay: Motion Picture Society of India, 1949), p. 456. However, very few cinema halls exhibited them; in 1954 it was estimated that not more than 5% of cinemas showed US films. *Filmfare* (India), 12 November 1954, p. 3.

4 In 1955, out of 285 films produced countrywide, 126 were in Hindi. V. Doraiswamy (ed.) *Asian Film Directory and Who's Who* (Bombay: 1956), p. 326.

5 By the end of the 1970s the Tamil (105) and Malayalam (123) industries were producing

as many films as the Hindi (122). E. Barnouw and S. Krishnaswamy, *Indian Film* (New York: Oxford University Press, 1980), pp. 294–5.

6 Ibid, pp. 127–9.

7 In 1963 it was estimated that there was one cinema for every 86,400 people. *Indian Motion Picture Producers' Association Silver Jubilee Souvenir 1938–63* (Bombay: IMPPA, 1963), p. 175. The corresponding figure for the US was 10,500.

8 Peter Brooks, *The Melodramatic Imagination: Balzac, Henry James, Melodrama, and the Mode of Excess* (New Haven, CT: Yale University Press), 1976.

9 Rosie Thomas, 'Indian cinema: pleasures and popularity', *Screen*, vol. 26, nos. 3–4, (1985), pp. 116–31.

10 Ibid, p. 130; see also Gaston Roberge, *Chitrabani: A Book on Film Appreciation* (Calcutta: Chitrabani, 1974).

11 I have used R. K. Yagnik, *The Indian Theatre: Its Origins and Later Development Under European Influence, with Special Reference to Western India* (London: Allen and Unwin, 1933), pp. 92–117, for the following account.

12 Ibid, p. 110.

13 Christine Gledhill, 'The melodramatic field: an investigation', in Christian Gledhill, (ed.), *Home Is Where the Heart Is* (London: British Film Institute, 1987), p. 21.

14 For example, Paul Willemen's emphasis on traditional aesthetics and 'Hindu' conceptions lacks any conception of historical dynamics. 'Notes/arguments/ hypotheses', in Paul Willemen and Behroze Gandhy (eds), *Indian Cinema* (London: British Film Institute, 1980 and 1982), pp. 33–8.

15 'Every year, the major American blockbusters are remade almost shot by shot, but in an Indian setting'. Ibid, p. 33.

16 *Devdas*, made by New Theatres, Calcutta, is the sole non-Bombay production discussed here. Its influence on Hindi cinema makes analysis of it indispensable.

17 Brooks, *The Melodramatic Imagination*, p. 4.

18 A. K. Ramanujam details a number of Oedipus-type tales for India, the closest of which privileges the mother's point of view. 'The Indian Oedipus', in Lowell Edmunds and Alan Dundes (eds), *Oedipus: A Folklore Casebook* (New York: Garland, 1983), pp. 234–61.

19 Ramanujam notes that the withdrawal or renunciation of the son in the face of the father's aggression is a characteristic element of stories relating to father–son conflicts (ibid, pp. 244–8). Vijay Mishra has used the term 'renunciation' to identify character types motivated variously by a 'higher sense of duty' and 'self-pity', but does not look at the implications of this category for narration, in 'Towards a theoretical critique of Bombay cinema', *Screen*, vol. 26, nos. 3–4, (1985), p. 140.

20 There seems to have been a shift in the 1970s to narratives of male friendship (*dostana*). See Thomas's remarks, 'Indian cinema', p. 125.

21 For the priority of the mother–son relationship and the various representations it gives rise to, see Sudhir Kakar, *The Inner World: a Psychoanalytic Study of Childhood and Society in India* (Delhi and New York: Oxford University Press, 1978), especially ch. 3.

22 Cf David Bordwell's argument that, unlike the detective film, melodramatic narration tends to be omniscient and highly communicative, thereby privileging spectatorial knowledge: see *Narration in the Fiction Film* (London: Methuen, 1985), p. 60.

23 As suggested by Steve Neale, 'Melodrama and tears', *Screen*, vol. 27, no. 6 (1986).

24 I refer to the code of enigma, used by Barthes to analyse the classical realist text in the West. Roland Barthes, *S/Z* (London: Jonathan Cape, 1975).

25 Of course this would be true of most classical narrative. It is the absence of enigma – as narrational mechanism rather than as a mystery for the narrative to solve – which

would distinguish the Hindi commercial narrative. Thomas appears to address this distinction when she notes that the Hindi cinema emphasises 'a moral disordering to be (temporarily) resolved rather than an enigma to be solved' ('Indian cinema', p. 130).

26 In some instances, the widow is considered a 'fallen woman', her husband's death interpreted to mean that she had not been entirely true to him. See Veena Das, 'Social construction of adulthood', in Sudhir Kakar (ed.), *Identity and Adulthood* (Delhi: Oxford University Press, 1979), pp. 97–8.

27 The displacement described here is analogous with Geoffrey Nowell-Smith's usage of the notion of conversion hysteria to suggest how repression is articulated in melodrama. See 'Minnelli and melodrama', in Bill Nichols (ed.), *Movies and Methods*, vol. II (Berkeley, CA: University of California Press, 1985), p. 194.

28 In his study of American family melodrama, Thomas Elsaesser has noted: 'Just as in dreams, certain gestures and incidents mean something by their structure and sequence rather than by what they literally represent, the melodrama often works . . . by a displaced emphasis, by substitute acts, by parallel situations and metaphoric connections': 'Tales of sound and fury: observations on the family melodrama', ibid, p. 180.

29 Barthes's semic code may be helpful in this context: 'a shifting element which can combine with other similar elements to create characters, ambiances, shapes, and symbols': *S/Z*, p. 17.

30 The group nature of the performance here and the song's telling of a religious story resembles the performance of narratives called *deval*. See Komal Kothari, 'Myths, tales and folklore: exploring the substratum of cinema', in 'Indian Popular Cinema: Myth, Meaning and Metaphor', *India International Centre Quarterly*, special issue, vol. 8, no. 1, March 1980, p. 33.

31 The mode of address and audience positioning described here is akin to that of the fairly recent (about 150 years old) and still extant folk–theatrical form known as *khyal*. Ibid, p. 36.

32 I am referring to a textual operation here, rather than to a gendering of spectatorial position.

33 '. . . the domain of operative spiritual values which is both indicated within and masked by the surface of reality . . .': Brooks, *The Melodramatic Imagination*, p. 5.

8 Avenging women in Indian cinema

Lalitha Gopalan

That there has been an escalation of violence in contemporary Indian cinema is now a well worn cliche. *The Illustrated Weekly of India* cashed in on this truism by publishing a roundtable discussion between filmmakers, critics and stars that explored the 'correlation between violence in films and violence in society and the various implications of the nexus'.[1] The discussion attentively dwells on film as a mass cultural product, but fails to offer any specific link between a particular film or genre and its effects on society. What also remains unacknowledged in this discussion is how contemporary films feed off the crisis of legitimacy of the Indian state, a crisis that unleashed an open display of the state's coercive powers and was precipitated most visibly after the state of emergency between 1975 and 1977. Even if it is debatable that the state of emergency was the origin of the crisis of legitimacy of the Indian state, at the very least we can speculate that it did set in motion contestations of power and authority which have made pressing a more thorough exploration of hegemony, citizenship, community, nationalism and democracy in India. In short, discussions of violence have to consider how films replete with avenging women, gangsters, brutal police forces, and vigilantes stage some of the most volatile struggles over representation that shape our public and private fantasies of national, communal, regional and sexual identities.

A brief examination of three more features from the Indian press published in the late 1980s and early 1990s will show further how contradictory some of the discussions of violence in contemporary Indian cinema are. Firoze Rangoonwala names the near-decade between 1981 and 1992 'the age of violence'.[2] Assembling Hindi films with vigilante resolutions from both 'parallel' cinema – Govind Nihalani's *Ardh Satya / Half Truth* (1984) – and the commercial industry, he identifies a marked shift towards escalating violence in this period. Rangoonwala does not comment on the social impact of these films, as the roundtable discussion tended to do, but directs his sharpest criticism at popular cinema for having 'succumbed to a hackneyed formula'. Arguably, dismissing formula-ridden popular cinema, however hackneyed it may be, unwittingly ascribes to it the authority to standardize cinematic codes and narratives and, in turn, contradicts a widely held view that Indian cinema randomly picks up storylines only finally to deliver *masala* films. M. Rahman offers a less disparaging report of the Indian film industry in the 1980s. He sets out the workings of an emerging 'formula' in Hindi cinema inaugurated by N. Chandra's film *Pratighat / Retribution* (1987) and soon followed by *Sherni* (Harmesh Malhotra, 1988), *Khoon Bhari Mang* (Rakesh Roshan, 1988), *Khoon Bahaa Ganga Mein* (Pravin Bhatt, 1989), *Commando* (Babbar Subhash, 1988), *Bhraschtachar* (Ramesh Sippy, 1989), and *Kali Ganga* (Raj N. Sippy, 1990). The common theme of these films, according to Rahman, is their portrayal of women as 'hardened, cynical, vengeful creatures'.[3] For his report, Rahman interviews director Chandra as well as prominent actresses like Hema Malini, Dimple and Rekha, who have all played avenging women. While Chandra suggests that these violent films are generated in response to the voracious viewing habits of an audience that wishes to see something different from stock male 'action' films, the actresses argue that screenplays with dominant and powerful women are a welcome break from stereotypical roles as submissive and dutiful mothers and wives. Another critic, Maithili Rao, also identifies this emerging trend in the industry, again inaugurated, she argues, by Chandra's *Pratighat*, a trend that she calls the 'lady avengers'.[4] Arguing that the films 'reflect the cultural schizophrenia in our society', Rao reproaches them for being 'hostile to female sexuality' and for passing themselves off as 'victimization masquerading as female power'. Yet Rao's feminist critique addresses neither Rahman's discussion with the director and actresses of *Pratighat* nor the tremendous box-office success of these films in general.

This essay proposes that these contradictory and diverse readings of 'aggressive woman' films are provocative enough to warrant another look at the films' visual and narrative goriness. I will argue that a different reading of the configurations of femininity and violence staged in these films will uncover the contours of their appeal. My reading strategies are indelibly shaped by a feminist film theory that argues for formal textual analysis as a means to understand the articulation of sexual difference in cinema. Although it tends to focus heavily on Hollywood productions, feminist film theory remains useful for at least two reasons: first, deploying it for an analysis of Indian cinema interrogates a monolithic conception of 'national cinema' and opens up the possibility of exploring points of contact with international filmmaking practices; and second, its nuanced theorization of scopophilia and spectatorship holds up extremely well for the films discussed here. Despite my general move to place Indian cinema in the context of international filmmaking practices, I do want to argue, provisionally at this point, that the national specificity, or 'Indianness', that we might attribute to these films emerges from the ways in which the censorship regulations of the Indian state shape and influence them as cinematic representations. We must acknowledge and theorize the presence of the state when discussing the relationship between films and spectators.

In the critical reception of these films the term 'formula' is bandied about to belittle the structures of repetition between films. But this term only partially accounts for the viewer's pleasure. This essay explores above all how it may be equally possible that we are not only drawn to the formulaic use of visceral images in these films, but also to the circuits of intertextual relay between and among them. I find it pertinent to call on the concept of 'genre', which allows us to place assertions that these films are different from male action films alongside critical evaluations which may condemn the films for cunningly representing female victims as vigilantes. Only the concept of genre will allow us simultaneously to address, on the one hand, the Indian film industry's investment in standardized narratives for commercial success and, on the other, the spectator's pleasure in these genre films with their stock narratives structured around repetition and difference. While it is a legitimate line of enquiry to gather and marshal production details to verify the historical emergence of a genre, I prefer here to employ textual analysis of different films in order to unravel their particular structuring of repetition and difference and to demonstrate their generic workings.

If we examine Rahman's loose cluster of films which treat the figure of a 'dominant' woman, and in which the critic groups together a film close to the bandit genre, *Sherni / The Lioness*, with a film close to the police genre, *Zakmi Aurat / Wounded Women* (Avtar Bhogal, 1988), we can distinguish a genre of films that I will call, following Maithili Rao, 'avenging women'. These films open with family settings which, according to Hindi film conventions, appear 'happy' and 'normal', but with a difference. There is a marked absence of dominant paternal figures. The female protagonist is always a working woman with a strong presence on screen. These initial conditions are upset when the female protagonist is raped. The raped woman files charges against the perpetrator, who is easily identifiable. Court rooms play a significant role in these films, if only to demonstrate the state's inability to convict the rapist and to precipitate a narrative crisis. Miscarriages of justice constitute a turning point in the films, allowing for the passage of the protagonist from a sexual and judicial victim to an avenging woman.

The general features of these narratives and the production of horror in their rape scenes point to a close similarity to the rape–revenge narratives of Hollywood B films, especially horror films.[5] Critical writing on Hollywood rape–revenge films, particularly Carol Clover's work, suggests that the marginal status of these films, in contrast to mainstream Hollywood, permits them to address some of the unresolved and knotty problems of gender and spectatorship that are carefully regulated and managed by the mainstream. In moves that are useful for my own work, Clover turns to the sadistic and masochistic pleasures evoked by these horror films to suggest that B films are the 'return of the repressed' in mainstream Hollywood. Focusing on B horror films, where low production values are coupled with sex and violence, Clover argues that these films displace the woman as the sole site of scopophilic pleasure and open possibilities of cross-gender identification through the sadomasochistic pleasures encouraged by these films. She concludes:

I have argued that the center of gravity of these films lies more in the reaction (the revenge) than the act (the rape), but to the extent that the revenge fantasy derives its force from *some* degree of imaginary participation in the act itself, the victim position, these films are predicated on cross-gender identification of the most extreme, corporeal sort.[6]

Instead of privileging the revenge narrative or the rape scenes as Rao does, it is more useful to explore, following Clover, how the narrative nuances of this genre are predicated on a cinematic logic that draws these two elements together. Rape scenes are not unusual in Indian cinema. They are, however, frequently subject to censorship rulings on the grounds of their irrelevance to the main narrative and the unseemly pleasure they evoke.[7] Yet rape scenes in avenging women films are indispensable to their narrative, repeatedly evoked as evidence in a court room sequence or repeated as a traumatic event experienced by the victim. In other words, the centrality of the rape scenes in the narrative heightens their intimate relationship to the subsequent revenge plot where, once again, there is a replay of negotiations between sex and violence.

While *Pratighat* is frequently cited as an originary moment in the avenging women genre, the combination of rape and revenge was already evident in B. R. Chopra's *Insaaf Ka Tarazu / Scales of Justice* produced in 1980. The latter's initial box-office success can be partly attributed to the heroine of the film, Zeenat Aman. *The Encyclopaedia of Indian Cinema* describes the conditions of reception that shaped this film:

> This notorious rape movie followed in the wake of growing feminist activism in India in the 70s after the Mathura and Maya Tyagi rape cases, the amendment to the Rape Law and the impact of, e.g., the Forum Against Rape which offered legal assistance to rape victims.[8]

References to the feminist movement are obviously one of the determining features structuring the reception of this film, but its notoriety points to a different route of analysis in which we should consider how this film relies on our knowledge of these rape cases as a point of entry into fantastical stagings of our anxieties about women, sexuality and law, anxieties that in turn are set off, but not resolved, by anti-rape campaigns.[9] *Insaaf Ka Tarazu* unquestionably stands out as one of the early experiments in rape–revenge narratives.

This film opens with a rape scene. A colour sequence showing us a medium shot of a screaming woman in a sari rapidly cuts to a black-and-white shadow play. The silhouette of a man first chases and then disrobes this woman. Another male figure enters the scene and a fight begins between them. The film returns to full colour when the potential rapist is fatally stabbed. The following credit sequence is a montage of stills from religious and tourist sites in India with the soundtrack playing the title song of the film. These two sequences juxtapose rape with representations of India. This association with India is further played out in the film by naming the female protagonist Bharati – the feminine name in Hindi for India. These first scenes suggest female rape as an allegory of a beleaguered nation-state, a suggestion which, however, is not developed further in the film.

The second rape sequence in the film is distinguished from the opening sequence by the continued use of colour footage and the absence of a male saviour. Using a calendar art print of a woman in bondage in the victim's (Arti's) bedroom as a reference point, the sequence allows glimpses at a rape scene that includes both coercion and bondage. Furthermore, the scene offers us another point of identification with the victim's younger sister, Nita, who accidentally walks into Arti's bedroom during the rape. Arti files charges against the rapist, Gupta. A number of social encounters between Gupta and Arti preceding the rape, combined with Nita's confused testimony, are employed in the court room to suggest that Arti was not raped but consented to have sex with Gupta. The court finds Gupta not guilty of rape.

The court's verdict in Arti's rape case comes as no surprise to the spectators, for the film mobilizes this doubt throughout the scene. For instance, Nita's testimony is crucial to this case but the defence lawyer convincingly argues her inability to tell the difference between coerced and consenting sexual relationships. The film frames Nita as a horrified voyeur witnessing a primal scene, infusing the scene in this way with both fear of, and pleasure in, sexual knowledge instead of recognizing it as sexual violation pure and simple. The sadistic–voyeuristic pleasure also surfaces here through the art print on the bedroom wall. The viewer might expect the print's subject to be identified with the aggressor, a traditional strategy. Instead, it shores up confusion between the representation of rape and rape itself – thus eroticizing the scene of violation and escalating our masochistic identification with this scene. Privileging Nita's relationship to the scene, the film also exposes, and depends on, our inability as spectators to tell the cinematic difference between a scene of sexual consent and rape.

Notwithstanding the relationship between Nita's credibility as a witness and the court's verdict, Nita's ambivalence presses upon another aspect of the film's narrative – the unfolding of the revenge plot. The film delays and reserves its revenge scenario until it can represent an unambiguous rape scene. It is only after Gupta proceeds to rape the virginal Nita in his office that Arti's revenge is allowed. At the film's climax Arti shoots Gupta, circumventing a judicial verdict on Nita's case. The film closes with another court scene where this time the judge abdicates his office for failing to deliver justice in earlier rape cases. Closing the rape–revenge narratives around a court scene or a figure representing the state is now a standard feature of this genre and stands in sharp contrast to the male vigilante genre where the figure of the state is repeatedly undermined, for example in *Nayakan / Don* (Mani

Rahman, 1987). Although it took seven years for *Insaaf Ka Tarazu* to produce a 'spin-off', in the form of *Pratighat*, the film nonetheless established some of the basic conventions that squarely locate it as the inaugural moment in the avenging woman genre.

Pratighat consolidates some of the basic strains of this emergent rape–revenge narrative. The film revolves around corrupt politicians and the ongoing crisis over law and order in a small town. The female protagonist, Lakshmi, is a college teacher who lives with her lawyer husband and his parents. The film opens with several scenes of hooliganism orchestrated by Kali, a *lumpen* youth leader, in Lakshmi's town. These scenes lead us through Lakshmi's conversion from an ordinary, disinterested citizen into an active intervenor in Kali's reign of terror. Her complete conversion to an avenging woman hinges on a crucial scene when she openly confronts Kali by filing a criminal suit against him and then refuses to withdraw it, even when he threatens to harm her. As the stakes continue to rise in their confrontation, Kali finally resorts to a gendered resolution: he disrobes Lakshmi on the street in front of her house, with all her neighbours and family watching in silence. This violation establishes the primary conditions for Lakshmi's revenge on Kali and his gang, and at the same time seals her estrangement from her husband. Lakshmi is rescued from this scene of public humiliation by Durga, whose own life has been scarred by Kali's violence – she was gang raped by Kali's men, and her husband tortured to death – and who nevertheless continues to galvanize opposition to Kali. Lakshmi moves into Durga's home, recovers, and receives support for her own revenge plan.

Pratighat displaces the conventional representation of the rape scene by recon-figuring it, both visually and narratively, as a disrobing sequence. Ironically, while Kali declares that disrobing is a part of the Hindu tradition, evoking the *Mahabharata*, cinematically the film disengages with all of the conventional representations of rape. The entire disrobing scene is spliced as a medium-length shot, and in the final moment of complete nudity the film switches to colour negative, conveying the full extent of this violation in Indian cinema. In moving away from the standard representation of rape scenes, *Pratighat* draws our attention to the usual proximity of scenes of rape and disrobing in Hindi cinema, and thus interrogates the ethics of a 'full view' normally circumscribing such scenes.

The scene of revenge where Lakshmi confronts Kali is also framed with narrative references to Hindu mythology and filmic gestures pointing to mythological films from the Madras film industry as well as the *Ramayana* and *Mahabharata* television serials.[10] Clad in a red sari, Lakshmi garlands and anoints Kali at a public meeting and then repeatedly strikes him with an axe originally intended as a gift to him. The final killing scene is edited by juxtaposing shots of Kali's larger-than-life cardboard cutout with the onstage altercation between Lakshmi and Kali, fight scenes between Kali's men and Lakshmi's students, and colour negative stills from the original disrobing scene. The cardboard cutout intertextually evokes the art print in *Insaaf Ka Tarazu*, playing on the unrepresentativeness of the depiction of rape in the former film, and suggesting that Lakshmi's aggressive attack in *Pratighat* is equally horrific. Moving the narrative focus away from a single killing scene to a general murderous chaos replays the film's own themes in which rape is located alongside other social crimes like hooliganism and corruption.

Two contradictions must be noted. Even as the film is critical of rape, rape scenes figure periodically in the narrative, signalling in each instance the consolidation of criminality and vigilantism and the increasing displacement of the state's role in law and order. Similarly, criminalizing rape, the conceit employed in this film, appears to identify the film with a progressive legal position, but this does not take account of the sadistic–voyeuristic pleasure prompted by the film's representations of rape. Kali's death may bear a formal resemblance to the disrobing scene, but is not subject to the same censorship regulations that underscore sexual representations in Indian cinema. *Pratighat*, nevertheless, irks us with the limits and possibilities of equating rape and revenge scenes, and thus coaxes us into reconsidering the masochistic underpinnings of the rape scenes in this genre. While the film relies on our maso-chistic identification in the rape scene to fully play out its horrifying potential, the sadistic dimensions of this very scene propel the revenge plot and remind us that the ensemble of elements in the rape scene is always a volatile marriage between sex and violence.

There are several reasons for *Pratighat*'s success, but its ability to figure horror in the revenge sequences opened the gates for other permutations and combinations of rape and revenge. The full import of horror in revenge scenes is further developed in Avatar Bhogal's *Zakmi Aurat / Wounded Women*, released in 1988. Retaining the rule of targeting 'modern' women as victims – a fashion model in *Insaaf Ka Tarazu* and a college teacher in *Pratighat* – *Zakmi Aurat* picks a policewoman as its protagonist. With the rape scene occurring early in the narrative, the turning point emerges when the judicial system refuses to convict the rapists, in spite of policewoman Kiran Dutt's own testimony. Abandoning legal recourse, Kiran Dutt joins forces with other rape victims in the city. Together the women come up with a fitting revenge plan: to ensnare the rapists and castrate them.

Kiran's gang rape is edited as a fight sequence that closes around a conventional representation of rape. The rape scene returns to the bedroom familiar from *Insaaf Ka Tarazu*, but with a twist. Refusing to linger on Inspector Kiran Dutt's body as the rapists strip her, the film focuses instead on the rapists as they tear off her jeans and fling them up at the ceiling fan. The rape scene climaxes in a series of shot/reverse-shots of fetishized objects – the ceiling fan and a medium closeup shot of Kiran's screaming face.

The sequence of shots employed in the gang rape of the female police officer creates the basic template for the castration revenge scenes. Again, peripheral details, like the doctor's operating gown, her mask and the overhead lamp, are excessively in focus and fetishized. The camera cuts off the entire abdominal region of the man, refusing to zoom in on a cloaked genital area. Rapid freeze frames of men's faces, and ninety-degree shots of the overhead lamp in the operating theatre signal the ongoing process of castration. This equivalence between the gang rape and castration scenes, suggested by the repetition of shot/reverse-shots of a face and an overhead object cinematically attempts to balance rape and revenge.

Critics have lambasted this film for offering an improbable resolution to a rape scenario; however, such a reading assumes that films have an indexical signification to political reality instead of examining how their narratives repeatedly stage various fantastical possibilities of these very same realities for the spectator.[11] One of the crucial constitutive features of this genre is its vociferous staging of 'reality' through familiar references: shots of real newspapers, photographs of Gandhi on courtroom walls, footage of the Indian flag, and so on. *Zakmi Aurat* relies more extensively on these elements than other films: the opening sequence shows us actual newspaper reports of various rape cases in India, and the film draws an obvious link between the Kiran Dutt character and Kiran Bedi – a well-known woman police officer in Delhi. These authenticating details appear to be strategically placed to heighten our viewing pleasure of the unravelling horror plot, reeling us in to scenes of escalating horror that culminate precisely at the very moments when the film plays on its uncanny resemblance to extra-cinematic icons and events. In general, these narratives may not directly respond to, or satisfy demands for, justice in particular rape cases, but they do stage scenes of resolution that remain beyond state legality and expose the spectator's complicity in the terrifying rape sequences.

Defending the spectatorial pleasures ensuing from *I Spit on Your Grave* (Meir Zarchi, 1977), a film that bears an intimate relationship to *Zakmi Aurat*, Carol Clover writes: 'what disturbs about *I Spit on Your Grave* is its perverse simplicity, the way it closes all the intellectual doors and windows and leaves us staring at the *lex talionis* unadorned'.[12] Clover's comment is aimed at up-market films like *The Accused* (Jonathan Kaplan, 1988), in which, leaving little space for the rape victim to articulate her torment, the legal process takes over the narrative and substantially closes off the possibility of direct vigilante action. Clover's defence of Zarchi's film bears on my own reading of *Zakmi Aurat* in which, despite the film's narrative simplicity, the problems attending the visual representation of revenge in these films are precipitated. As we have seen, films in this genre rely on convincingly meting out vigilante revenge that must equal, or even surpass, the horror of rape. While this equation produces ongoing narrative tensions, visual representations of rape in Indian cinema also remind us of the authority of censorship regulations, and suggest the possibility of sadomasochistic pleasures structuring these rape scenes.

I have argued elsewhere that, despite overt protests at film censorship, the Indian film industry is crucially dependent on state censorship in the cinematic generation of sadomasochistic pleasure.[13] The female body is always the object in focus, and is repeatedly subjected to a withdrawing camera that banks on an intimate relationship between the psychic laws governing taboos and the state laws of censorship. Until the emergence of the revenge plot in these movies about rape, rape scenes in Indian cinema appeared to be substitutes for sex, relentlessly eroticizing violence. It comes as no surprise that the criticism levelled against these films is sparked by a suspicion that violent sex is merely being flaunted as rape, a suspicion that also guides censorship regulations.

To mitigate against and ward off such criticism, revenge scenes in these films have to be equally horrific in order to allow us to read clearly the scenes of violent sex as rape *retroactively*. The narrative and visual machinations of this genre thus revolve around the problem of balancing rape and revenge: *Pratighat* settles rape by evoking figures of Hindu Shakti goddesses and by killing the rapist, whereas *Zakmi Aurat* resorts to an anatomical equation by suggesting castration as an act of revenge, thus escalating the horror of rape by visually locating the castrated male body in an analogous position to the raped female body. Settling rape through castration points to a feminist Utopia where, at least momentarily, the easy economic equation between the penis and phallus resolves the differences between gender and power that are constantly complicated by, and subjected to, the symbolic difference between the penis and phallus. The question is, while revenge narratives in this genre seek continuously to 'match' the horror of the rape, can they ever succeed?

Zakmi Aurat brings to a head the entire problem of visually and narratively matching rape with revenge through its absurd logic of five rapes to fifteen castrations, a logic that heralds a moratorium on this genre in the configuration I am describing. At the same time, *Zakmi Aurat* spawned films like *Aaj Kie Aurat / Today's Woman* (Avtar Bhogal, 1993) and *Damini* (Rajkumar Santoshi, 1993), where the narratives not only emphasise the difference between the raped woman and the avenger, but also return to exhausting the possibilities of pleasure in violent rape scenes.[14] Even while revenge narratives, as Rahman informs us, provide female stars with more dominant roles because women's access to avenging power in these films is intimately predicated on rape as a violent litmus test of gender identity, rape scenes are never neatly cordoned off from Indian cinema's extensive use of the woman's body as a stand-in for sex, as a crucial site of scopophilic pleasure. Faced with these contradictory demands, the avenging woman genre emerges as a giddy masculine concoction. The rape scenes provide the narrative ruse for revenge while also providing the spectator with a conventional regime of scopophilic pleasure. Revenge allows female stars to dominate the screen, but the genre demands that the violent assertion of masculine power in the form of rape is the price to be exacted for such power. Clearly, at the periphery of this genre, where the interlocking narratives of rape and revenge are less than minimally finessed, the gratuitous deployment of rape does not sufficiently dislodge or displace conventional representations of women in Indian cinema, nor does it appease Rao's suspicions that these films are hostile to women's sexuality.

Located within the larger rubric of other violent action films produced in the same period, the more provocative feminist aspects of the rape–revenge films are most apparent in their narrative closures. In these, the avenging woman's taking up of power is always limited by the arrival of the police; this finale differs markedly from the more assertive vigilante resolutions of masculine genres like the gangster and bandit films. Given, also, their prolonged judicial sequences revolving around the rape cases, the appeal of these rape–revenge narratives, then, arguably rests on their ability to stage all the anxious points that attend the relationship between patriarchy and the state. If the social imaginary promotes a unity between symbolic law and the state, rape cases inject a dissonance between these sites of authority to remind us that 'issues' of honour and shame are only provisionally resolved through legal proceedings. For the victim, the state's betrayal in rape cases is accompanied by patriarchal abandonment and, together, these 'disappointments' are consolidated as the turning points that enable the shift to the revenge narrative. Faced with an orderless universe, the 'avenging woman' film proceeds on a transgressive vigilante path, inciting masculine anxiety about the phallic female, and opening up the representational circuit for women on the Indian screen. But this unfettered feminine power is finally undercut, in the films, by reeling in the authority of the state, and by revealing the avenging woman's own overwhelming investment in the restoration of the known social imaginary. The casting of women as embodying and sustaining tradition recycles an old stereotype in Indian films; however, the forced closure in this genre only provisionally irons out the anxieties between patriarchy and the state.

While the conventional narrative closure and the precarious necessity of rape in these films both seem to limit the radical potential of the revenge narratives, they cannot completely regulate the series of unstable desires and identities set in motion by the ongoing dynamics of rape combined with revenge. This matter of the subversive qualities of rape–revenge narratives, both at the level of cinematic form and in the realm of the spectator's pleasure, leads us to some tangled issues which have plagued feminist film theory. Laura Mulvey's classic essay 'Visual pleasure and narrative cinema' argued that Hollywood style at its best (and all the cinema which fell within its sphere of influence) offers pleasure for the masculine spectator by enacting a conventional heterosexual division of labour in its narrative structure between active male and passive female. Challenges to Mulvey's essay, besides her own revision through melodrama, have been mounted by feminist film theorists as they move into Hollywood's other genres, particularly B films that include horror, slasher and pornographic elements. Focusing on the less-than-best cinematic styles of B films that are directed at, and have, a loyal female audience and incorporate a heady combination of sex and violence, recent feminist film theory has been forced to reconsider the dynamics between identification and pleasure, particularly sadomasochistic pleasure. Arguing for the presence of sadomasochistic pleasure in violent pornographic films, Williams writes:

> . . . it seems to me preferable to employ the term *sadomasochistic* when describing the perverse fantasies that inform these films. While still problematic, the term

at least keeps in play the oscillation between active and passive and male and female subject positions, rather than fixing one pole or the other as the essence of the viewer's experience. At the same time, it does not allow us to forget, as some celebrations of masochisms (e.g., Studlar or Samois) do forget, where ultimate power lies.[15]

Drawing on Williams's economic articulation of sadomasochism, it appears that the rape–revenge scenes in the avenging woman genre similarly rely on the generation of sadomasochistic pleasure, a pleasure that unwittingly challenges, however provisional it may be, the straightforward sadistic impulses of the depiction of rape in Indian cinema. Because rape scenes are inextricably meshed with the revenge plot in this genre, the masochistic dimensions of the rape scene far outweigh its conventional sadistic associations, while at the same time the unfolding revenge plot provokes the spectator's sadistic investments in revenge and punishment. Interweaving sadism and masochism through different filmic moments, this genre upsets the normalizing fetishistic economy with the fragmented woman's body as the central object. But complicating these generic pleasures is the ongoing tussle between every Indian filmmaker and the state over censorship. As a result, it is precisely through overt submission to censorship regulations that the commercial film industry parodies the authority of the state, a relationship that is not unlike the masochist's relationship to patriarchal law. We may have to consider, therefore, the possibility that the rape–revenge device might provide yet another ruse to circumvent censorship, one which resorts, once again, to the woman's body. At the same time, though, tightening the rape–revenge equation, as these films seem to do, unwittingly opens possibilities for cross-gender identifications. The contradictory forces of Indian commercial cinema beg for a reconsideration of the other identifications available in this heady combination of sex and violence. I would suggest, responding in part to the debates on violence in Indian cinema which cast these representations solely in terms of their regressive effects on society, that violent scenes circumscribed by cross-cutting genre features and pressures can, in surprising ways, challenge patriarchal gender constructions. While rape–revenge narratives may not be completely suitable as Utopian feminist models, in their engagement with the female star system in Indian cinema and the feminist movement, as well as through the foregrounding of feminine aggression in their mise-en-scene, they do stage the contradictory contours of sexual identity and pleasure. I would suggest that, in this context, the scenes of circumscribed, intertextual, and crosscut violence in these films constitute one of the crucial axes of spectator interest.

Before we commit ourselves to the idea that all roads to female aggression inevitably lead us to rape scenes in Indian cinema, it is worth remembering that this tight relationship between rape and revenge is a recurrent feature in Hindi cinema.

Whatever peculiar production rationale helps to fortify this link, the yoking of rape with revenge cannot be disconnected from the modes of address structuring Hindi cinema: a national audience is always already its imagined addressee. In other words, its desire to command a national audience severely shrinks Hindi cinema's ability to stray from a successful, yet conventional paradigm.

However an appraisal of other regional cinemas, in particular of Telegu films with the actress Vijayshanti in the leading role, demonstrates that there are other contours to cinematic female aggression, ones without the routine rape scene. Dispensing with rape scenes, these films allow aggression to shadow desire. These films also lend themselves to a rich reading of regional and global cinematic issues. For instance, as Telegu films they are in constant dialogue with political dramas – a forte of the Telegu film industry – challenging the masculine rule of this genre. As female-centred action films, they recall 'Fearless Nadia's' stunt films from the 1930s to the 1950s, and their representation of female agility reminds us of a long lineage of films and television shows, up to and beyond *Charlie's Angels* (TV series, 1976–1981). In addition, as films initially made in Telegu and subsequently dubbed into Hindi and Tamil, they raise interesting issues about the new economics of dubbing that have gained a national market for regional cinemas.

Rumours and reports from the industry claim that Vijayshanti is one of India's highest paid female stars whose cachet at the box office is greater than that of most of her male counterparts. However, she too has had her share of rape–revenge narratives – *Pratighat*, for instance, is a remake of a Telegu film *Pratighatan* (T. Krishna, 1986), which has Vijayshanti cast as the avenging woman – and is not altogether protected from playing the submissive wife, as in *Eeshwar* (K. Vishwanath and Rajesh Malik, 1989). Nevertheless she manages to corner some of the most spectacularly aggressive roles in Indian cinema. Vijayshanti's own self-representation does not rest on emulating other heroines but, as she puts it: 'I always have to kick and pound the villains to pulp. That's why I'm called the Amitabh Bachchan of Andhra Pradesh.'[16]

So far, when examining rape–revenge narratives, I have generally steered away from considering the influence of the female star economy, choosing instead to focus on textual analysis. But, despite their different directors, Vijayshanti's films – for example, *Tejaswini* (N. Chandra, 1991), *Adavi Rani* (Kodanda Rami Reddy, 1992), *Rowdy Inspector* (B. Ghopal, 1991), and *Streetfighter* (B. Ghopal, 1994) – hold together as if to constitute a genre in their own right. They thus challenge my own marginalization of the female star economy in my previous readings of the avenging woman films. Each of Vijayshanti's films upturns several conventional associations between femininity and aggression, but all too often their narratives tend to characterize female aggressiveness as a feature belonging exclusively to the pre-Oedipal phase. Kodi Ramakrishna's *Police Lock-up* (1992), on the other hand, refuses any narrow casting of female aggressiveness and, in turn, allows for an intriguing relationship between law and desire.

The narrative takes the following route: Vijaya (Vijayshanti) is an upright police

officer who arrives in the town of Vishakpatnam to investigate a political assassination. She has to contend with corrupt policemen and a conniving and ambitious
chief minister, Panjaraja, whom we know is responsible for the assassination.
Panjaraja accuses her of being a terrorist and Vijaya is thrown into jail. A second
storyline now unfurls: Shanti, Vijayashanti's double role, is the wife of a zealous
police inspector, Ashok, who is frequently transferred because of his honesty. Shanti
is obviously cast as Vijaya's alter ego: meek, clad in a sari, devoted to her husband
and pining for a child. It is precisely this guilelessness that lands her in jail one curfew
night. The police throw her into Vijaya's cell and the two see each other for the first
time. Unlike stories of lost sisters and brothers that recur in Indian films, this scene
does not draft in mothers and fathers to claim kinship between the two women.
Instead, it moves quickly through the respective events that brought the two women
to jail. The crucial detail that lends credibility to Vijaya's story of her capture is
Shanti's encounter with a dying journalist who, mistaking Shanti for Vijaya, passes
on details of yet another assassination scheme. Shanti suggests that they switch places
so that Vijaya can complete her investigation and arrest the corrupt chief minister.
Vijaya reluctantly agrees, and the following morning leaves with Ashok, now passing
as his meek wife. The film now gallops along, plotting Vijaya's pursuit of the Chief
Minister. We see her move effortlessly from sari to jeans, from submissive daughter-
in-law to strong and masterful police official. Through various twists and turns that
include the notorious international assassin John, the film ends in a temple courtyard
where Vijaya and Ashok annihilate the villains. The wily politician is the last to go;
Vijaya blows him up with his own bomb, strapped on with a belt, reminding viewers
of the way Rajiv Gandhi was killed. The film closes with Vijaya and Shanti embracing.

Departing radically from both the rape–revenge narratives and male action films,
Police Lock-up reconfigures the relationship between power, authority and gender,
opening up a wide range of fantastical possibilities for feminist identifications. There
are many obvious scenes of positive identification secured in the film. For instance,
a series of slow-motion shots, the film introduces Vijaya as a police officer driving
her jeep in thus breaking away from the routine logic of passage from victim to
avenger in the rape–revenge genre. The film ungrudgingly celebrates her ability and
success as a police officer by showing us elaborate details of her work: there are
several fight scenes where both guns and kung-fu fighting styles are exhibited; her
acumen and confidence with technology are shown more than once. My own
favourite scene is when Vijaya, dressed as Shanti, uses a video camera to shoot an
exchange between Panjaraja's hoodlums. She then replays this scene in slow motion
and decodes their conversation through lip reading in order to discover where
a kidnap victim is hidden. These scenes suggest the presence, possibility and
intervention of female control over modern sites of technology which are all too
frequently represented as male prerogatives. Collectively, these details easily
constitute the bedrock of any feminist primer on positive identifications, but they
fit too neatly and are too far from the messy economies of identification and desire

that cinematic spectatorship thrives on. What we do see in *Police Lock-up* is a woman's excessive investment in the law, a law that we often mistrust for the ways in which it gives feminism short shrift.

The cornerstone of this film's innovativeness, however, is its deployment of the double role. Indian cinema has long been fascinated with double roles and utilizes them both to recognize and to bank on a star's popularity. When female double roles surface, for example in Ramesh Sippy's *Sita aur Gita/Sita and Gita* (1972), the narrative revolves around the separate lives and identities of twins, and conventionally closes on family romance: lost siblings, cast as opposites, find each other, find their parents, and so on. In sharp contrast, *Police Lock-up* refuses to recuperate the family: Vijaya and Shanti are not lost-and-found twins, and their resemblance is never resolved narratively in the film. Demonstrating that the two women effectively and easily pass for each other – Vijaya as the submissive wife and Shanti as an aggressive officer – the film mobilizes change in each woman and closes with a less polarized distinction between the two. Obviously the blurred distinction between them draws this film dangerously close to the horror film genre on twins.[17]

Rejecting a narrative closure around biological kinship, this film wrings out the full effects of masquerade. Vijaya's competency is asserted through her ability to masquerade not only as Shanti, but also as a telephone line repair man and as the killer John at various points in the film. Masquerade controls and mobilizes this film's narrative.

Joan Riviere's conceptualization of masquerade continues to abet theorizations of cross-gender identifications that attend the female spectator when viewing a masculine-ordered universe in Hollywood cinema.[18] Among all the available appropriations of her work in film theory, John Fletcher's reworking stands out for his return to the signifying form of the film as a potential site of masquerade. He writes:

> The importance of Riviere's conception of the masquerade is that it constitutes a transgressive doubleness, an inscription of alternative wishes. The potential for a critical distance from the mythemes of femininity (passivity, responsiveness, deference, flattery, etc.) is lodged already within it and the narratives it might generate.[19]

Reconsidering these insights for the film in hand, it can be said that masquerade functions at different levels in *Police Lock-up*. The film is clearly located within the male action film genre where restoration of law and order dominate the narrative. Usurping the standard male hero's role, that is, masquerading as a police officer, Vijayashanti plays this role to the full. The film supports her masculinization completely, for instance, by holding off song and dance sequences exclusively around her. The placing of Shanti into the narrative as an upright inspector's wife, provides the perfect foil for Vijaya's aggressive public self. Together the two roles, private and public, demonstrate Vijayashanti's ability to perform across different and competing terrains. Doubleness is further supported by naming the two characters from different parts of the star's full name, thus 'assuring' the masculine subject, as proposed by Riviere, that behind the mask lies this powerful phallic figure that unites both halves of polar screen personalities.

The double role in this film also actuates a different fantastical staging of desire. The lack of parental origin as a reason for their resemblance unhinges the film, preventing it from closing around a cosy sibling unity, while simultaneously unleashing the possibility of desire for the other. For instance, when Shanti suggests they switch places, the scope of this offer clearly extends to her spouse. We see Vijaya effortlessly passing for Shanti in her home, even masquerading in her love for Ashok. It is only later in the film that Ashok reveals that he suspected that Vijaya was not Shanti when she rejected his sexual demands. Of course, the film suspends all knowledge of the exact moment of his discovery, leaving open the possibility of a sexual interaction between Ashok and Vijaya. The switch thus opens the possibility of Ashok being exchanged as a sexual object between them.

We have seen the 'male version' of this arrangement first proposed by Levi-Strauss, ingeniously resurrected by Lacan, and then revised by feminists.[20] Eve Sedgwick's reformulation in *Between Men* shifts the exchange of women between men from a heterosexual matrix to a homosexual one.[21] Sedgwick proposes that women are exchanged between men to avert, ward off and occlude the articulation of homosexual desire for each other, while simultaneously oppressing women and producing homophobia. These terms seem uncannily reversed in *Police Lock-up*, raising the possibility that Vijaya and Shanti's full-scale switching is driven by a desire for each other, however narcissistic this may appear. This reading is further endorsed by the final moment of the film where we see them embracing, a closure that displaces and postpones heterosexual resolutions.

Although Vijaya has been the focus of most of the dramatic moments in the film, Shanti, too, provides dissonance in the plot, despite her conventional representation of passive femininity: she not only initiates the idea of the switch but also remains extremely loyal to her role as Vijaya in spite of arduous conditions in the jail. But the film also elaborately informs us that Shanti's anxiety about having children has absurd effects on her behaviour: she daydreams about phantom children, upsets her husband's work routine by demanding his presence at various fertility rituals and, above all, she has a pathological attachment to a dog whom she treats as her child.

I am reminded here of Edmund Leach's stimulating essay 'Animal classification and verbal abuse', where he argues for a close correspondence between the human classification of animals, verbal abuse and incest taboos.[22] There is an unrelated, yet similar, take on domestic pets by Avital Ronell in an interview where she expounds on the Bush family and pets after Millie's 'autobiography' was published. She comments:

> I remember telling people, 'Watch their rapport to the dog, because here is where they articulate things that are taboo, that are unconscious'.[23]

Shanti's attachment to Caesar, and her attempts to anthropomorphize, cast aspersions on the fertility of this heterosexual unit, particularly on her husband and his ability to reproduce. Furthermore, her incapacity to differentiate between dog and child in many scenes, a difference that conventionally marks so many human sexual, dietary and verbal taboos, casts asunder all normative images of a reproductive human family, and even anticipates the remarkable switch suggested and promoted by her. The film encourages her attempts to humanize Caesar by providing the dog, on more than one occasion, with subjective point-of-view shots. Notably, Caesar supports her switching places with Vijaya without a bark of protest, and, unlike Ashok, he can spot the difference between the two women. The exchanging of husbands and the circulation of fetishized objects, such as dogs, between them allows us to read these movements as representing circuits of desire between Vijaya and Shanti, thwarting our expectations of the normative heterosexual closure to most tales about twins. Curiously, this intimate bond between Vijaya and Shanti permits representations of other kinds of transgressions: Ashok's uncle is indisputably cast as a stereotypical homosexual, and surfaces as a symptom of the film's nascent homophobia; and Panjaraja, the chief minister, schemes to have his own daughter kidnapped to gain political ground, a motive that violates most conventions of paternal affection.

The film galvanizes one of the most common signs of love used in Indian cinema to stage desire: a song-and-dance sequence spliced together as a dream sequence from Shanti's point of view. Triggered by Vijaya's visit and finding herself pregnant, Shanti longs to go home, but instead lulls herself to sleep by singing a song. This sequence is set around a pregnancy ritual, and she begins a duet with her husband, but soon substitutes him with Vijaya, and the song closes around their embrace. Like the final embrace of the film, here, too, the heterosexual convention of these songs in Indian films is subverted. In the absence of any clear performative declaration of a lesbian identity in the film, which might allow for a more straightforward reading of a lesbian desire plot, I propose that *Police Lock-up* approximates a female buddy film, allowing and encouraging the staging of lesbian fantasies. As a police narrative, the film shadows and masquerades the male action genre to the hilt, while surreptitiously displacing the conventional expectations and resolutions present in its masculine counterpart.

In sharp contrast to the avenging woman genre, where the inept law and order system allows for the avenging plot to unfold with a closure that forcibly reintegrates the woman into the social and civic order, *Police Lock-up* and other Vijayashanti films harbour a less antagonistic relationship to the law. Indeed, located directly within the law, the female protagonist is constantly settling law and order problems produced by corrupt politicians and other policemen, a relationship with the state that is unabashedly accommodating. Nevertheless, as we have seen with *Police Lock-up*, Vijayashanti films raise some of the most knotty and unresolved problems attending representational struggles around femininity, violence and the state in Indian cinema.

Acknowledgements

A version of this paper was presented at the Department of South Asian Regional Studies, University of Pennsylvania and I have greatly benefited from all the thoughtful comments and challenging questions raised on that occasion. I wish to thank Robert Schumann, Sandhya Shetty, and Nalini Natrajan for their generous comments on previous drafts. Finally, thanks to Itty Abraham who has been there at every turn offering his critical eye and support.

Notes

1 'Imaging you', *The Illustrated Weekly of India*, 29 May–4 June 1993, pp. 24–37. The participants included N. Chandra, Prakash Jha, Javed Akhtar, Meenakshi Seshadri and Maithili Rao.

2 Firoze Rangoonwala, 'The age of violence', *The Illustrated Weekly of India*, 4–10 September 1993, pp. 27–9.

3 M. Rahman, 'Women strike back', *India Today*. 15 July 1988, pp. 80–2.

4 Maithili Rao, 'Victims in vigilante clothing', *Cinema in India*. October–December 1988, pp. 24–6.

5 See Carol J. Clover. *Men, Women, and Chain Saws: Gender in the Modern Horror Film* (Princeton, NJ: Princeton University Press, 1992); Peter Lehman. '"Don't blame this on a girl": female rape–revenge films', in Steven Cohan and Ina Rae Hark (eds), *Screening the Male: Exploring Masculinities in Hollywood Cinema* (New York: Routledge, 1993). This explicit resemblance to Hollywood B movies throws up a set of new issues: it draws limits to 'national' styles of cinema, forcing us to consider the exchange and appropriation of cinematic styles across national boundaries. Every 'national' cinema has, of course, to contend with Hollywood hegemony, but if the points of contact between Indian and Hollywood film are the much maligned, yet often experimental, B films, a host of fascinating questions are raised in relation to taste and the distribution networks of B films in the Third World.

6 Clover, *Men, Women, and Chain Saws*, p. 154.

7 See Aruna Vasudev, *Liberty and Licence in Indian Cinema* (New Delhi: Vikas, 1978) on censorship regulations.

8 Ashish Rajadhyaksha and Paul Willemen, *Encyclopaedia of Indian Cinema* (New Delhi: Oxford University Press. 1995), p. 416.

9 For a useful treatment of the public discussion of rape and the women's movement, see Ammu Joseph and Kalpana Sharma, 'Rape: a campaign is born', in Ammu Joseph and Kalpana Sharma (eds), *Whose News?: the Media and Women's Issues* (New Delhi: Sage Publications, 1994). pp. 43–50.

10 *Ramayana* (Ramanand Sagar, 1986–1988) and *Mahabharata* (B.R. Chopra and Ravi Chopra, 1988–1990).

11 Farhad Malik, 'Fact and fiction', *Cinema in India*, August 1981, pp. 5–8.

12 Clover, *Men, Women, and Chain Saws*, p. 151.

13 Lalitha Gopalan, 'Coitus interruptus and the love story in Indian cinema', in Vidya Dehejia (ed), *Representing the Body: Gender Issues in Indian Art* (New Delhi: Kali for Women, 1997).

14 Also see *Khoon Bhari Mang*.

15 Linda Williams, *Hard Core: Power, Pleasure, and the 'Frenzy of the Visible'* (Berkeley, CA: University of California Press, 1989), p. 217.

16 Interview with Vijayshanti, *Filmfare*, July 1993.

17 Horror films about twins, similarly, do not possess the cushion of a family romance and play on all the horrific aspects of twin identities. The most competent film in this genre is David Cronenberg's *Dead Ringers* (1988), which takes on both Peter Greenaway's avant-garde film *A Zed & Two Noughts* (1985) and Bette Davis's *Dead Ringer* (Paul Henreid, 1964) to render a techno-horror film that borders on incest.

18 Joan Riviere, 'Womanliness as a masquerade', in Victor Burgin, James Donald and Cora Kaplan (eds), *Formations of Fantasy* (London: Methuen, 1986, pp. 35–44, p. 35. Mary Ann Doane's essays are good examples of this kind of appropriation. See Mary Ann Doane, 'Film and masquerade: theorizing the female spectator', in *Femmes Fatales* (New York: Routledge, 1991); 'Masquerade reconsidered: further thoughts on the female spectator', in *Femmes Fatales*, p. 33.

19 John Fletcher, 'Versions of masquerade', *Screen*, vol. 29, no. 3 (1988), p. 55.

20 Claude Levi-Strauss, *The Elementary Structures of Kinship*, trans. James Harle Bell, John Richard von Stumer and Rodney Needham (Boston: Beacon Press, 1969). For a pithy elaboration of Levi-Strauss and Lacan, see Jane Gallop, *The Daughter's Seduction: Feminism and Psychoanalysis* (London: Macmillan, 1982).

21 Eve Kosofsky Sedgwick, *Between Men: English Literature and Male Homosocial Desire* (New York: Columbia University Press, 1985).

22 Edmund Leach, 'Anthropological aspects of language: animal categories and verbal abuse', in Eric H. Lenneberg (ed.), *New Directions in the Study of Language* (Cambridge, MA: MIT Press, 1964), p. 23.

23 Avital Ronell, interview, *Re/Search*, no. 13 (1991), p. 142.

9 Narratives of resistance: national identity and ambivalence in the Turkish melodrama between 1965 and 1975

Nezih Erdoğan

One of the first Turkish feature films, *Mürebbiye/The Tutor* (Ahmet Fehim, 1919)[1] was banned by the allied forces which had occupied Istanbul just after World War I. It was adapted from Hüseyin Rahmi Gürpinar's novel of the same title, published in 1898. *Mürebbiye* tells the story of a French woman who seduces the members of a snobbish family she works for. Apparently the text was meant to give a comical illustration of the upper classes' infatuation with French culture. But the film was released in the context of the occupation of Istanbul by the allied forces, and by then the focus was on the corrupt French tutor who, more or less, represented western woman. Domestic film circles read *Mürebbiye* as Turkish cinema's 'silent resistance' to occupation.[2] What is more interesting is that the censor for the allied forces banned the film on the same grounds.

Woman as the site of production of meaning is one of the issues that I will discuss in this essay. For now, I would like to point out that the expression 'silent resistance' is somewhat problematic here. To the Turkish eye, the cinema was a western form of entertainment right from the start. Sigmund Weinberg, a Polish Jew of Romanian nationality, launched the first regular public screenings in Istanbul in 1896. These were Lumière shorts, *L'arrivée d'un train en gare de la Ciotat* (1895) among them. Weinberg also made some documentaries and was reputed to be an 'expert' in cinematography. Soon, companies such as Lumière, Pathé, Gaumont and Ciné Théâtrale d'Orient began to distribute French, American, German and Danish films. In the beginning, the audience for these films consisted mostly of the non-Muslim minorities who lived in Pera (now Beyoğlu), a district of Istanbul marked by a western lifestyle. D. Henri screened films in a pub named 'Sponeck'; Matalon in the 'Lüksemburg Buildings'; and Camdon, probably a Lumière man, in 'Varyete Theatre' — all places with western names. In addition, publicity was printed in French, German, Armenian and Greek but not in Turkish. Pera was posed as an object of desire for the Muslim upper class and, partly, for the intelligentsia at a time of modernization fuelled by western-oriented policies; and the cinema seems to have served as the latest desiring machine — the films that were shown presented glamorous scenes from various European centres, and filmgoing itself had the charm of being a western-style ritual.[3]

Mürebbiye is not the only example of a national cinema that produces a discourse of resistance while a general perception of cinema itself was already constructed entirely in western terms. And it is not surprising that, as far as national cinemas are concerned, any formulation of resistance is overshadowed by images of mimicry. Turkish popular cinema, Yeşilçam, whose death was announced in the early 1980s, had been frequently criticized for imitating other cinemas, and repeating other films.[4] Back in 1968, the film magazine *Yeni Sinema* (*New Cinema*) noted that more than half of the 250 films made that year were adaptations – plagiarisms, to be more precise – of foreign box-office successes.[5] Given this fact, one can easily deduce an identity crisis; but what are we to make of an identity which is in permanent crisis? And what kind of national identity can be formed from a cinema renowned for its failures rather than its successes, or for its endless efforts to mimic others rather than to produce films that are 'Turkish to the core'?

In this essay I will examine the dynamics through which Turkish popular cinema describes a national identity, and attempt to demonstrate how the specificity of this identity can be seen in the very way it mimics and resists others. Cinema, as a desiring machine, produces a discourse which operates on a social level, involving psychical processes with subject effects. I will argue that these psychical processes are characterized by ambivalence (for example, mimicry and resistance) which provides a ground for the 'identity in crisis' I referred to above. In this respect, I will make use of postcolonial theory, particularly its formulation of the ambivalent nature of colonial discourse and the way it operates on the social unconscious. However, I am not going to offer an analysis of colonial discourse as such; rather I will focus on 'the discourse of the national identity as derivative of colonial discourse' as articulated by Yeşilçam.[6] Indeed, Turkish popular cinema is one popular site where such an 'identity in crisis' has been experienced for decades.

My study covers the period when commercial cinema enjoyed its heyday – that is, between the mid 1960s and mid 1970s – producing an average of two hundred films per year. *Konfeksiyon* films, as they were called, were made in a rush to meet a continuously increasing demand.[7] Not only did they entertain the domestic audience, they also became very popular in other Middle Eastern countries, such as Iran, Iraq and Egypt. Production declined dramatically after the 1980s, and today only about ten Turkish films reach cinemas each year. This is primarily due to the US film distribution companies that now control exhibition mechanisms in Turkey, and secondly to the gap between the audience and the inaccessible discourse of current Turkish films, many of which follow the conventions of European art cinema. The new Turkish cinema has lost its audience to television channels which repeatedly show old popular films – the frequency of commercial breaks suggests that these films still appeal to a mass audience, still contribute to popular imagery.

The first three decades of Turkish cinema were marked by the domination of a single man, Muhsin Ertuğrul, who was, and is still, widely criticized for transferring the stylistic devices of theatre to cinema. This period came to an end in 1953, when a number of filmmakers initiated a somewhat different practice. Ayşe Şasa, a veteran scriptwriter, calls this the period of the 'illiterates', in that they were neither aware of, nor interested in, the artistic possibilities of cinema. Craftsmen of rural and lumpen origin now ruled Yeşilçam. They did not hide their commercial interest in the films from which they made big profits. Şasa maintains that the period of the 'illiterates' in Turkish cinema was undervalued because of its low-quality films: its potential of growing a genuine cinematic 'seed' was underestimated, as was 'the poetry that was hidden in this artless authenticity'.[8]

The mid 1960s witnessed the beginning of a debate about national identity in Turkish cinema. A group of writers from various branches of literature gathered around the film magazine *Yeni Sinema*, and founded the Turkish cinematheque (with some help from Henri Langlois). They argued that a national cinema with international concerns was impossible within Yeşilçam, which was associated with worn-out formulas, plagiarism, escapism and exploitation. While *Yeni Sinema* published interviews with film directors such as Godard, Renoir and Antonioni, and translations from theoretical works examining cinema in relation to other arts, screenings organized by the cinematheque gave a particular audience access to canons of European art cinema. When one looks back at this scene, one can see a programme aiming at an art cinema. If, in Europe, art cinema developed as a resistance to the increasing domination of Hollywood, in Turkey, Yeşilçam appeared as the first obstacle to be tackled: alternative modes of production were sought, and festivals and competitions held to promote short films.[9]

When the Asiatic mode of production championed by the novelist Kemal Tahir became a popular issue in the late 1960s, a close friend of his, the then film critic and promising film director Halit Refiğ, elaborated a concept of national cinema: films are made by money coming *from* the people, so they must be made *for* the people, one way or another. Since it is impossible to reach the people of Turkey via western forms, a cinema which considers the people's characteristics and needs must be developed within Yeşilçam, which has already formed its audience. Refiğ insisted that Yeşilçam relied less on a capitalist mode of production than on a labour-intensive one, and urged film writers and producers not to turn their backs on it. He used ironic language when criticizing the elitist approach of the cinematheque group:

> To sum up, cinema [according to the cinematheque group] is a universal art. The criteria for the evaluation of this art are provided by the West. To be able to make a good film, one must do whatever a western filmmaker would do. There is no point in taking an interest in Turkish films as they do not subscribe to western criteria . . . and one must fight to have the Turkish audience develop a sympathy for and love of films coming from the West.[10]

In 1967 the major film directors of the time refused to respond to a questionnaire on the role of criticism prepared by *Yeni Sinema*, and that was the end of relations between filmmakers and the cinematheque.[11] We might represent the differences between Yeşilçam and the projected New Cinema as follows:

New Cinema	Yeşilçam
western	domestic
art cinema	popular cinema
model: European art cinema	model: Hollywood
to create	to produce
auteur policy	star system
alternative modes of production	capitalist mode of production
festivals, competitions	production–distribution–exhibition

Inevitably, the sharp conflict in this set of oppositions was occasionally resolved by some directors. Yilmaz Güney, for instance, produced popular, commercially successful films which were also hailed by the cinematheque group. At the beginning of the 1980s, New Cinema began to introduce its first films to the domestic audience (and to international film circles), but it could not get out of the domain of Yeşilçam entirely. At first *Yeni Sinema* attempted to win over some established directors, Lütfi Akad and Yilmaz Güney among them. Then came a generation of young filmmakers who tried hard to differentiate their films from those of popular cinema; although they made these films in Yeşilçam, they sought recognition from international art cinema institutions. In Yeşilçam, stars were used to brand the film product; the New Cinema directors also worked with stars but, following auteur policy, the director was inscribed as the 'creator' of the film. Audiences began to read authorial credits, such as 'an Ali Özgentürk film', 'an Ömer Kavur film'. In addition, the New Cinema assumed the point of view of European art cinema (which includes the European audience) in that it produced representations of Turkey either as an 'impenetrable other' (*Hazal* [Ali Özgentürk, 1979]; *Bedrana* [Süreyya Duru, 1974]; *Kuma/The Concubine* [Atif Yilmaz, 1974]) or as a phantasmic western country (*Piano Piano Bacaksiz/Piano Piano My Little Boy* [Tunç Basaran, 1990]; *Seni Seviyorum Rosa* [Isil Özgentürk, 1992]; *Yengeç Sepeti/The Crab Basket* [Yavuz Özkan, 1995]; *Gizli Yüz/The Secret Face* [Ömer Kavur, 1991]. It is interesting to note that a British film critic, reporting from the Istanbul Film Festival in 1992, describes the films as 'pretentious allegories drawing on influences from Buñuel to Bergman'.[12]

The mid-1970s saw Yeşilçam enter another crisis, while New Cinema continued to seek its audience by way of international festivals and other such events. Thomas Elsaesser makes a similar observation about German cinema in the early 1980s:

the Germans are beginning to love their own cinema because it has been endorsed, confirmed and benevolently looked at by someone else: for the

German cinema to exist, it first had to be seen by non-Germans. It enacts, as a national cinema now in explicitly economic and cultural terms, yet another form of self-estranged exhibitionism.[13]

To echo Elsaesser in a slightly different context, for Turkish art cinema to exist, it would have to be 'endorsed, confirmed and benevolently looked at' by some one else. But unlike German cinema, with a few exceptions, it never enjoyed such recognition. What was expected from German cinema was, for instance, the sophisticated, self-reflexive films of Fassbinder. This has not been the case for Turkish cinema: *Susuz Yaz / The Dry Summer* (Metin Erksan, 1964) and *Yol* (Yilmaz Güney, 1982), which won prizes at major festivals, illustrate the harsh circumstances of rural life stricken by poverty, absurd moral values, oppressed individuals, and so on. Roy Armes's comment on the relationship between the Third World cinema and the intelligentsia is relevant here:

> But the processes of their education and the advent of national independence will have made them very aware that they cannot become western filmmakers. Hence they will tend to prove their identity by plunging deeply into local tradition, myth and folklore. The result is all too often an ambiguous cinema which is too complex in form for local audiences and too esoteric in substance for western spectators.[14]

That 'they cannot become western filmmakers' needs further elaboration. I want to demonstrate that fetishism and, relatedly, fantasy complicate things further. Indeed, Turkish film directors are very well aware that they cannot become western filmmakers; but the fetishistic disavowal of difference keeps them moving in the same direction (to adapt the famous 'I know very well, but nevertheless . . .', 'I am very well aware that I cannot become a western film maker, but nevertheless . . .'). The problem is not in knowing but in doing, as Slavoj Žižek maintains:

> They know very well how things really are, but still they are doing it as if they did not know. The illusion is therefore double: it consists in overlooking the illusion which is structuring our real, effective relationship to reality. And this overlooked, unconscious illusion is what may be called the ideological fantasy.[15]

Turkish art cinema deserves a more detailed analysis, but I want now to return to Yeşilçam and to demonstrate that the dissemination of colonial discourse is not exclusive to New Cinema. I will concentrate upon melodrama as a popular genre which plays on desire, providing us with invaluable insight into the ambivalent nature of national identity.

As Thomas Elsaesser observes, family melodrama,

> dealing largely with the same Oedipal themes of emotional and moral identity, more often records the failure of the protagonist to act in a way that could shape the events and influence the emotional environment, let alone change the stifling social milieu. The world is closed, and the characters are acted upon, and each other's sole referent, there is no world outside to be acted on, no reality that could be defined or assumed unambiguously.[16]

Steve Neale notes that 'melodramas are marked by chance happenings, coincidences, missed meetings, sudden conversions, last minute rescues and revelations, *deus ex machina* endings'.[17] Melodrama, in short, is perfectly suited to Yeşilçam, which sticks to narrative traditions inspired by legends, fairy tales and epics (rather than by, say, tragedy, which emphasizes the inner conflicts and transformations of its characters). While, in its beginnings, western melodrama recorded the 'struggle of a morally and emotionally emancipated bourgeois consciousness against the remnants of feudalism',[18] Yeşilçam exploits melodrama in articulating the desires aroused not only by class conflict but also by rural/urban and eastern/western oppositions. Immigration from rural areas to big cities is still a social phenomenon with significant economic and cultural consequences. The possibilities of crossing from one class to another and from village to big city provide the ground upon which melodrama plays and activates its machinery of desire. Hence the formulation: lower class/rural = East/local culture vs upper class/urban = West/foreign culture.

The Yeşilçam melodrama repeatedly returns to the 'boy meets girl' plot: they unite, they split, they reunite. In one particular variation, the boy from the urban upper class and the girl from the lower class have an affair and then the boy leaves the girl. The girl finds him again, but learns that he no longer wants her. She comes back in disguise (urban, rich, sophisticated) and the boy, having failed to recognize her, falls in love. This time the girl takes her revenge and leaves him. In the end, her identity is revealed and the boy learns his lesson. The upper class, which is fixed as the object of desire here, is encoded with its western attributes.[19] Luxurious American cars, blondes wearing revealing dresses, crazy parties and whisky all connote moral corruption, and construct an iconography of the West.[20] This is in sharp contrast with the virtues (simplicity, loyalty, correctness and chastity) of the woman from the rural area/lower class.

In a recurrent plot, the heroine is raped/seduced and immediately deserted by a man whom she already loves. She has a baby and brings it up under reduced circumstances, and then somehow becomes rich. Towards the finale, having come to appreciate the heroine's virtues, the long-lost lover, now father, returns, but the heroine's pride delays the reunion (*Sana donmeyeceğim/I Will Never Return to You* [Mehmet Dinler, 1969]; *Ayşem/Ayşe Mine* [Nejat Saydam, 1968]; *Kinali Yapincak/ Golden Red Grape* [Orhan Aksoy, 1968]). In *Dağdan İnme/Came Down From the Mountains*

(Metin Erksan, 1973), the male hero is struck by the appearance of an extremely attractive woman he meets at a party. She is actually a villager, desperately in love with him. *Taşra Kizi / The Girl From the Province* (Arsevir Alyanak, 1964) tells the story of a girl who comes to Istanbul from a small town. She moves into the house of an old family friend, who turns out to be her father. This film, like many others, exemplifies how melodrama resolves conflict using the Father figure (as father, police chief, judge, boss) as its agent.[21] In many instances the authoritarian Father plays the benefactor, and sides with the girl against the spoiled son. There are, of course, some contradictory variations (for example, the rich father making friends with two young men who turn out to be his daughters' boyfriends). Variations, however, do not negate the argument that the Father regulates the economy of desire and power. The message, which is of course addressed to the lower-class / rural subject, is that the upper class will be able to survive only if the lower class helps. Possibilities for identification in these films are a matter of justifying the audience's (especially the female audience's) desire for, and wish to be desired by, the upper class. Yeşilçam melodramas thus offered a sense of legitimacy to people like the squatters who had migrated from rural areas into the cities.

Plagiarism, of which Yeşilçam has often been accused, is by no means a simple issue. The technical and stylistic devices of Yeşilçam differ radically from those of Hollywood and European cinema. Lighting, colour, dubbing, dialogue, shooting practices, point-of-view shots and editing create a very specific cinematic discourse in even the most faithful of adaptations. In trying to meet a demand for two hundred films a year, production practices had to run at great speed; and thus by default a visual tradition of shadowplays, miniatures, and so on was revived. To save time and money, shot / reverse-shot and other point-of-view shots were avoided as much as possible. This meant the domination of frontal shots: characters mostly performed facing the camera. This made full identification impossible and gave way to empathy instead. Yeşilçam was a hybrid cinema: it produced a cinematic discourse blending Hollywood-style realism with an unintentional Brechtian alienation effect.

Characters who were never depicted as individuals, and who could not act but were 'acted upon', reinforced the melodramatic effect. Given such circumstances, it is not difficult to see why split identities have always been convincing for, and appealing to, the audience. The Yeşilçam character can trick her lover into believing that she is someone else, taking on various successive identities. What was once a poor, uneducated girl with a strong accent can instantly become an attractive, sophisticated lady of manners. A girl from the lower class can adapt herself to the rules of the high society she has just joined without any trouble. These are, of course, narrative reproductions of Pygmalion and Cinderella. If we can hazard that splittings are mobilized by presenting the upper class / West to the lower class / East as an object of desire and identification, then splitting is a symptom which betrays Yeşilçam's own conception of national identity. Ambivalence (narcissism / aggression), identification and fantasy are the basic terms of the logic of this conception. Splitting, as a matter of fact, provides the ground for ambivalent psychical positionings of the subject in relation to its object of desire, and transition from one identity to another takes place in the realm of fantasy: after the poor young girl is discovered by the owner of a night club, she quickly becomes a rich and famous singer. The huge efforts required to achieve success (private education from a non-Muslim instructor, music lessons, training, rehearsals) are either shown in a rapid succession of scenes or are ignored entirely.

I want now to examine a film which, I believe, focuses the problem of national identity as derivative of colonial discourse. *Karagözlüm / My Dark Eyed One* (Atif Yilmaz, 1970) is not a typical or normal melodrama; even its plot is different from the ones so far described. Rather it is a limit-text, which stands at the margins of the logic of melodrama, and this is why I think it is capable of representing Yeşilçam melodrama perfectly.

Azize (Türkan Şoray) is a fisherman's daughter who enjoys singing while she works in the fish market. She happens to meet Kenan (Kadir Inanir), an idealistic composer who disdains all music other than western classical. Teasing him for his pretentious cultural preferences, she names him 'Chopin'. As in many melodramas, Azize is then discovered by the owner of a music hall, and becomes a famous singer, finding herself in an entirely different network of sociocultural and economic relations. Kenan, having failed to find a decent job, begins work as a waiter at the same place. They eventually fall in love. Kenan drops classical music in favour of composing popular songs for Azize ('I retire from Chopinhood'). He mails his work anonymously to her, never revealing his identity. Two Hollywood producers who happen to hear her singing one night offer to co-star Azize with Rock Hudson in a film ('The Favourite of Maharajah') on the condition that she will bring her 'unknown composer' along with her to Hollywood. She is delighted with the idea that she will enjoy worldwide fame, but her mysterious, hitherto unknown composer (Kenan disguised as an old man) shows up, and not only declines the offer but also accuses her of 'being adrift in a Hollywood dream'. He deserts Azize and gets engaged to Semra, the daughter of a rich family. Azize, having discovered that 'one who wants to have everything, loses what she already has', quits her job and goes back to selling fish. But, in the end, Kenan reappears and they are reunited.

The film is very quick to establish the opposition between East/popular culture and West/elite culture. In the scene following the opening, Kenan's close friend, Orhan, advises him to drop 'this *kefere* [infidel's] music which is a pain in the neck', and perform his art for a larger audience in order to make a fortune from his talent. Once Azize starts working at the music hall she cannot enjoy the new life she is expected to lead. When the vacuum cleaner goes dead in a power cut, she and her assistant happily use brooms. They are almost embarrassed to use mechanical appliances for any kind of housework that can be done manually. Technology not only marks a class conflict here, it also serves as an icon for a western lifestyle.

Figure 9.1 Azize dances: *Karagözlüm/My Dark Eyed One* (Atif Yilmaz, 1970). Akün
Film. [All images in this chapter are taken from video frame grabs]

But the dream sequence is most significant since it reveals the 'intention of the
text'. In order to go to Hollywood, Azize has to locate her unknown composer; but
Kenan is none too happy with her enthusiasm, and is reluctant to give away his
secret. As he tries to make up his mind he falls asleep and has a dream. In the dream
we see the chamber of the maharajah. Azize enters the scene and begins to dance
in front of a man whom we are not allowed to see (Figure 9.1). Then Kenan sneaks
into the chamber through the back door, and becomes furious when he sees Azize
dancing for someone else (Figure 9.2). In response, Azize puts out her tongue in
mockery. But what strikes Kenan most is that right behind Azize, accompanying her
on the flute, he sees himself, dressed in Indian clothes (Figure 9.3). Kenan produces
a bomb (a molotov cocktail) from the pocket of his coat and throws it right into the
middle of the chamber (Figure 9.4). The bomb explodes and Kenan awakes. He has
made his decision: he will not let Azize go to Hollywood. When Kenan detonates
the bomb we do not see any damage done: we do not see the palace falling into
pieces, we do not see anybody killed, and we do not hear any screams. We see only
a smokescreen and then, in closeup, Kenan awakening in dismay. What has broken
down is not the content of the dream but the fantasy screen itself.

Figure 9.2 Kenan sees Azize: *Karagözlüm.*

As Mahmut Mutman stresses, colonial discourse and orientalism play on sexual difference. Psychic processes (fantasy, castration, fetishism, aggression) which mobilize the discourse, enable the representation of Woman as a cultural construct: 'Muslim woman stands where the political, the economic and the cultural "values" meet: her culturally specific embodiment is the commodity that is exchanged with other commodities'.[22] This applies to *both* sides (colonized and colonizer) of colonial discourse. In Turkish, *anavatan* and *anayurt*, which might be translated as 'mother-land' and 'mother country', are terms which explain how Woman comes to represent values attached to the concept of nationhood. And this is precisely what *Karagözlüm* does through the agency of Kenan: Chopin/the unknown composer is asked to trade Azize for a brilliant career (she dances to his music). Azize, a word of Arabic origin, means 'dear' or 'beloved' in Turkish and can easily be associated with the common usage *Aziz Vatan* (beloved country). The molotov cocktail was an icon of the militant Left in the 1970s, frequently used in demonstrations against the growing US hegemony. It was considered an unsophisticated, cheap, easy-to-produce, easy-to-use combat weapon, a suitable device for a 'people at war with imperialism'. What seems problematic for my analysis at this point is that Kenan's

Figure 9.3 Kenan in Indian clothes: *Karagözlüm.*

dream actually serves as a screen onto which 'Hollywood' projects its fantasy. It is also the very dream Kenan refers to when he accuses Azize of being adrift in a Hollywood dream.

Through his music, Kenan fixes his beloved as an object of desire, and then exhibits her body (that is, hands her over) to Hollywood. More importantly, the splittings of Kenan verify the ambivalence of colonial discourse: there is a Kenan (the flute player) who accompanies Azize with his music, a Kenan (the white male hero) who is struck by what is going on in the scene and explodes the bomb, and finally a Kenan who dreams all of this. I suggest that the dream sequence forms the kernel of the entire film. The splittings that take place within it are parallel to the diegetic ones: the flute player is the unknown composer, now unmasked; the one who bombs the palace is the waiter; and the one who dreams is a Kenan who retired from 'Chopinhood' in favour of Azize. But who is the maharajah? Although we see very little of him, he is a pivotal figure around which the rest of the characters revolve. Motionless, he is watching Azize dancing. It seems he controls the space with his gaze. He can see Azize and the flute player, and vice versa. He cannot see the waiter (or the audience), and although the waiter cannot see his face Kenan is

Figure 9.4 Kenan throws the bomb: *Karagözlüm*.

very well aware of his presence. So the maharajah also functions as a 'borderline', separating the waiter and the audience from Azize and the flute player. The audience identifies first with the dreaming Kenan and then with the waiter. When Kenan throws the bomb, he puts an not only end to the dream, but also to the voyeuristic pleasure of the maharajah. The audience of the exotic films of Hollywood shares the erotic experiences of the Oriental despot and then identifies with the white male hero who bursts into the palace and takes the girl away from him. In this connection, the explosion has a double effect which brings us back to the problem of split identities: Kenan tears apart the fantasy screen of 'Hollywood', yet identifies with it by playing the white male hero who is already a part of this same fantasy. Therefore, *Karagözlüm* offers us a dual set of relationships which reveal the actual fantasy of the colonized – to share the colonizer's fantasy. This is made possible by a subtle reversal: the narrative switches positions and the colonized becomes someone other than Kenan. Aggression takes place elsewhere; neither the word 'maharajah' nor the setting is Turkish, but it is still Oriental.

Azize and her father ride to the fish market on a shabby motorcycle they have named Apollo. In 1970, the production date of this film, the reference is clearly to the US moon landing. To name an old motorcycle after Apollo is a parody intended as mockery, but as Fredric Jameson emphasizes in a different context, 'the parodist has to have some secret sympathy for the original' and 'there remains somewhere behind all parody the feeling that there is a . . . norm'.[23] And *Karagözlüm* re-establishes western norms by illustrating cultural deviations. Throughout the film we hear three sorts of music, representing three levels of culture: classical western music (Kenan – the norm), traditional Turkish popular music (Azize – the settlement), and popular dance music (Semra – the corrupt).[24] Kenan has to sacrifice classical music (the norm) for Azize and the values she represents (the popular); when he thinks he has lost her to Hollywood, he decides to marry Semra (the corrupt).

My observation is supported by another film. In *Sana Tapiyorum/I Worship You* (Aram Gülyüz, 1970), Ayşe (Zeynep Değirmencioğlu) studies ballet at a dance school. In order to meet her expenses, her mother works as a singer in a night club, which utterly embarrasses Ayşe. When the rumour is spread that her mother is more or less a prostitute, Ayşe is cut by her classmates and teachers. She drops out of school under pressure and, at the same time, is informed that her mother is dangerously ill. The doctors say that she will die unless she is sent to Switzerland for an operation. Ayşe is desperate because she cannot afford to pay for the operation. Her mother's boss offers her money, but she would have to dance in his night club in return. When Ayşe furiously refuses the offer, he asks ironically whether her body is more sacred than her mother's life, remarking that her mother did the same thing in order to be able to pay her tuition fees. At this, Ayşe agrees to start working in the night club. Ayşe's classmates and teachers appreciate the sacrifice she has made for her mother and decide to help her. In the meantime, Ayşe locates her long-lost father, who was once a famous brain surgeon and is now an alcoholic; and after a climactic speech persuades him to perform the operation. In the final scene we see Ayşe taking the leading role in a ballet performance and all the characters in the audience, especially the owner of the night club regretfully weeping. Her body, as in many Yeşilçam melodramas, is a metaphor for postponement and sacrifice. Once again, Woman provides the ground for an exchange of values. The body which represents the cultural values of the dance school (the norm) is not more sacred than the Mother. It must be sacrificed for the Mother and submitted to the night club. Only then will the Mother survive and the Father assume his identity.

As I have tried to demonstrate, colonial discourse and its derivatives operate in a vast area, and neither nationalism nor any other sort of anti-western practice can easily avoid reproducing them. For Yeşilçam, the moment of colonial discourse is the moment of transgressing the boundaries it has defined. Yeşilçam depicts the West pejoratively. However, it suppresses the fact that the social class which represents the West is represented in phantasmic scenes where everything can be vindicated and thus desired unashamedly.

It must, nevertheless, not be forgotten that Yeşilçam melodrama stages a real ambivalence in the sense that reversals work both ways. It imposes the cultural values attached to national identity as necessary and temporary deviations. One must conform to them for now so as to acquire the norm (that is the West) in the future. To be able to be Chopin one day, one must be a waiter or an unknown composer now – because Azize is at stake; to be able to go back to the dance school one day, one must work in a night club – because mother is ill and money is required for the operation.

When the Hollywood producers burst into Azize's dressing room to meet her, the owner of the music hall cannot figure out what they want. 'They want the bill', Azize guesses, and points to Kenan, who happens to be there. 'Pay it to the waiter', she suggests. Kenan's intervention prevents Azize from going to Hollywood, so Hollywood does pay the bill to Yeşilçam in a way. Yeşilçam seems determined to demand payment, only it cannot avoid reproducing colonial discourse once again, since it fixes national identity precisely in this problematic moment.

Acknowledgement

An earlier version of this essay was presented at the Theory, Culture and Society Conference, Berlin, August 1995. I wish to thank Mahmut Mutman and Stephanie Donald for their comments.

Notes

1 The majority of the films cited in this essay were not released in English-speaking countries. I am, however, adding my own English translation of the original titles to give an idea of their content.
2 Nijat Özön, *Fuat Uzkinay* (Istanbul: TSD, 1970) cited in Giovanni Scognamillo, *Türk Sinema Tarihi 1896–1986* (Istanbul: Metis, 1987), p. 28.
3 Nilgün Abisel gives a detailed account of how intellectuals debated the tension between foreign films and cultural identity in her work *Türk Sinemasi Üzerine Yazilar* (Ankara: Imge, 1994).
4 Yeşilçam is a street in Istanbul where film production companies gathered until a decade ago. It also denotes a specific system of production–distribution–exhibition that dominated the Turkish cinema between the late 1950s and mid-1980s.
5 'Ikilem yanliş konunca', *Yeni Sinema*, nos 19/20 (June/July 1968), p. 3.
6 I borrow this expression from the title of a book by Partha Chaterjee, *Nationalist Thought and Colonial World: a Derivative Discourse* (Minneapolis: University of Minnesota Press, 1993).
7 Daytime 'women only' screenings were part of a strategy developed by the movie theatres to regulate this demand.
8 Ayşe Şasa, *Yeşilçam Günlüğü* (Istanbul: Dergah, 1993), p. 30.
9 Ece Ayhan, a famous poet, evaluated the contributors to a short film competition: 'This Young Generation of honour has chosen to work away from Yeşilçam in order not to fall prey to it'. 'Simurg', *Yeni Sinema*, nos. 19/20 (June/July 1968), p. 10.

10 Halit Refiğ, *Ulusal Sinema Kavgasi* (Istanbul: Hareket, 1971), p. 47 [author's translation].

11 'We refuse to collaborate with the Turkish cinematheque and its publication *Yeni Sinema* for their hostility to the Turkish cinema in general and Turkish filmmakers in particular'. Memduh Ün, Atif Yilmaz, Metin Erksan, Lütfi Akad, Duygu Sagiroglu, Alp Zeki Heper, Osman Seden, Halit Refiğ, *Yeni Sinema*, no. 4 (July 1967), p. 34 [author's translation].

12 John Gillett, *Sight and Sound*, vol. 2, no. 4 (1992), p. 5.

13 Thomas Elsaesser, 'Primary identification and the historical subject: Fassbinder and Germany', *Cine-Tracts*, vol. 3, no. 3 (1980), p. 52.

14 Roy Armes, 'Twelve propositions on the inaccessibility of Third World cinema', in Christine Woodhead (ed.), *Turkish Cinema: an Introduction* (London: Turkish Area Study Group Publications, 1989), p. 7.

15 Slavoj Žižek, *The Sublime Object of Ideology* (New York and London: Verso, 1989), pp. 32–3.

16 Thomas Elsaesser, 'Tales of sound and fury: observations on the family melodrama', in Bill Nichols (ed.), *Movies and Methods*, Volume II (London: University of California Press, 1985), p. 177.

17 Steve Neale, 'Melodrama and tears', *Screen*, vol. 27, no. 6 (1986), p. 6.

18 Elsaesser, 'Tales of sound and fury', p. 168.

19 At this point Yeşilçam gets closer to Indian melodrama. Ravi Vasudevan gives an instance of a female character who was sentenced to death for murdering a man but thinks she is already guilty 'of having adopted customs alien to their land' (*Andaz/A Sense of Proportion* [Mehboob Khan, 1949]). 'The melodramatic mode and the commercial Hindi cinema: notes on film history, narrative and performance in the 1950s', in this volume.

20 Mehmet Açar notes that the innocent girl is always offered a western drink, often whisky, when she is to be seduced, 'Felakete çeyrek kala', *Sinema* (February 1996), p. 88.

21 I thank Mahmut Mutman for drawing my attention to this issue.

22 Mahmut Mutman, 'Pictures from afar: shooting the middle east', *Inscriptions*, no. 6 (1992), p. 15.

23 Fredric Jameson, 'Postmodernism and consumer society', in Hal Foster (ed.), *Anti-aesthetic: Essays on Postmodern Culture* (Port Townsend, WA: Bay Press, 1986), pp. 113–14.

24 It must be noted that, like many other Turkish films, *Karagözlüm* borrows its title from a popular song.

Part IV

Contemporary world cinema and critical theory

10 The open image: poetic realism and the New Iranian Cinema

Shohini Chaudhuri and Howard Finn

When Mohsen Makhmalbaf's *Safar e Ghandehar/Kandahar* was screened at London's Institute for Contemporary Arts in Autumn 2001 it drew sell-out audiences, as it did in other European and North American cities. The film's success, partly due to its timely release, also reflects an enthusiasm internationally for Iranian films which has been gathering momentum in recent years. This essay focuses on one characteristic of 'New Iranian Cinema' which has evidently intrigued both critics and audiences, namely the foregrounding of a certain type of ambiguous, epiphanic image. We attempt to explore these images, which we have chosen – very simply – to call 'open images'. One might read these images directly in terms of the political and cultural climate of the Islamic Republic which engendered them, as part of the broader ongoing critical debate on the relationship of these films to contemporary Iranian social reality. Our intention, however, is primarily to draw structural and aesthetic comparisons across different national cinemas; to show, among other things, how a repressed political dimension returns within the ostensibly apolitical aesthetic form of the open image.

The term 'image' encompasses shot, frame and scene, and includes sound components – open images may deploy any of these elements. Open images are not necessarily extraordinary images; they often belong to the order of the everyday. While watching a film one may meet them with some resistance – yet they have the property of producing virtual after-images in the mind. Although their effects are ambiguous, the images exhibit identifiable signs and techniques, and this essay provides a classification of the open image, drawing on concepts from Pier Paolo Pasolini's theory of poetic realism, Paul Schrader's notion of the arrested image – stasis – as a cinematic signifier of transcendence, and Gilles Deleuze's theory of the time-image. We will sketch out the historical emergence of the open image in Italian neorealism and its reflexive turn in the French New Wave, and then apply our account of the open image to particular films drawn from the New Iranian Cinema.

The influence of Italian Neorealism and the French New Wave on Iranian cinema is commonly asserted – and hotly contested. Within Iran, this trend in critical debate might appear as another 'injection' of cultural imperialism, which the revolutionary regime has sought to resist by curtailing imports of first world cinema and actively promoting appreciation of films from the developing world.[1] However, we will argue that it is with reason that critics invoke Italian and French antecedents, because of the crucial role these cinemas played in the historical formation of the open image.

Those who oppose the 'hackneyed' references to neorealism in discussions on Iranian cinema tend to overemphasize Italian Neorealism's so-called 'realist' aspects.[2] This use of reality as a yardstick to measure Neorealism, whether it be in terms of its social content or its aesthetics has resulted in the dominant framing of the middle and late works of Luchino Visconti, Federico Fellini and Michelangelo Antonioni as 'post'-neorealist. We prefer to emphasize a poetic conception of neorealism and, consequently, argue that these directors do not represent a break with Italian Neorealism; rather, they bring forward poetic qualities which were inherent in Neorealism from the beginning.[3]

This poetic conception is articulated in Pasolini's 1965 essay 'The cinema of poetry'. Pasolini claims that filmmakers imbue the 'image-signs' they use with their personal expression as well as giving them general meanings.[4] These signs can eventually acquire conventional meanings (as they have in Hollywood codes), constituting a 'cinema of prose'. At the other extreme is the 'cinema of poetry', made possible by the cinematic counterpart of free indirect discourse in literature: the 'free indirect subjective'. Here, the filmmaker's viewpoint becomes one with the character's. Pasolini refers to instances in *Deserto Rosso/Red Desert* (1964), in which Antonioni's viewpoint merges with that of the neurotic heroine Giuliana. The colours and objects around Giuliana are transformed in accordance with her psychological state – a cart of fruit turns grey to reflect her uncertainty, an industrial workshop dominated by the colour of bright red plastic directly materializes her sense of danger. We no longer have the objective shot (which corresponds to indirect discourse) nor the subjective shot (direct discourse), but *a vision which has liberated itself from the two* – the free indirect subjective.

Pasolini traces the free indirect subjective (and with it the cinema of poetry) from Roberto Rossellini and the founding works of Italian Neorealism. Compared to the overdetermined narrative image-sign system of the cinema of prose, the images that constitute the cinema of poetry are infinite in possibility, but can be identified in terms of the cinematic style or means by which they are achieved. Pasolini notes a few of the characteristics of these free indirect subjective images under the heading of 'obsessive framing': the close juxtaposition of shots showing slightly different viewpoints of the same object; the static shot of a scene in which characters enter and leave the frame; the stillness of a shot upon an object. The free indirect subjective image is rooted in the diegesis (the character and narrative perspective) and the obsessive vision (psychology/aesthetic) of the filmmaker, yet such images cannot be straightforwardly deciphered as a revelation of either a character's psychological state or that of the filmmaker.[5] Instead the unresolved tension between the two viewpoints – character and filmmaker – creates an ambiguity, a space in which the image appears to emerge from somewhere other. This 'other' perspective is often, as in Antonioni's films, felt to reside in the camera itself, particularly in those scenes where the camera continues recording empty reality after people and identifiable human consciousness have departed – the camera as the uncanny eye of surveillance. Commenting on Pasolini's theory of the free indirect subjective, Deleuze refers to this emphasis on a 'reflecting consciousness' distinct from that of both character and director as a 'camera consciousness . . . a properly cinemato-graphic *Cogito*'.[6] However, we would prefer to stress not an imagined source of subjective or subjectless viewpoint, but rather the otherness of the images as objects, as intrusions of the real.

A common characteristic of the open image is stasis. An obvious indication of this in several of the Iranian films to be discussed is the use of the long-held freeze-frame as closing image: *Nun va Goldun/Moment of Innocence* (Mohsen Makhmalbaf, 1996), *Nama-ye Nazdik/Close-Up* (Abbas Kiarostami, 1989) and *Sib/The Apple* (Samira Makhmalbaf, 1998) all end on a freeze-frame and they all freeze characters mid-action – that is, in overt movement. As a cinematic device this can probably be traced back to the influence of the famous closing freeze-frame of Antoine running towards the sea in François Truffaut's *Les Quatre cent coups/400 Blows* (1959) – the New Wave film closest in sensibility to New Iranian Cinema. One of the few attempts to elaborate an aesthetic of stasis remains Schrader's *Transcendental Style* (1972). Among the key characteristics of what he calls 'transcendental style' are the following:

- The everyday: a meticulous representation of the dull, banal commonplaces of everyday living, involving understated acting and dedramatization.
- Disparity: an actual or potential disunity between man and his environment, which culminates in a decisive action.
- Stasis: a frozen view of life, which does not resolve the preceding disparity but transcends it.[7]

What Schrader calls the 'stasis shot' within his stylistics of the transcendental style is close to our conception of the open image within the stylistics of Neorealism, insofar as both involve the fracturing of the everyday by something 'other.' (Dedramatization and disparity, too, have a bearing on the production of open images, as we shall see.)

An aesthetic of stasis appears paradoxical given that an essential component of cinema is movement. Cinema can be seen as opposed to the photograph: even though it is constituted by still photographs, these are not perceived as such in the act of viewing, although they may be extracted (as distinct frames). As Jean Mitry, among others, has noted, the photographic image has a melancholy relationship to its referent:

> The photograph of a person retains the impression of his presence. It constantly refers back to him. His going away merely reinforces the impression that this image is the only testimony of what his physical appearance was at a particular moment in his existence.[8]

In the cinematic image this 'testimony' is desired yet paradoxical, out of reach (because the moving image is always moving beyond the particular moment). We would argue that the stylistics of 'transcendental' stasis common to the open image is, in part, an attempt to imbue the moving image with the photographic aura. Following Henri Bergson and William James,[9] we can presume that it is inevitable that the moving image of real-time duration will be broken down by memory into discrete images of moments and then synthesized or reconstructed into a privileged static image or a series of quasi-static images. Memory privileges the fleeting motionless image over direct visual representation of duration.

The photographic aura accrues to the cinematic image of stasis as an 'always already' recollected image. The image from a film that impresses itself upon our consciousness constantly refers back to its *presence*. Echoing Mitry, the fact that we are no longer watching the film, the fact that we saw it five hours or five years ago, 'merely reinforces the impression that this image is the only testimony' not only of the 'appearance' of the film, but of *our experience* of watching the film 'at a particular moment' of our existence. The static image thus finds itself embroiled in notions of presence, absence and death, especially when it is experienced in cinema – that is, in relation to moving images, and to duration. It is the aura of the fixed, static image which throws the passing of time, of existence, into relief; and all these existential terms suggest that the religious underpinning of Schrader's 'transcendental style' – an anathema to most film theorists – is impossible to repress.

In the examples from Iranian cinema to be discussed, stasis (arrested images, the fixed long-shot, the freeze-frame or images of empty spaces) will be seen as auspicious for open images, but not invariably so. Although Schrader equates stasis, austerity and what he terms the 'sparse' with transcendental style, he points out that the long-take stasis films of avant-garde art, usually depicting objects in real time (as in the minimalist cinema of Michael Snow or today's video installations), fail to evoke the transcendental effect. Such an effect is only produced by stasis as a break within 'realist' narrative: for an image to be 'arrested' it must previously flow.[10]

Likewise, we contend that the open image only has meaning as a deferral of an otherwise implied narrative closure. It is this context that gives rise to viewer resistance to stasis, experienced as boredom; though boredom might be an integral part of the aesthetic experience – for the diachronic arts, especially film, the occasional 'space' of boredom is a way in which real-time duration is defamiliarized and then made retrievable to the reconstructed imaging of memory. It may be the *longueur* that facilitates the 'opening' of image in narrative. The experience of

resistance, of boredom, may be transformed into the experience of the transcendental, of ecstasy. In Schrader's words: 'When the image stops, the viewer keeps
going, moving deeper and deeper, one might say, into the image. This is the "miracle"
of sacred art.'[11]

Deleuze's writings on cinema, *Cinema 1: The Movement-Image* (1983) and *Cinema 2:
The Time-Image* (1985), investigate the opening out of the image in direct images of
time; not external, chronological time, but the time of concrete duration. These
direct time-images are characterized by a lack of causal links. Movement-images, on
the other hand, are defined by causal links. In Deleuze's neurological terminology,
movement-images show 'sensory-motor' connections between stimulus and
response. Something is seen, for example, and an action, perception or feeling is
given as a reaction.[12] The time-image is created when such sensory-motor links in
the image are suspended or broken. When the situation no longer extends into
action, films give rise to pure optical and sound situations. Something has become
'too strong' in the image, something which cannot be reduced to what happens or
what is perceived or felt (by the characters).[13] The break between movement-images
and time-images is not clearcut, but generally time-images belong to cinema's
'postclassical' phase. Time-images are connotative rather than denotative, imbuing
objects with a number of associations. Deleuze suggests they might have political
implications: 'It is precisely the weakness of the motor linkages, the weak connections', he writes, 'that are capable of releasing huge forces of disintegration',
producing images of process, of transformation; such images are not an obscurantist
turning away from the political, but the open-ended politicization of the image.[14]
This argument has become relevant again in the light of the controversy surrounding
the (a)political trajectory of the New Iranian Cinema.[15]

   In Deleuze's account, Italian Neorealism is the film movement that most
epitomizes the break between the movement-image and the time-image. This break
came about, he claims, for reasons both internal and external to cinema. External
circumstances were provided by postwar devastation, reconstruction and diaspora.
As cities were demolished and rebuilt, wastelands (such as derelict and disused out-
of-town sites) proliferated, and people became displaced from their settings, the
determinate environments associated with the movement-image became blurred.
After World War II, circumstances internal to cinema made it ready to respond to
these external conditions, particularly in postfascist Italy. The sensory-motor links
between motivation and action gave way to new forms, such as the meandering
journey, which accorded more with the transformed landscapes. Cinema gave rise
to images of indeterminate settings – 'any-spaces-whatever'[16] which became pure
optical and sound situations.

   When we turn the emphasis from Neorealism's 'realism' to its poeticism and its
production of pure optical and sound situations, the ground on which the common
view of Neorealism stands begins to shift. No longer can we see it simply in terms

of its commitment to record 'reality'. All those features which justified that view
– its association with nonprofessional actors, contemporary social and political
topics dealing with ordinary people, combining fictional drama with documentary,
and location shooting – must be put into contact with something else. The settings
retain their reality, but they are no longer situations that disclose actions as they
would in traditional realism. Instead, they open onto thought, dream, memory and
feelings of *déjà-vu*, as the action 'floats' in the situation. Viewers no longer perceive
a sensory-motor image to which they respond by identifying with the characters.
Instead, they undergo 'a dream-like connection through the intermediary of the
liberated sense organs'.[17]

Rather than extending into movement, the pure optical and sound image enters
into relation with a virtual image, and 'forms a circuit with it', as if it has linked up
with an image we recall from somewhere else.[18] But it is most effective when our
memory falters and we cannot remember: as Bergson realized, 'attentive recognition
informs us to a much greater degree when it fails than when it succeeds', and the
same applies to cinema.[19] When the present optical perception fails to make a link
with either a motor-image or a recollection-image, 'it enters into relation with
genuinely virtual elements, feelings of *déjà-vu* or the past "in general" (I must have
seen that man somewhere . . .), dream images (I have the feeling that I saw him
in a dream . . .)'.[20] This opening-out of the image seems to occur regardless of
the content – the images may be of 'everyday banality' or 'exceptional limit-
circumstances', but their predominant optical and sound situations, Deleuze writes,
are 'subjective images, memories of childhood, sound and visual dreams or
fantasies'.[21]

The discussion so far is pertinent not only to work that is generally termed 'post'-
Neorealist, but also to the key Neorealist films such as Rossellini's war trilogy,
Vittorio De Sica's *Ladri di Biciclette/Bicycle Thieves* (1948) and Visconti's *La Terra
Trema/The Earth Trembles* (1948). There is a formalism and a penchant for
aestheticized stasis in Visconti's vision – and a corresponding deployment of devices
that would come to be associated with the poetic post-Neorealism of Antonioni and
Pasolini (such as fixed shots as characters enter and exit the frame). Thus, *La Terra
Trema* exploits the effects of documenting social reality and combines this with
fictional (re)construction by way of a formalist aesthetic, a combination prefiguring
– amongst much else – the most widely-recognized strategy of the New Iranian
Cinema, from Kiarostami's *Close-Up* to Samira Makhmalbaf's *The Apple*.

The 'reality effects' in *La Terra Trema* would be nothing without the visual
stylization and theatrical staging that characterize each shot. The film makes striking
compositions out of the natural surroundings – with views of the rocks which
enclose the harbour and the image of the women, their black shawls billowing in
the wind, standing on rocks, straining seaward for the brothers' return. The film
keeps returning to the view of the rocks, which might be seen as an attempt to

anchor the story in a specific locale – the rocks being signs of a distinctive, recognizable place, However, silhouetted in the dusk they become ambiguous and, in our associations, break free from their geographically-specific moorings and also from their symbolic moorings (where they represent the isolation of the village from the outside world). They are no longer the rocks of a particular harbour in Sicily, but (to adapt the Deleuzian term) 'any-rocks-whatever'.

This brings us to another aspect of Neorealism's break with traditional realism. While the latter is characterized by determined spaces, neorealism loses the specific geospatial coordinates of a given locale and rearranges the references. Deleuze contends that one can refer to 'Riemanian spaces' in Neorealism, where the 'connecting of parts is not predetermined but tan take place in many ways'.[22] Landscapes or cityscapes attain a hallucinatory, crystalline quality that looks forward to later Antonioni (the trilogy, *Red Desert, Zabriskie Point* [1969]) or the Zone in Andrei Tarkovsky's *Stalker* (1979). Such spatial indeterminacy is a feature of the New Iranian Cinema, in which a character's quest traverses the labyrinthine pathway of either city streets (*Badkonak-e Sefid/The White Balloon* [Jafar Panahi, 1995], *Dayereh/The Circle* [Jafar Panahi, 2000]), the tracks of villages/rural areas (*Khaneh-ye Dust Kojast/Where Is My Friend's House?* [Abbas Kiarostami, 1987], *Zir-e Darakhtan-e Zeytun/Through the Olive Trees* [Abbas Kiarostami, 1994], *Bad Mara Khahad Bord/The Wind Will Carry Us* [Abbas Kiarostami, 1999]), or passes over barren mountainous landscapes (*Takhteh Siyah/Blackboards* [Samira Makhmalbaf, 1999], *Zamani Barayé Masti Asbha/A Time for Drunken Horses* [Bahman Ghobadi, 2000]). Alternatively, characters may navigate the labyrinthine topology of the liminal space where equally barren city and rural environments meet (*Ta'm-e Gilas/A Taste of Cherry* [Abbas Kiarostami, 1997]). The circuitous quest makes even the most concrete places fleetingly uncanny – both for the character and for the viewer.

Deleuze refers to the 'dispersive and lacunary reality' in Rossellini's *Paisà* (1946), where locales fragment into unstable configurations.[23] This feature is carried further in Antonioni, where the Deleuzian 'any-space-whatever' is constituted from geometrical blocks of whites, shadows and colours – starting with almost empty urban riverbank shots in *Netteza Urbana* (1948), and the deserted stadium in *Cronaca di un Amore/Chronicle of a Love* (1950), going on to the final scene showing the rendez-vous point devoid of protagonists in *L'Eclisse/The Eclipse* (1962) and the industrial landscapes of *Red Desert*. These emptied or disconnected spaces obtain a relative autonomy from the surrounding narrative, enabling them to become open images.

The neorealist locations inspired by the indeterminate environments created by the postwar situation attract a new type of protagonist who – because images no longer obey sensory-motor rules – tends to see rather than act. For this reason, as Deleuze suggests, the role of the child, who mostly looks on in wonder or confusion while unable to intervene, becomes significant.[24] In this development, where the child's gaze and the pure optical and sound image meet, Italian Neorealism is clearly the crucial turning point (for example, Rossellini's *Germania Anno*

Zero / Germany Year Zero [1947] and De Sica's *Bicycle Thieves*). It is a development which will be vital for some of the most powerful open images in New Iranian Cinema and helps to explain its many child protagonists (*Where Is My Friend's House?*, *The White Balloon, The Apple*) in terms other than those of sentimental humanism.[25]

The French New Wave adapted much of the image repertoire created by Neo-realism, but gave the images a reflexive spin, an effect that can also be seen in New Iranian Cinema. The French directors specialized in images of movements that falsify perspective, taking further a tendency already assumed by Neorealism (and which gave rise to its disconnected spaces). With reference to a Deleuzian analysis, two salient characteristics can be briefly noted here: first, the 'irrational' cuts (which have disjunctive rather than conjunctive value), typified by Godard; second, the 'crystal image', which recurs across the French New Wave films, but is best typified by Alain Resnais.[26]

    As already mentioned, the pure optical and sound situation, instead of extending into movement, enters into relationship with a virtual image (thought, dream, memory or *déjà-vu*). A crystal image occurs when an actual optical image and a virtual image form a circuit and coalesce or exchange places.[27] The most familiar instance of the crystal image is the mirror. A famous example is in *Citizen Kane* (Orson Welles, 1941) where we see Kane passing between two facing mirrors; as the mirror images recede infinitely, the actual and the virtual become indistinguishable. Alternatively, the crystal image may have what Deleuze calls 'an internal disposition', like 'a seed in relation to the environment'.[28] Here the crystal image has a *mise-en-abyme* structure, where the seed is the virtual image crystallizing the environment ('environment' denotes both the physical landscape and the diegetic reality of the film). The paperweight that falls from the dying man's hand as he utters the word 'Rosebud' in the opening of *Citizen Kane* is an example of such a crystal image, the paperweight being the 'seed' or *mise-en-abyme* of the environment, Xanadu (and also the uncertain 'seed' of the story itself).

    Deleuze argues that the crystal image is the true 'genetic moment' of pure optical-sound situations, which 'are nothing but slivers of crystal-images'.[29] In Resnais's film *L'Année dernière à Marienbad / Last Year in Marienbad* (1961), the hotel (indeed the whole film) is a crystal, maze-like, mirroring infinite probabilities. The film-within-a-film (characteristic of so many Godard and New Wave films) is a type of crystal image, including the film which takes its own process of making as its object – but, as Deleuze implies, this work in the mirror must be 'justified from elsewhere' if it is to succeed (that is, the self-reflexivity must not be in and for itself).[30] It is no surprise therefore that the film-within-a-film should so often provide the context for open images in New Iranian Cinema (*Close Up, Through the Olive Trees, Salaam Cinema* [Mohsen Makhmalbaf, 1995], *A Moment of Innocence*). The overt reflexivity of Iranian cinema is not merely a borrowing of Brechtian devices via Godard and the French New Wave, but rather something integral to its form and always 'justified from elsewhere' by the neorealist diegesis.

In the following sections, we will show how Iranian cinema has developed, for its own purposes, elements drawn from the stylistic theories and practices discussed above, resulting in a recognizable aesthetic structured around the privileging of open images. Some of these elements correspond very closely to what we have already seen in (post)neorealism, while others develop the stylistics of the open image to a new degree, bringing into being new distinctive types. By refocusing existing debates in terms of the open image, we ensure that cinema's 'poetic realism', so often obscured, is kept in view.

The majority of recent Iranian films are structured by a 'quest' through a realist location. But such classical neorealist locations are stylized – naturalistic specificity of location giving way to poetic universalism. Moreover, as the quest becomes a meandering circular itinerary, so location breaks down into disconnected spaces: *A Taste of Cherry, The Wind Will Carry Us, The Circle*, even *The White Balloon* and *The Apple*, display variations of this process. In Kiarostami's *Where Is My Friend's House?*, schoolboy Ahmad mistakenly takes his friend Mohammad's homework book. Knowing that the teacher will expel Mohammad if he does not do his homework in the correct book, Ahmad sets off to return it, although no one can tell him where Mohammad lives. The quest will never be completed; Ahmad running up and down the zigzag path between villages stands for the whole structure of the film: the meandering, or indirect, journey form. The film's cinematography has the effect of erasing the precise co-ordinates (the villages Koker and Poshteh in Northern Iran) and instead gives rise to disconnected spaces in which the various sensory-motor linkages begin to come apart.

The way in which characters become lost in the liminal zone between disconnected spaces takes on an overtly political aspect in Samira Makhmalbaf's *Blackboards* and Ghobadi's *A Time for Drunken Horses*. In these films the narrative is driven by its characters' attempts to cross the border between Iran and Iraq, but the landscape gradually dissolves into disconnected spaces: 'border' ceases to be an identifiable, recognizable place and instead signifies a nightmarish unstable zone of inexplicable military atrocity. The idea for *Blackboards* began with the landscape: when Samira Makhmalbaf was walking in Kurdistan with her father, she was struck by the harsh infertility of some parts of the landscape, and selected these for her film's location.[31] They give an overwhelming impression of inhospitality, with red, stony, steep ascents; a hint of menace is underscored by the film's use of offscreen sound to indicate helicopter surveillance and border patrols. The treatment of landscape in the film places a neorealist emphasis on the relationship between characters and their lived-in surroundings, where characters are 'moulded' in the image of the environment.[32] The recalcitrance of the landscape rubs off on the characters: the obdurate, weatherbeaten old patriarchs and the hardy boy smugglers. The itinerant teachers are out of place in this landscape – and they look it, ungainly with their blackboards, searching for pupils, when nobody wants to be taught. As a result of this 'free indirect' relationship between character and landscape (where the vision of the landscape is filtered through that of the character), poetic open images are possible in every scene. But it is not only the teachers who are displaced; eventually, as they near the border, all the Kurdish characters in the film become 'lost', 'disconnected' from the landscape, and the landscape itself dissolves into disconnected spaces of desolation.

This disconnection is reflected in the editing of *Blackboards* as well as in its mise-en-scene. Whereas Hollywood editing ensures spatial continuity from shot to shot, the editing in this film tends to present a given scene as disconnected fragments of space. This, too, highlights the instability of space, spatial disruption and disorientation. For example, in one conversation scene (between a teacher and an old man who asks him to read a letter), the camera alternates from one character to the other, with each character occupying a separate frame; but unlike the Hollywood shot/reverse-shot structure, there is little common space from shot to shot. This kind of spatial system is characteristic of the House of Makhmalbaf films discussed here. Instead of cutting from a spatial whole to a part, sequences are often entirely constructed from parts, especially in the many scenes taking place before closed (or partially closed) doorways. Here the doorway functions as an internal frame, marking the barrier to our vision, and emphasizing the selectiveness of what we see. There are closeups of disembodied women's hands giving directions, handing out soup or watering flowers (*Moment of Innocence, The Apple*) from behind doors that are barely ajar. Thus, the disconnected spaces of Iranian cinema also gesture to concerns about the limits of what can be shown (from a non-Iranian perspective, it is tempting to read this allegorically as referring to censorship restrictions).

Both the fixed long shot and the long take are typical components of an aesthetic of 'stasis' as outlined by Schrader, and typical vehicles for the open image. The zigzag path on the hill between villages in *Where Is My Friend's House?* is an exemplary open image. We see Ahmad's tiny figure running up and down across the hillside three times in the film, mostly in a static framing and in long shot. The distant view and length of the take in the absence of any conventional action force us to concentrate on the image and absorb the abstraction imposed on the environment. Kiarostami had the path specially built for the film (and planted a tree on the top of the hill), which reflects his concern for not just recording reality, but making it carry certain poetic resonances. Some of these are symbolic (aside from resonances specific to Persian culture, the tree on the top stands for friendship, while Ahmad's zigzagging symbolizes the hurrying-around in modern life, Kiarostami says).[33] However, the static long shot frame and its duration give the cinematic image an openness in excess of its closed symbolism, allowing it to connect with virtual images in the mind.[34]

Kiarostami's *Through the Olive Trees* concludes with a long take showing a young peasant, Hossein, following the girl, Tahereh, to whom he has proposed marriage. The two figures wend their way through an olive orchard and along zigzag paths across a valley, finally disappearing into almost invisible dots in the distance. Because of the real-time, fixed point-of-view determination of the scene, making us strain to follow the two speck-figures on a path, we scrutinize the moving image as if it were a photograph containing the sublime object, the veiled secret. This is an important quality of the open image and an aspect of its residual photographic aura.

As discussed earlier in relation to Schrader, in a film where every image is equally open there can be no openness; the term becomes meaningless due to the lack of distinguishing qualities and contrast. This is also true of the individual image: the open image must contain a level of closure, of limitation, which enables the openness to reveal itself and, by the same token, allows the play of universality and particularity to show forth. This seems to be how Kiarostami approached, technically, the universalizing of Hossein and Tahereh in the final scene of *Through the Olive Trees*: by holding the viewer in an extreme way to the image, both temporally (four minutes) and spatially (long and wide shot of one scene), the eventual release of interpretative desire is all the more pronounced. Kiarostami comments:

> The film-maker has carried the film up to here, and now it is given up to the audience to think about it and watch these characters from very far away. I like the last shot because of its openness. Until that moment social differences were dividing these two people, but as human beings they were equal. The class system separated them, but in nature and in long shot I felt that these two could get closer to their real selves, that is to their inner needs, without giving any value to the social norms.[35]

In the process of becoming extradiegetic archetypes, Hossein and Tahereh continue to be inflected with what seem to be, for Kiarostami, the three primary levels of being: the personal level of love; the social level of class difference; the existential level of nature. The universalizing never loses sight of the particular.

When Ahmad undertakes his quest in *Where Is My Friend's House?*, many obstacles and detours are put in his path, mostly by interfering or unhelpful adults. The bewilderment of the child in the world of adults is key to the film's emotional power. Kiarostami has said that the actor was chosen because of his gaze, a decision which revives the child's role as a witness in Italian Neorealism.[36] One might have expected him, therefore, to exploit this by having many facial closeups expressing precisely this bafflement; but although the image of Ahmad's startled face is one we are likely to take away from the film, there are not many closeups. Instead Kiarostami prefers medium closeups, moving out to extreme long shots, blocking direct identification with Ahmad's gaze and instead making the viewer work through a 'free indirect subjective'[37] relation between the gaze of the character and a given image, between the child's gaze and the gaze of the film.

The most bewildering sequence in the film, both for Ahmad and for the viewer, is the wander through the narrow streets of Poshteh. The set is a labyrinth, a crystalline or Riemanian space, but one which creates more anxiety than those in Italian neorealism, for here the meandering structure of the film in general, and this sequence in particular, directly confronts what Deleuze calls the child's motor-helplessness in the adult's world. The anxiety and helplessness of the child lost in the forbidding labyrinth is encapsulated in the film's title, a plea to which nobody has a proper answer. Everyday signs become mysteriously ominous: a man, dwarfed and bent over by the bundle of twigs he is carrying, looks like a walking bush; brown trousers on a washing line are a false sign (Ahmad believes, mistakenly, that they belong to his friend). Ahmad stumbles from one dead end to another, following the ambiguous and imprecise directions that denizens of the village give him; meanwhile we hear off-camera sounds – the sudden mewing of cats, a dog barking, the distant clacking of a passing train, all the more puzzling and ambiguous for their absence in the scene. When, finally, Ahmad encounters an old carpenter, his quest is suspended: the carpenter takes him on a tour of the doors and windows of the village. Sensory-motor linkages in the image come utterly apart here: not only is there no extension into action *per se*, but the scene itself ceases to make sense. Dream-like sensations descend on the viewer as the narrative enters this extraordinary lull. What takes hold instead is optical play: teasing glimpses of kaleidoscopic projections of light on the walls of the old houses. These, supposedly, are all cast through windows and doors from lit interiors, but the bizarre positioning of some of this shadow-play gives the lie to such a rational explanation. This image of the play of light is not reducible to realism, but is a reflexive motif on the technology that projects the images that we see.

In classical Hollywood narrative the protagonist becomes the moral yardstick against which we measure all the other characters in a film; he is the character with whom we most identify, and we can do this because he is presented as sympathetic, despite his foibles. The presence of unsympathetic characters, central to many Iranian films, marks a divergence from the Hollywood norm but connects with a development out of Italian Neorealism represented especially by Antonioni. In an added self-reflexive ambiguity many of these central characters are film directors: seemingly insensitive and aloof manipulators of their casts – Mohsen Makhmalbaf taking this even further by 'playing himself' as the manipulative director in *Salaam Cinema* and *A Moment of Innocence*. This blocking of identification relates to the muted performances Iranian directors draw from their actors, especially from adults, an ambiguity of acting register closer to Neorealism and Rossellini than to the uniform flatness of Bresson or Ozu; a dedramatization that creates space for the intensification of images. In Deleuzian terms, when identification with characters does take place, the sensory-motor arc remains intact – there is a connection between what is seen and a motor reaction (our identification with that character in that situation). The failure of identification with characters snaps the sensory-motor chain, and liberates the senses: we become more receptive to other aspects of the film. In particular, it facilitates connections with virtual images which will return in the viewer's memory.

In Kiarostami's *The Wind Will Carry Us*, the unsympathetic central character is the film producer protagonist, Behzad, who is insensitive and irresponsible in his attempts to exploit the rural village he has come to film. In a disturbing scene, Behzad on a hillside kicks over a tortoise – there are some conventional reverse-shots of the character looking down on the back of the tortoise, though it is the tortoise and its movement which is the dominant real-time image (filling the image-frame), beyond any conventional point of view or narrative requirements. Behzad loses interest and walks off but we (to our relief) see the desperate tortoise managing to right itself and continue on its way. As with similar scenes in Antonioni, a reductive explanation is possible: when Behzad kicks over the tortoise he gives expression to the way in which his individual alienation (bourgeois, urban) necessarily separates him from existence itself (nature). Such alienation (at the three levels of personality, class and the existential) is manifest in the very arbitrariness of his cruelty and the fact that it is unthinking curiosity rather than intentional cruelty – he does not stay to extract sadistic pleasure from the upturned tortoise's plight. But Behzad is not hero, villain or victim; identification with him and his act remains disconnected, open, as does the image of the tortoise – obsessively framed in excess of the narrative requirement – or to put it in Pasolini's terms, a poetic image infuses a prosaic narrative with its ambiguity.

Open images are a feature, of film endings, closing scenes which try not to close down a narrative but rather open it out to the viewer's consideration, to 'live on' after the film itself has finished. A striking example is in Kiarostami's *A Taste of Cherry*, where the central character, Mr Badiei, plans to commit suicide in the evening, but must find someone who will come the following morning to bury him. Towards the end of the film Badiei takes an overdose and lies down in his self-dug grave. The screen goes completely black for a few seconds. Suddenly the film cuts from darkness to light, from film to grainy video stock. Characters that we saw earlier are now seen waiting around, like actors on a film set, while motifs from the film (marching soldiers counting in unison) are repeated *vérité*-style.

This change to grainy video stock to give a *vérité* effect is a common feature of New Iranian Cinema. An early example is Kiarostami's use of video for the real trial scene of the 'fake Makhmalbaf' case in *Close-Up*. In *A Taste of Cherry* the documentary effect is subverted. The *vérité* coda does not assert, in Brechtian fashion, that the foregoing film is just a representation, because the fuzzy imaging of the video reality seems far stranger than the tangible diegetic reality of the preceding narrative; instead, the intrusion of this uncanny real marks a shift to the poetic. The switch from night and death to day and life, far from resolving the narrative, creates an ambiguity, an openness, as if we are now watching images of life after death – whether or not our central character actually died or not. Following the blacked-out image, the temporal relation between the coda and the preceding narrative is thrown into confusion, as is the relation between diegesis and metal diegetic documentary. The coda – evoking dream or *déjà-vu* – is not a recollection or flashback but a merging or shortcircuiting of past and present, forming a crystal image.

While *A Taste of Cherry* ends with 'documentary' in video, Samira Makhmalbaf's *The Apple* uses videocam for its documentary beginning, thus setting up the whole film as a Deleuzian crystal image. The film follows the adventures of two girls who have spent most of their lives locked up at home under their father's watchful eye. The first image shows an outstretched hand watering a plant. This shot documents the everyday, yet makes it abstract – the stationary camera waits for the hand to enter the frame. The shot composition is austere, almost abstract – flat, with the camera axis perpendicular to the background. It is a form of abstraction which does not remove the everyday, but opens it into dimensions other than the everyday. It raises possible symbolic meanings relating to the narrative – the plant is in the open, receiving the sun, unlike the housebound girls. Yet the image resists any one-to-one correspondence between the sign and meaning.

The story for *The Apple* is taken straight from Tehran television news, and uses the family members concerned to act as themselves – but the director introduces significant props, such as the dangling apple and mirror, into her reimagining of the events. Several open images in this film come from scenes which make use of these symbolic props. This is because their intrusion into the reconstruction of events that took place in actuality only a few days before produces an uncanny effect; the irreducible quality alluded to above never vanishes. Makhmalbaf began filming even as the events were happening – her documentary section, using video, shows the girls at the welfare centre while the reconstruction of the girls' release into the outside world started only four days after it happened. As a result, the whole film becomes a crystal image, but one in which the work in the mirror is put in the scene in a peculiarly uncanny fashion, for not only are the symbolic props a constant reminder that this is a fictional reconstruction, but they directly materialize the twins' process of coming to terms with the outside world. They, like the film, examine themselves in the mirror (given to them as a present by the social worker). Even the apple, which is such an overdetermined symbol in the Judaeo-Islamic-Christian cultural inheritance, becomes detached from those particular moorings to configure the twins' curiosity about the world.

Mohsen Makhmalbaf's *A Moment of Innocence*, a film which films itself in the process of its own constitution, contains particularly intricate crystalline open images. Makhmalbaf plays himself as the (unsympathetic) director of a film which looks reflexively at his own past – and might be said to reconstitute that past. For there is a significant disparity between the past as it happened and the past which is recollected in the film. In the former, Makhmalbaf, an Islamic revolutionary, aged seventeen, tried to disarm one of the Shah's policemen, was shot by him, and subsequently imprisoned in a Pahlavi jail. By contrast, the film (made long after

Makhmalbaf renounced his revolutionary fervour) represents the policeman as a sensitive man, in love with a mysterious woman who seemed to ask him for the time, or for directions, at every opportunity. It also tells us that this woman was Makhmalbaf's cousin and accomplice (whose flirtation is merely to distract the policeman while Makhmalbaf stabs him with a knife); the two revolutionaries are in love with each other, and together they want to save the world using any means – including violence. In the film's reconstruction of history, the ideal of saving the world through love is contrasted with the means of violence – this is the version that the youngsters are asked to reenact, but their failure to reenact this version introduces yet another alternative (nonviolent) reality, which calls into question Makhmalbaf's attempt to reconstitute – and manipulate – the past. The young actors do not wish to take up arms against each other – the 'Young Makhmalbaf' repeatedly sobs and throws away the knife that he has been directed to thrust into the policeman's side. The 'Young Policeman' refuses to draw his gun. In the climax of the film-within-a-film, the 'Policeman', on impulse, offers the woman the flower which he had been instructed not to give her, and 'Makhmalbaf' in turn donates to the policeman the flatbread under which he was supposed to conceal the knife; the film closes with this image of exchange, the veiled woman caught in between, arrested in a freeze-frame.

The fusion of reality and its poetic remake in *A Moment of Innocence* develops into a very complex crystal image, in which no component is entirely independent from any other – this has the antirealist consequence that characters who have never met before act as if they knew each other intimately. For all the film's intricate design, the components in the film do not just slot neatly inside each other – they open onto each other, overlapping. In this respect the film, like so many Iranian films (*The Circle, The Wind Will Carry Us, A Taste of Cherry*), structurally resembles the musical round – which, according to Deleuze, is an instance of a crystal – with its rhythmically-modulated repetitions. In *A Moment of Innocence*, the first scene of the policeman strand ends when a woman happens to come by and asks him the time. 'It happened just like that!' exclaims the policeman as she walks away. We then cut to the Makhmalbaf strand, where the part of the cousin is allocated to the young actor's own cousin. When, finally alone, she calls into a shop where the clocks have all stopped, then walks towards the rehearsing policemen, the encounter we saw before is repeated. This time we recognize the woman, and realize that the two scenes/ strands have not been taking place in sequence (which is how we have experienced them), but simultaneously. The narrative then takes up the policeman strand from exactly where it was left before, but the repetition has underlined the words 'It happened just like that!' with a new ambiguity.

There are political implications in this use of the crystal image as a round, which, Deleuze writes, describes 'the rising and falling back of pasts which are preserved.'[38] As the round progresses, more and more alternative realities are negotiated and put into contact with the past 'as it happened'; the actual images are made to confront virtual images, generating multiple fictional possibilities. As such, *Moment of Innocence* utilizes the properties of the open image (crystalline ambiguity, indeterminacy) in a way that subtly undermines the Islamic regime itself. That regime, which temporarily banned the film, states that there is only one reality; but even in the one, the film points out, there are many.[39] The shop where the clocks are frozen signals the arrest of linear time, the severing of sensory-motor links, and the release of subjective possibilities.

The freeze-frame which ends *Moment of Innocence* suspends within its single image the competing determinants of Islamic fundamentalism, revolutionary idealism, terrorism, law and order, adolescent romance, unrequited love, revenge and pacifism. The freeze-frame 'arrests' the precise 'moment' where history and its attempted re-enactment interpenetrate – that is, the past (the original terrorist act of the young Makhmalbaf and accomplice) is transfigured by the present (the actors' refusal to repeat the original violent act). The original terrorists' act, the original lovelorn policeman's naive response, the actors' spontaneous refusal of violence, and the middle-aged protagonists' witnessing of this refusal in the re-enactment, are no longer separate moments in time but are all joined to constitute the moment of innocence. Although there is a synthesis of past and present and of the competing ideologies in this moment, this image, there is no resolution, no closure. Instead the viewer is left to read the freeze-frame tableau and the contradictions held within it as an open image.

It might be argued that the tendency towards the allegorical evident in New Iranian Cinema pulls the films' open images towards narrative determinism. *The Apple*, for instance, can be read in terms of feminist allegory. In the concluding scene, the blind, chadored mother wanders out of the house, into the alleyway, and reaches for the dangling apple. The final shot freezes her with the apple firmly in her grasp (an allegory about women seizing opportunities). The imprisonment of the girls may be a code, enabling the film to pass the censor, for the restrictions imposed on women in Iran. Nonetheless, neither the allegorical-symbolic nor the documentary elements/codes have hegemony, and the closing freeze-frame of *The Apple* is an open image in that it 'suspends' interpretation between competing narrative codes.

A groundbreaking Iranian film in terms of popular (commercial) international success was Panahi's *The White Balloon*. This is the story of a seven-year-old girl, Razieh, meandering around a few Tehran streets on her way to buy a goldfish for New Year, and losing her money. It displays all the characteristics we have come to expect – a play with real-time duration, natural locations, a repetitive, cyclical structure, and a child protagonist on a quest. Because of its popularity in the West, critics – inside and outside Iran – have taken issue with the film, alleging that it does not reflect Iranian political reality (claiming that it provides propaganda for western audiences instead). This often bitter debate has been replayed with almost every subsequent Iranian film (more recently, critics have been charging that the films are too negative.) In terms of our classification of the open image, *The White Balloon* suggests that even in a film that appears to be completely apolitical, there is in fact a political aspect, and this relates to the forms we have been discussing. At the end of the film Razieh and her older brother, Ali, recover their 500-toman banknote with help from an Afghan balloon seller. Razieh and Ali then, without thought, abandon their saviour, buy the goldfish and return home. The film ends with the clock ticking down to the New Year, an ominous offscreen explosion, and a freeze-frame: the Afghan refugee boy with his white balloon.

The Afghan boy is in every sense 'marginal' to the narrative – this is, of course, the point. He has barely figured in the film, neither has the white balloon. And, one might add, neither have the Iranian political situation nor the question of Afghan refugees in Iran. Yet *The White Balloon* is the title of the film and this is the final image – one that, by its very unexpectedness and the fact that it is a long-held freeze-frame, announces itself as the crucial image of the film, a static image we are given the necessary time to 'read'. Identification with (the now unsympathetic) Razieh's quest is called into question; the implication is that the Afghan refugee will not be going home to celebrate the New Year – he has no home. But the image is too ambiguous, too 'strong', to be reduced to one level of interpretation. The freeze-frame of the Afghan boy and his white balloon feeds back into and modifies the whole preceding 'charming' narrative, the entire chain of images. The best open images 'open up' the films in which they appear (turn the films into crystal images) and open films 'out' to the world, rendering the absent political reality present.

We would not argue that ambiguity or indeterminacy are inherently radical – indeterminacy can itself be politically determined in opposing ways – but we would argue that Iranian filmmakers have utilized the open image to circumvent a particularly strict form of censorship and to point to the plurality of truth and experience in a political context where a repressive notion of one truth is imposed by the state. The dogmatic constructions of reality associated with the Iranian state have, of course, their equivalents elsewhere. The appeal of New Iranian Cinema in the West may have less to do with 'sympathy' for an exoticized 'other' under conditions of repression than with self-recognition. The open images of Iranian film remind us of the loss of such images in most contemporary cinema, the loss of cinema's particular space for creative interpretation and critical reflection.

Notes

1 General Department of Cinematographic Research and Relations, *Post-Revolution Iranian Cinema* (Tehran: Ministry of Ershad-e Eslami, 1982), p. 8.

2 See Mir-Ahmad-e Mir-Ehsan, 'Dark light', in Rose Issa and Sheila Whitaker (eds), *Life and Art: the New Iranian Cinema* (London: British Film Institute, 1999), p. 113.

3 Sam Rohdie makes a similar point when, tracing connections between Rossellini and 'post'-neorealism, he argues that the 'reality' Italian Neorealism reflects is the 'reality' of film language; its experimentation with language implies concerns beyond the merely

representational. Sam Rohdie, *The Passion of Pier Paolo Pasolini* (London: British Film Institute, 1995), pp. 15–16.

4 Pier Paolo Pasolini, 'The cinema of poetry', in Bill Nichols (ed.), *Movies and Methods*, vol. I (Berkeley, CA: University of California Press, 1976), p. 544.

5 Ibid., pp. 552–3.

6 Gilles Deleuze, *Cinema 1: The Movement Image*, trans. Hugh Tomlinson and Barbara Habberjam (London: Athlone Press, 1992), p. 74.

7 Paul Schrader, *Transcendental Style in Film: Ozu, Bresson, Dreyer* (New York: Da Capo, 1972), pp. 39, 42, 49.

8 Jean Mitry, *Semiotics and the Analysis of Film*, trans. Christopher King (London: Athlone Press, 2000), p. 31.

9 Henri Bergson, *Matter and Memory*, trans. N.M. Paul and W.S. Palmer (New York: Zone Books, 1991); William James, *Principles of Psychology*, Volume I (London: Macmillan, 1890).

10 Schrader, *Transcendental Cinema*, p. 160.

11 Ibid., p. 161.

12 Deleuze, *Cinema 1*, p. 70.

13 Gilles Deleuze, *Cinema 2: The Time-Image*, trans. Hugh Tomlinson and Robert Galeta (London: Athlone Press, 1994), p. 18.

14 Ibid., p. 19.

15 Controversy over the politics of internationally successful Iranian films reflects ideological tensions amongst intellectuals in Iran and in Iranian exile circles. For criticism of Kiarostami and the 'festival film' see, for example, Azadeh Farahmand, 'Perspectives on recent (international acclaim for) Iranian cinema', in Richard Tapper (ed.), *The New Iranian Cinema: Politics, Representation and Identity* (London: I.B. Tauris, 2002), pp. 86–108. This debate has also had some impact amongst non-Iranian critics. The often unenthusiastic reviews of Iranian films in *Sight and Sound* during the 1990s tended to characterize the films as sentimental and apolitical. See, for example, Simon Louvish's review of *The White Balloon, Sight and Sound*, vol. 6, no. 1 (1996), p. 57 and subsequent responses in the letters pages: vol. 6, no. 3 (1996), p. 64; vol. 6, no. 4 (1996), p. 64.

16 Deleuze, *Cinema 2*, p. 5.

17 Ibid., p. 4.

18 Ibid., p. 48.

19 Ibid., p. 54.

20 Ibid., pp. 54–5.

21 Ibid., p. 6.

22 Ibid., p. 129.

23 Deleuze, *Cinema 1*, p. 212.

24 Deleuze, *Cinema 2*, p. 3.

25 There are, of course, many reasons for the predominance of child protagonists in Iranian film: censorship codes relating to the depiction of women, as has been extensively discussed elsewhere; the long-standing role of the Centre for the Intellectual Development of Children and Young Adults (associated most notably with Kiarostami); the important crosscurrents between Iranian and Indian film – the impact of Neorealism in Iran undoubtedly bears the influence of Satyajit Ray (especially *The Apu Trilogy* [1955–9]).

26 Deleuze, *Cinema 2*, p. 248.

27 Ibid., p. 69.

28 Ibid., p. 71.

29 Ibid., p. 69.

30 Ibid., p. 77.

31 Samira Makhmalbaf, interview with Jahanbakhsh Nouraei, *Iran International*, vol. 8, no. 1 (2000), p. 17.

32 For the neorealist exposition, see Giuseppe De Santis, 'Towards an Italian landscape', in David Overby (ed.), *Springtime in Italy: A Reader on Neorealism* (London: Tantivy Press, 1978), p. 126.

33 Abbas Kiarostami, interview with Robert Richter, *Kinder und Jugendkorrespondenz*, no. 42 (1990), p. 24.

34 David Bordwell sees Kiarostami as ironizing his own practice of using static images in the film-within-the-film of *Through the Olive Trees*, 'gently mocking this minimalism' with shots that activate 'angular depth and offscreen space' and 'throw into relief the static, planimetric images in the film that the characters are shooting'. David Bordwell, *On the History of Film Style* (Cambridge, MA: Harvard University Press, 1997), pp. 262–3.

35 Kiarostami, interview with Nassia Hamid, *Sight and Sound*, vol. 7, no. 2 (February 1997), p. 23.

36 Kiarostami, talking after the screening, National Film Theatre, London, 21 June 1999.

37 Pasolini, 'The cinema of poetry', pp. 551–3.

38 Deleuze, *Cinema 2*, p. 93.

39 The religious underpinning of these images referred to earlier does not, in our view, compromise their dissident potential. This religious underpinning is not synonymous with state religion or any other hegemonic versions of reality.

11 Signs of angst and hope: history and melodrama in Chinese fifth-generation cinema

Ning Ma

Although different methodologies have been used in the study of film genre as a sociocultural process of meaning production conditioned by economic imperatives, artistic conventions, institutional regulation and audience participation, they all turn on a complex configuration of the relationship between the discursive nature of meaning production, its underlying power structure and the formation of subjectivity. They also attempt to relate the formal exposition of the identity of historically specific genres to various forms of identity politics in terms of the binary logic of self/other, conscious/unconscious, masculine/feminine and individual/state. In this respect, the critical studies of Chinese film genres by Chris Berry, Nick Browne and E. Ann Kaplan are exemplary.[1] And yet, with the accelerating pace of globalization in recent years, genre production is increasingly influenced by the paradigms of the postmodern and the postcolonial that challenge any essentialist definition of genre based on binary logic. With the emergence of the 'post' paradigm come new questions: how should we analyze the form and meaning of genre films whose claim to authentic representation rests less on a manifestation of the national psyche or the collective unconscious than on what Fredric Jameson calls the 'logic of impersonal transnational capital'?[2] What role can locally produced genre films play in the global cultural economy characterized by what Arjun Appadurai calls 'disjunctures and flows'?[3] And what kind of subjectivity, if any, do genre films, which often assume a simulated, hybrid and fractal form, construct for a global audience?

The process of globalization has affected Chinese film production in recent years. While most Chinese filmmakers have used generic formulas first tried in Hong Kong or Hollywood to win the support of the domestic audience, the key figures of fifth-generation cinema, with the backing of transnational capital and the patronage of international art cinema, have tried to revamp the established genres in Chinese cinema, such as melodrama and historical film, for global consumption. Their films not only won critical acclaim but also generated a lot of debate on the form and meaning of these films and the role they have played in global cultural politics.

While some China-based nativist critics have criticized and denounced these films as a new type of orientalist discourse that legitimates western hegemony over a demonized China, many cosmopolitan critics, most notably Sheldon Lu, have celebrated them as a new, transnational, Third World cinema noted for its oppo sitional politics.[4] And yet, despite this critical difference, all of these scholars agree that post-1989 fifth-generation cinema has turned the specificity of Chinese culture and history into a highly marketable generic product for global consumption. As such, an adequate analysis of this cinema has to take into consideration the specific generic conventions deployed in individual films, the intertextual relations they embody, the complex power relations that structure their production, and the subject-identity they help to construct in the process of reception.

In this essay I shall address the issues raised above by conducting a genealogical analysis of post-1989 fifth-generation cinema as an exemplary instance of the problematics of transnational genre production. I will first examine the local and global conditions underlying this genre production and the discontinuity and difference it embodies in relation to the dominant Chinese melodramatic discourse. I shall argue that a Foucauldian analysis of post-1989 fifth-generation films as a culturally specific discursive field of power relations can enable us to see them as a new form of 'crosscultural melodrama' noted for its articulation of democratic politics in symbolic response to various totalizing discourses and processes shaping the postmodern world we live in. I shall then illustrate the key features of this new crosscultural melodrama with reference to the concepts of 'effective history' and 'intersubjective history' found in continental European thinking. In the process, I shall also argue that fifth-generation filmmakers' reinvention of melodramatic aesthetics in their transnational film production can also be seen as an attempt to reconstruct a historically specific subject-identity which will have an important role to play in the global cultural politics of the twenty-first century.

Fifth-generation cinema first presented itself as a rejection and critique of the established genres in classical Chinese cinema and its underlying melodramatic aesthetics. The rediscovery of the aesthetic and critical value of melodrama, as in Zhang Yimou's *Judou* (1990) and Chen Kaige's *Farewell My Concubine* (1993), occurred in the post-1989 era when the conflict between sociopolitical forces unleashed during the initial stage of reform had already come to a head and the subsequent actions taken by the state against the student movement for democracy had brought with them profound political and ethical consequences.

Because of rigid ideological control and censorship, film production critical of the state became almost impossible in the post-1989 era. However, thanks to the new policy of developing a western-style market economy, which allowed local talents to be employed by transnational capital, commercially oriented genre production financed by transnational capital based in Hong Kong and Taiwan for the international art cinema market offered itself as an option. Of all genres, melodrama was favoured by fifth-generation filmmakers, partly because of its ability to link the personal with the political in gripping stories of crime and passion in which the desire for poetic and social justice is irrepressible; and partly because of the progres-sive role the genre played in Chinese cultural politics. Thus the fifth generation's belated interest in melodrama can be seen as a highly contingent historical event premissed on the Chinese government's brutal suppression of the 1989 democratic revolution and its subsequent embrace of transnational capital.

The process of globalization pioneered by transnational capital had not only brought changes in the institutional and economic aspects of Chinese genre production, but also enabled filmmakers to introduce new melodramatic conven-tions and modes of audience participation in their filmmaking. As such, a close examination of the discontinuity and difference of fifth-generation genre production from the melodramatic aesthetics of both western and Chinese cinema is necessary. Melodrama as an aesthetic mode or cinematic genre has been theorized by scholars such as Peter Brooks, Thomas Elsaesser, Geoffrey Nowell-Smith and others as a highly theatrical bourgeois art form in which issues of justice and ethics are often raised in a domesticated narrative space within which unfolds an Oedipal scenario centred on issues of individual desire and identity in relation to patriarchal law.[5] With the increasing pace of globalization, issues concerning the crosscultural nature of melodrama as a modern aesthetic mode and its influence on non-western cinemas and the woman's film have also been put on the critical agenda.[6]

Classical Chinese cinema, as I have argued elsewhere, embodies a melodramatic imagination which is culturally and historically specific, in that it is closely linked to the moral economy of Confucian ethics and constitutes a symbolic response to the sociopolitical effects of the transplantation to China of various forms of western modernity, from capitalism to Marxism.[7] Born around the 1911 republican revo-lution under the influence of western melodrama, Chinese melodramatic discourse is highly hybridized, exhibiting different forms in different periods, ranging from the family ethics films of the 1920s and the leftist films of the 1930s to Xie Jin's melodrama of the Mao and post-Mao periods. Features such as cultural specificity, historicity and hybridity that characterize Chinese melodrama as a crosscultural form also problematize the dominant psychoanalytic conception of melodrama in the West and any attempt to use binary logic to characterize melodrama as belonging to a particular class, gender or culture.

The dominant position Xie Jin's melodrama occupies in mainstream Chinese cinema has to do with a skilful use of western melodramatic conventions within a culturally specific narrative paradigm in which the articulation of individual desire and subject-identity is conditioned by the deployment of a set of symbolic divisions valorized by the traditional Chinese patriarchal order.[8] The popularity of this melodrama, despite glaring evidence of its incoherence and contradictions, is due to an ingenious use of moral expressivity which not only constitutes a discursive field wherein the established power relations can be reversed, but also helps to construct a group-oriented subject-identity in line with the traditional Chinese symbolic order in response to rapid sociopolitical changes brought about by reform and an open-door policy.

Focusing on the sociohistorical inscription found in Xie Jin's melodrama, Browne has characterized it as a form of political melodrama that differs from western melodrama in terms of its ethical–political conception of the individual and her relationship to the state as a matter of justice in both private and public spaces.[9] In Xie Jin's melodrama, the issue of justice is not posed in terms of individual freedom and rights, but as a set of conventions, social relations, and transactions within the group. Furthermore, premissed on a definition of the self in relation to the social as a fully public matter, this political melodrama embodies a mode of historical experience which, Browne argues:

> inscribes 'subjectivity' in a position between the expectation of an ethical system (Confucianism) and the demands of a political system (socialism), a condition that typifies the Chinese dilemma of modernization. The form's principal significance lies in the affective dimension of the self's relation to the social order, catalyzing two affective regimes that are acted out in the narrative as intensified performances of betrayal, disappointment, or defeat.[10]

Xie Jin's political melodrama, and the popularity it enjoyed among the local audience, can be seen as a powerful sign of the aspirations and frustrations of the people caught in the process of reform and modernization.

Transnationally financed post-1989 fifth-generation melodrama forms a complex intertextual relationship with this dominant melodramatic discourse. As the work of Jenny Lau, W.A. Callahan, Shuqin Cui, and E. Ann Kaplan demonstrates, post-1989 fifth-generation films are noted for their foregrounding of culturally specific notions of gender and gendered perspectives, melodramatic treatment of Oedipal desire and conflict, dazzling display of Chinese sexuality and ethnicity, allegorical readings of Chinese culture and history, and symbolic responses to traumas of various kinds – ranging from the cultural revolution of 1966 to the democratic revolution of 1989.[11] Furthermore, as instances of the transnational production of ethnicity catering to the needs and desires of the international art cinema audience, this form of melodrama could be read, as Rey Chow argues, from a postcolonial perspective as the sign of 'a cross-cultural commodity fetishism' and 'exhibitionism' that projects a subalternized and exoticized China under 'the gaze of orientalist surveillance'.[12] However, a close analysis of the specific generic conventions deployed in these films, and of the ways in which they facilitate audience participation in meaning production, shows them to constitute a new form of crosscultural melodrama noteworthy, in sharp contrast to Xie Jin's melodrama, for its articulation of democratic politics.

A major difference between this new crosscultural melodrama and that of Xie Jin is its dramatization of the disastrous consequences of the assertion of individual freedom and rights through the deployment of an orientalized Oedipal story and its exploration of patriarchal law as that of 'big brother' in modern China. Zhang Yimou's *Judou* (1990), for instance, tells a story about a fatherless son, Yang Tianqing, who not only sires a son through an illicit love affair with his uncle's wife Judou (Gong Li) but also takes over his uncle's booming business, with dire consequences. The film highlights the identity problem Yang Tianqing's nuclear family faces due to the imposition of 'big brother' law by the village elders. The form and function of this new law is explored in *Raise the Red Lantern* (1992) in terms of a feminine version of the Oedipal story: a fatherless girl named Songlian is forced to marry Master Chen as his fourth concubine and aspires to the position of matriarch, with disastrous results. Focusing on female rivalry set inside a walled-in family compound with watch towers and a death chamber, the film reveals in vivid detail how female desire and sexuality are controlled by visual surveillance, hierarchical ordering and violent repression. Touches of realism and contemporaneity are added in *The Story of Qiu Ju* (1993), which is about a peasant woman's courageous attempt to sue the village chief, Wang, for causing injury to her husband's reproductive organs in a row. The dramatization of the destructive effects of the patriarchal suppression of individual rights centres on Qiu Ju's pregnant body.

The orientalized Oedipal story in Chen Kaige's films is concerned with the formation of aberrant personalities due to an excessive use of symbolic and physical violence sanctioned by the Chinese patriarchal order. A melodrama about the lives of two Peking opera actors, *Farewell My Concubine* (1993) focuses on the role played by institutionalized violence in turning Chinese males into feminized subjects. The law of the father as that of big brother reveals itself most effectively in the ways in which symbolic and physical violence are executed. A melodramatic story about family succession set during the Republican revolution, *Temptress Moon* (1996) not only examines the sociohistorical factors contributing to the problem of the feminization of Chinese males, but also traces the spectacular rise of patriarchal law as that of big brother in modern China. Opium smoking has not only weakened the male members of a big feudal family in China, but has also claimed both the male and the female heirs as its latest victims, so that a feminized brother chosen by the family elders becomes the new patriarch. *The Emperor and the Assassin* (1999) offers a scathing critique of the Chinese patriarchal order by retelling a historical narrative about the first emperor of China and the sociopolitical system he established more than two thousand years ago. It is an epic-length historical film in which narrative focus is placed on the contradictory relationship between the first emperor and his mother and her illicit lovers on the one hand and, on the other, his special relationship with Zhao Nu, a friend since childhood whom he treats as a sister. The film reveals that it is through the brutal killings of his mother's illicit lovers, including his own father who serves under him as prime minister, and of all those who know about his illegitimate birth, that his ambitious plan to unify China and to place it under totalitarian rule is achieved.

Discontinuity and difference can also be found in the ways in which history figures in these post-1989 films. In Xie Jin's melodrama, history functions largely as an objective and inexorable process embodying a progressive moral framework which not only helps the viewer to make sense of the melodramatic conflicts depicted but is also instrumental in bringing the narrative to closure. In post-1989 fifth-generation films, history most often manifests itself in terms of the consequences and effects of the patriarchal suppression of individual assertion, dramatized in a narrative full of sudden reversals and ironic twists. There is also an attempt to reintroduce the ancient yin–yang view of history as an eternal flux, or the Nietzschean notion of the eternal return, to problematize the conventional progressive view of history.

Such a treatment of history is similar to Michel Foucault's notion of effective history in his genealogical analysis of how power works in the production of historical knowledge.[13] According to Foucault, effective history differs from traditional history in that it rejects notions of continuity, objectivity, totality and closure. History becomes 'effective' to the degree that 'it introduces discontinuity into our very being – as it divides our emotions, dramatizes our instincts, multiplies our body and sets it against itself'.[14] Effective history seeks to 'uproot its traditional foundations' by showing that 'the forces operating in history are not controlled by destiny or regulative mechanisms but respond to haphazard conflicts'.[15] In effective history, the world we know cannot be subjected to a simple configuration where events can be reduced to their essential traits and final meanings. Furthermore, effective history can invert the relationship traditional history establishes between proximity and distance and between abstract concepts and concrete historical existence. It does not aspire to be a handmaiden to philosophy by using such terms as 'the noblest periods, the highest forms, the most abstract ideas, the purest individualities', but seeks to become 'a curative science' by focusing on what is nearest and dearest, the human body as it is moulded by a great many distinct regimes, broken down by the rhythms of work, rest and holidays, poisoned by food or values; and by constructing resistance.[16]

Another important feature of effective history, according to Foucault, is its affirmation of knowledge as perspective. Historians usually hide or erase the elements in their historical writing which reveal their grounding in a particular time and place, their preferences in a controversy. Effective history is explicit in its perspective. It is not given to a discreet effacement before the objects and events it observes. It is highly selfconscious about historical writing as a perspectival use of documents for political purposes. It does not seek to establish laws but tries to highlight the power relations at work in the production of historical knowledge. As Foucault puts it, in effective history, 'knowledge is not made for understanding; it is made for cutting'.[17]

The key features of effective history can also be seen as the hallmarks of post-1989 fifth-generation melodrama. For instance, by elevating the notion of history as a vicious cycle or a wanton process to that of a formal organizing principle, the filmmakers in their representation of Chinese culture and history seek to foreground the theme of discontinuity through the use of melodramatic conventions of narrative reversals and twists. Subjectivity is achieved in these films through the deployment of an orientalized Oedipal story dramatizing the destructive effects of the patriarchal suppression of individual desire and subjectivity. The critique of totality finds its strongest expression in a symbolic use of the mise-en-scene elements to reveal a prison-like social environment within which individual characters live. The rejection of closure is clearly seen in the refusal to reward the good and punish the evil at the end of the narrative.

Post-1989 melodrama also aspires to be a curative science by focusing on the human body as it is split by unconscious desire, torn between family demands and social obligation, and moulded by different regimes. Concerned with the ways in which various totalizing discourses endorsed by the Chinese state affect the lives of ordinary people, the fifth-generation melodrama not only seeks to represent the human body as the inscribed surface of sociohistorical processes and the bearer of an impersonal and brutal force of social totality, but also resorts to the use of performative rhetoric of the body to highlight the destructive effects of the imposition of patriarchal law as that of big brother, upon which the new state is founded.

What is crucial to *Judou*, for instance, is the performative rhetoric articulated by Gong Li within the walled-in family compound with its dyeing pools, machines, stairways and cloths of white, red and blue. Abused by her husband and under the voyeuristic gaze of Yang Tianqing, Judou decides to let the latter see her bruised body as she bathes, and subsequently lures him into a productive love affair. Such is Gong Li's performance in lovemaking within the dyeing factory that it not only functions to confer legality and vitality on their love affair by integrating it into the reproductive cycle of the family business, but also adds new meanings to her body: it can be interpreted as a symbolic rendering of the workings of the libidinal economy of the female psyche on one level, and an objective reminder of the emergence of a booming private sector within a nominal socialist state in contemporary China on another. Thus it is no surprise to find that the destructive effects of the imposition on the characters of patriarchal law as that of big brother are first registered by her body. Fear of public opinion and sanction drives a pregnant Judou to use drugs to abort the second baby, only to have her reproductive organs damaged and her family business destroyed.

Such an effective use of the human body can also be found in other fifth-generation films. In *Raise the Red Lantern*, the performative rhetoric of the body is articulated in conjunction with mise-en-scene elements to dramatize the destructive effects of patriarchal ordering of female desire and subjectivity in terms of what the female characters and their servants do to their own and their rivals' bodies, The competition between the concubines to increase their attractiveness through makeup, hairstyle and dress, to achieve sexual arousal through body inspection and massage, and to increase their chances of becoming pregnant, eventually causes the death of two women and physical and psychological damage to the others.

Fifth-generation filmmakers also tend to adopt a highly perspectival and self-conscious mode of narration, foregrounding subjective reinterpretations of Chinese culture, history and identity as well as the consequences of character actions dictated by both external and internal forces. As effective history, these films are also about effects in search of causes, consequences in search of solutions. As symbolic responses to the tragic events in Beijing in 1989, the causes sought by the filmmakers are shown to be both internal and external, social and psychological, inferrable and yet indeterminate. In their films, those who have caused suffering to the characters turn out to be their own relatives or close friends. In *Farewell My Concubine*, for instance, the characters responsible for the symbolic castration and rape are Cheng Dieyi's mother and his closest friend in the Peking Opera Troupe. In *To Live*, the person who has caused the death of Fugui's only son turns out to be his former assistant in the shadow play troupe, now a Communist official returning home to work for the local community.

Such a perspectival approach to melodramatic narrative as effective history becomes more meaningful if we take into consideration Foucault's interpretation of events in effective history. According to Foucault, an event

> is not a decision, a treaty, a reign, or a battle, but the reversal of a relationship of forces, the usurpation of power, the appropriation of a vocabulary turned against those who had once used it, a feeble domination that poisons itself as it grows lax, the entry of a masked 'other'.

In effective history, the world as 'a profusion of entangled events' is ruled by 'the iron hand of necessity shaking the dice-box of chance'; and 'chance is not simply the drawing of lots, but raising the stakes in every attempt to master chance through the will to power'.[18] Thus it is necessary for us to examine how events are ordered and put into perspective in the process of narration. *To Live* opens in a gambling house where Fugui, the prodigal son of a rich family, is busy shaking the dice-box and raising the stakes in a deadly gamble with Long'er – without knowing that the game is rigged. Losing both his father and his family estate, Fugui gives up gambling to become a shadow play artist. As an epic-length melodrama in which the ups and downs of his life as an artist are closely related to drastic changes in power relations between hostile political forces, the use of performative rhetoric, in conjunction with a highly perspectival and self-reflexive mode of narration in the film, functions to dramatize the point that, although Fugui and the ordinary folks he entertains are given a new lease of life with each regime, they remain very much like the puppets in the shadow play theatre, whose actions are dictated by the will of the state.

In *Farewell My Concubine*, the eventful life of the two actors is re-enacted retrospectively in a dress rehearsal of the title play in an empty sports stadium, right after the end of the cultural revolution when the two actors have just been rehabilitated.

This re-enactment is clearly discernible as a sadomasochistic narrative of suffering and loss structured in terms of a shifting relationship between subject and object, masculine and feminine, active and passive, constructed along an axis of seeing and being seen that gives full play to the voyeuristic and exhibitionist tendencies inherent in film viewing theorized by Geoffrey Nowell-Smith.[19] This not only adds an extra dimension of psychic fantasy to the cinematic narration, it is also indicative of the kind of audience targeted by the film as a transnational commercial production. This sadomasochistic representation is also somewhat self-reflexive. The re-enactment of the actors' life story is watched by a gatekeeper, who constitutes the only member of the audience in the sports stadium. The presence of this lone figure, who professes to be a fan, not only foreshadows the theme of double confinement and imprisonment that recurs in the film, but is also a highly symbolic figuration of the 'will to power' that can manifest itself in different ways in world politics. Thus the search for causation in these films is also a search for new ways to understand and represent the workings of the Chinese patriarchal order as a specific configuration of the will to power in world history.

Discontinuity and difference can also be detected in the ways in which moral expressivity, formal excess and emotional appeal function in fifth-generation melodrama in relation to dominant Chinese melodramatic discourse. Xie Jin's melodrama, for instance, is noted for its excessive play with Confucian ethical codes and Communist political codes for moral clarification and expressivity. The function of the performative rhetoric is to articulate virtuous suffering, which arouses audience sympathy and contributes to the final vindication of the victim when a new regime comes to power. By contrast, moral expressivity in fifth-generation melodrama is typically articulated in terms of a critical exploration of the ways in which traditional ideologies shape the lives of the characters and contribute to their own suffering. Performative rhetoric is often used to dramatize the difficulty of the body split by unconscious desire, moulded by different regimes and manipulated by different totalizing discourses to make categorical moral and political statements. The emphasis on the difficulty of using a socioculturally constructed body to articulate clearcut moral meanings contributes greatly to an overwhelming sense of angst pervading post-1989 fifth-generation melodramas.

It remains to be asked how these films articulate moral meanings in an excessive way and where we can locate the Manichean conflict and the process of victimization and vindication that melodrama as a genre embodies, so that a sense of hope can be rekindled. In attempting to answer this, we can see more clearly how the filmmakers have tried to reinvent melodramatic aesthetics by introducing into their films a new mode of moral expressivity founded not so much on a psychoanalytically-based language of the body as on a language of the spirit.

The concept of the spirit or *Geist* developed in continental European think-ing about the morally oriented social and human sciences lays emphasis on the constitutive role played by ideas, mental processes, language and cultural formations as historically formed intersubjective structures in producing knowledge, culture and identity. While Foucault, following Nietzsche, uses a genealogical approach to human history as effective history in order to explore the complex relationship between knowledge and power in discursive practices, Hans-Georg Gadamer uses concepts such as effective history and the fusion of historical horizons in his hermeneutic approach to artistic production; and thus the *Geist* as intersubjectivity becomes the means by which the truth claims of an artistic discourse can be analyzed in the process of reception.[20] A more radical approach is adopted by Jürgen Habermas in his attempt to relocate the *Geist* as intersubjectivity in historically formed democratic institutions such as the public spheres that favour the use of communicative rationality rather than instrumental rationality as the means for constructing commonly accepted notions of truth, justice and ethics.[21]

The concept of the spirit as a historically formed intersubjective structure or intersubjective history informed by the writings of Gadamer and Habermas can help us understand better the process of moral clarification in fifth-generation melodrama as effective history, and the contribution this melodrama can make to democratic politics in China. This is because the combination of melodramatic and historical narrative discourses in post-1989 fifth-generation film production also creates various kinds of intersubjective spaces in which moral expressivity is achieved through a clash of different perspectives. In *Farewell My Concubine*, for instance, a culturally specific melodramatic discourse unfolds in terms of an ingenious play with traditional Chinese ethical terms such as right as *dui* (meaning a correct pairing or coupling in Chinese) and wrong as *budui* (an incorrect pairing or coupling) with regard to individual identity in gender, class and ethnic terms in various sociocultural contexts. These range from confusion over the difference between the gender of the actor and the gender of the role played, to the triangular problem between coupling onstage and coupling offstage involving the Manchu rulers, Japanese invaders, the nationalists and the Communists in modern Chinese history. And it is through a fusion of these different historical contexts or horizons that new interpretations of traditional notions of right as *dui* and wrong as *budui*, with regard to the life stories of the characters, can be constructed in the process of reception.

For instance, the attempt to resort to singular masculine power to shape history, which is foregrounded in the historical play about Bawang in the film, is counter-pointed by the tragedy of submissive femininity that infects all the characters in the Peking Opera Troupe. Whereas the historical play highlights the status of Bawang as a classical example of the will to power, the flashback story about the lives of the actors impersonating Bawang and his concubine delineates the two as victims of male aggression. While the disciplinary training the two actors have received before they reach stardom is shown to be administered for their own good, it is also responsible for their mental state and their suffering during the cultural revolution. Since the life stories of two actors are re-enacted retrospectively in a dress rehearsal, it becomes a contemporary version of the classical play about the assertion of masculine will to power. The question repeatedly raised in the narrative as to who is the real Bawang and who is his real concubine in different historical contexts also becomes an open one, inviting different answers from viewers in the process of reception.

The same can also be said about Zhang Yimou's *To Live*. An example of the intersection of the historical and the melodramatic discourses functioning as an intersubjective space in which moral meanings can be articulated in an excessive way occurs in the childbirth scene, when Fengxia's worker-turned-Red Guard husband stages an attack on Doctor Wang in the hospital corridor in order to get him to help with their emergency. It is ironic that days of starvation followed by a bout of overeating cause Wang's body to suffer digestive problems at the precise moment that Fengxia, who is under the care of ignorant Red Guard medical students, experiences a postnatal haemorrhage. Different perspectives are introduced in relation to Fengxia's bleeding body through the use of mise-en-scene elements. Previously married to a member of the Red Guard under the benign gaze of a portrait of Mao in Red Guard uniform, she now lies dying in a pool of blood, at the hands of Red Guards pretending to be doctors, another portrait of Mao over her hospital bed, while the real doctor is suffering from the attentions of her Red Guard husband in the corridor outside the ward. It is through an ingenious play with the concept of wrong as *budui* in Chinese in relation to different historical perspectives that moral expressivity is achieved.

The intersubjective spaces created in these films for moral clarification also constitute the very site where a subject-identity based on new ethical and political norms can be formed. This is because the combination of historical and melodramatic discourses not only generates different perspectives on modern Chinese culture and politics, it also creates a mirroring structure in the narrative that can send the spectator on a journey of self-discovery and self-knowledge. Placed at the centre of the intersubjective spaces is the cinematic representation of the suffering body with which audience identification is made either possible or impossible. The force of such a cinematic representation can be most strongly felt in various screen roles of Gong Li: as Judou, whose bruised body arouses feelings of sympathy among the audience; as Songlian, through whose eyes in *Raise the Red Lantern* the audience discovers the murders committed in the name of law and order; as a justice-seeking pregnant woman in *The Story of Qiu Jiu*, dressed in a man's suit and accompanied by her sister in the tricolour of blue, white and red; as the pregnant Juxian in *Farewell My Concubine*, who risks her life to protect her husband and suffers a miscarriage; as Zhao Nu, who has her face scarred for the cause of unification and eventually turns against the tyranny established by the First Emperor in China.

The mirroring structure deployed in these representations of the body introduces a highly selfconscious mode of viewing. Such a cinematic practice has its precedents in 1930s melodramatic films such as *Street Angel* (Yuan Muzhi, 1937) and *Crossroads* (Shen Xileng, 1937) made by leftwing filmmakers under the influence of Lu Xun, who first advocated the use of literature as a curative science by creating fictional characters to remind Chinese readers how ignorant and backward they are in a rapidly changing modern world.[22] Retelling the story by Lu Xun about being a film spectator under colonial conditions as a way of showing how 'selfconsciousness' is produced in the postcolonial 'third world', Rey Chow argues that this self-consciousness is also a consciousness of one's identity in a world constructed by the modern technological medium of visuality and the 'menaces' it brings to people brought up in traditional, literary culture in terms of various kinds of violence, ranging from military conquest to the colonization of the mind.[23] As she elaborates:

> Lu Xun discovers what it means to 'be Chinese' in the modern world by watching film. Because it is grounded in an apprehension of the aggressiveness of the technological medium of visuality, self-consciousness henceforth could not be separated from a certain violence that splits the self, in the very moment it becomes 'conscious,' into seeing and the seen. 'Being Chinese' would hence-forth carry in it the imagistic memory – the memorable image – of this violence. National self-consciousness is thus not only a matter of watching 'China' being represented on screen; it is, more precisely, watching oneself – as a film, as a spectacle, as something always already watched.[24]

However, the selfconsciousness exhibited by fifth-generation films does not simply represent a new national consciousness but a space of intersubjectivity, where the boundaries of gender, class, ethnicity or nationality can be transcended and contributions to democratic politics made. *To Live*, for instance, is noted for its ironic juxtaposition of the victor's view inherent in a historical discourse that foregrounds significant public events in modern Chinese history with the loser's view, in a melodramatic treatment that highlights the destructive effects which the totalizing discursive practices endorsed by the state have on the characters. While the film dramatizes Fugui's sufferings in various political campaigns ordered by government officials, it advocates not revenge but forgiveness. Furthermore, the deployment of an epic story, marked by sudden reversals and ironic parallels, also helps both characters and viewers to experience the plight of an excluded or persecuted other and to achieve a better understanding of the other as another human being in need of human rights protection.

The discursive space, within which the drama about selfconsciousness, self-knowledge and self-identity is staged, is also the intersubjective space where moral expressivity is articulated through a combination of historical and melodramatic discourses. While historical narrative discourse in fifth-generation cinema may function as a kind of historical documentation, it is also highly subjective and melodramatic, in a manner similar to Walter Benjamin's notion of history as intersubjectivity, of which he writes:

> To articulate the past historically does not mean to recognize it 'the way it really was'. It means to seize hold of a memory as it flashes up at a moment of danger. . . . The danger affects both the content of the tradition and its receivers. The same threat hangs over both: that of becoming a tool of the ruling classes. In every era the attempt must be made anew to wrest tradition away from a conformism that is about to overpower it. The Messiah comes not only as the redeemer, he comes as the subduer of Antichrist. Only that historian will have the gift of fanning the spark of hope in the past who is firmly convinced that even the dead will not be safe from the enemy if he wins.[25]

In his hermeneutic readings of history, Benjamin not only emphasizes the inter-subjectivity of historical writing, but also highlights its nature as the embodiment of a morally oriented Manichean conflict of biblical proportions. For that matter, the subject of history for him is also a melodramatic subject. The same can also be said about post-1989 fifth-generation films. To illustrate this, I shall focus finally on the dangers and hopes alluded to in films such as *To Live* and *Farewell My Concubine*. The danger highlighted in *To Live* is that of totalitarianism in various forms. The film opens in a gambling house controlled by Long'er, the owner of the shadow play theatre. While Fugui believes he is still a respected master and can do whatever he wants, including leaving the gambling table and changing the contents of the shadow play, he has been set up by the real master, Long'er, to lose everything. This opening sets the tone for the rest of the film, which shows that the sufferings Fugui and his family have to endure are more or less related to a social environment totally controlled by outside political forces.

While an overwhelming sense of angst and fear pervades this film, it also shows signs of hope. For instance, earlier in the film, after Long'er takes over Fugui's house, he nevertheless helps the latter to earn a living by offering him his own puppet kit. Towards the end of the film, although the puppets have been burned, the chest which held them is now a home for a new brood of chicks to be raised by Fugui's grandson. The whole family visits the tombs of the dead, talking about past traumas and future plans. The film ends with a long-shot of the surviving family members gathering together for dinner. The Red Guard son-in-law moves from his position at the table, screen right, as he prepares dinner for his bedridden mother-in-law Jiazheng (Gong Li), screen left; while the credits printed in blue roll from screen left to screen right. As a signifier of family reunion, the shot refers the audience to similar shots of family reunion at the end of many other Chinese melodramatic films. The symbolic use of tricolour also evokes in audience memories the three basic principles of liberty, equality and fraternity that inspired the French revolution – during which melo-drama as an aesthetic mode was born.

The melodrama in *Farewell My Concubine* unfolds within closed compounds of various kinds, from the sports stadium watched over by a lone gatekeeper to the heavily guarded Peking Opera school. Unable to endure the inhuman disciplinary training at the school, Cheng Dieyi tries to run away, only to find that the outside world is nothing but a larger theatrical stage surrounded by powerful patrons who desire his castration. The pervading sense of angst and fear has much to do with this double confinement in which characters either live in submission and conformity or commit suicide in despair. It also points to totalitarianism in its various forms as the main danger. The memories that flash up at a moment of danger in the film occur towards the end, when Duan Xiaolou addresses Cheng Dieyi as Xiao Douzhi in order to evoke in Cheng Dieyi memories of the days when they were fellow students in the Peking Opera school. This address also refers to character actions depicted in earlier scenes, where certain universal principles are embodied: liberty symbolized by the kites outside the Peking Opera school gates when Shitou the gatekeeper allows Douzhi and his pal to run away; equality symbolized by the sharing of quilts in a scene when Shitou, unlike other students, refuses to discriminate against Douzhi just because he was born in a brothel; and fraternity symbolized by the various kinds of help they offer each other in adverse situations. This address offers a discursive marker of a new form of subjectivity or subject-identity formed historically in relation to European Enlightenment ideals and values.

That totalitarianism is the ultimate danger is clarified further in *The Emperor and the Assassin*, in which European Enlightenment ideals are notable for their total absence. The theme of individual identity formed in relation to instrumental vision as the vehicle for self-discovery and self-knowledge is figured in Zhao Nu, who has her face disfigured in a scheme to win the confidence of the prince of the Yan State in North China in order to achieve political unification. Witnessing scene after scene of killing and massacre, she realizes that political unification can never be achieved through totalitarian means. To avoid further bloodshed, she helps Jingke to assassinate the First Emperor and is ultimately forced into exile. Textualized in the filmic body, as well as in the bodies of the main characters, in terms of scars and wounds, angst and fear, this symbolic response to a rapidly changing world shaped by the will to power becomes the most noticeable feature of this epic film.

The significance of post-1989 fifth-generation cinema lies in its attempt to create a new kind of crosscultural melodrama noted for its articulation of democratic politics in symbolic response to various totalizing sociohistorical discursive practices shaping our postmodern world. The form and meaning of this crosscultural melodrama can be illustrated with reference to the orientalized Oedipal story, deployed in individual films, that functions to dramatize the effects and consequences of the imposition of patriarchal law as that of big brother in China. The form and meaning of this melodrama can also be analyzed with reference to the concept of effective history, which rejects continuity, objectivity, totality and closure and aspires to be a curative science of the human body. Central to fifth-generation melodrama as effective history is a highly melodramatic representation of the body as the inscribed surface of sociohistorical events and the bearer of an impersonal and brutal force of social totality. This enables the viewer to interpret the functioning of Chinese patriarchal order as a specific configuration of the will to power in world history.

Moral expressivity in this new crosscultural melodrama is founded not so much on a psychoanalytically based language of the body as on that of the spirit. Understood as an intersubjective discursive space, this language of the spirit provides filmmakers with a valuable discursive space in which issues concerning truth, justice and ethics – issues affecting characters as well as audience – can offer new perspectives on the process of reception. The cognitive value of this transnational generic production has little to do with its manifestation of national psyche or the logic of transnational capital, but much to do with its use of intersubjective spaces for the articulation of democratic politics. Fifth-generation melodrama as effective history also gives heightened expression to people's fears and hopes, by representing the Manichean conflict featured in its melodramatic narrative as a conflict between totalitarianism and democracy in a global context, in which European Enlightenment ideals function as a basis not only for social justice but also for the construction of new subject-identities. This melodramatic aesthetic reinvented by the fifth-generation filmmakers will have an important role to play in the global cultural politics of the twenty-first century.

Acknowledgements

This essay is a revised version of a paper presented at the conference Cinema and Senses, at the University of New South Wales, Australia, in November 1998. I would like to thank Peter McGregor, Michael Helfand, Lucy Fischer, Sheldon Lu and other readers of my manuscript.

1   Chris Berry, 'Neither one thing nor another', in Nick Browne, Paul Pickowicz, Esther Yau and Vivian Sobchack (eds), *New Chinese Cinemas: Forms, Identities, Politics* (New York: Cambridge University Press, 1994), pp. 88–113; Nick Browne, 'Society and subjectivity: on the political economy of Chinese melodrama', in ibid, pp. 40–56; E. Ann Kaplan, 'Melodrama/subjectivity/ideology: western melodrama theories and their relevance to recent Chinese cinema', in Wimal Dissanayake (ed.), *Melodrama and Asian Cinema* (New York: Cambridge University Press, 1993), pp. 9–28.
2   Fredric Jameson, *Postmodernism or, the Cultural Logic of Late Capitalism* (London: Verso, 1991).
3   Arjun Appadurai, 'Disjuncture and difference in the global cultural economy', *Public Culture*, vol. 2, no. 2 (1990), pp. 1–24.
4   For a summary of nativist criticism, see Ben Xu, '*Farewell My Concubine* and its nativist critics', *Quarterly Review of Film and Video*, vol. 16, no. 2 (1999), pp. 155–70; Sheldon

Lu, 'National cinema, cultural critique, transnational capital', in Sheldon Lu (ed.), *Transnational Chinese Cinema* (Honolulu: University of Hawaii Press, 1997).

5 Peter Brooks, *The Melodramatic Imagination* (New Haven, CT: Yale University Press, 1976); Thomas Elsaesser, 'Tales of sound and fury: observations on the family melodrama', *Monogram*, no. 4 (1972), pp. 2–15; Geoffrey Nowell-Smith, 'Minnelli and melodrama', *Screen*, vol. 18, no. 2, pp. 113–18.

6 Christine Gledhill, 'Introduction', in Gledhill (ed.), *Home Is Where the Heart Is: Studies in Melodrama and the Woman's Film* (London: British Film Institute, 1987), pp. 1–39.

7 Ning Ma, *Culture and Politics in Chinese Film Melodrama: Traditional Sacred, Moral Economy and the Xie Jin Mode* (Monash University: PhD dissertation, 1992).

8 Ning Ma, 'Spatiality and subjectivity in Xie Jin's melodrama of the new period', in Browne et al. (eds), *New Chinese Cinemas*, pp. 15–39.

9 Browne, 'Society and subjectivity'.

10 Ibid., pp. 46–7.

11 Jenny Kwok Wah Lau, '*Judou* – a hermeneutical reading of crosscultural cinema', *Film Quarterly*, vol. 45, no. 2 (1991), pp. 2–10; and '*Farewell My Concubine*: history, melodrama, and ideology in contemporary pan-Chinese cinema', *Film Quarterly*, vol. 49, no. 1 (1995) pp. 16–27; W.A. Callahan, 'Gender, ideology, nation: *Judou* in the cultural politics of China', *East–West Film Journal*, vol. 7, no. 1 (1993), pp. 52–80; Shuqin Cui, 'Gendered perspective: the construction and representation of subjectivity and sexuality in *Judou*', in Lu (ed.), *Transnational Chinese Cinema*, pp. 303–20; E. Ann Kaplan, 'Reading formations and Chen Kaige's *Farewell My Concubine*,' in ibid, pp. 265–75.

12 Rey Chow, *Primitive Passion* (New York: Columbia University Press, 1995), p. 170.

13 Michel Foucault, 'Nietzsche, genealogy, history', in Lawrence Cahoone (ed.), *From Modernism to Postmodernism* (Cambridge: Blackwell, 1996), pp. 360–78.

14 Ibid., p. 370.

15 Ibid., pp. 370–1.

16 Ibid., pp. 371–2.

17 Ibid., p. 370.

18 Ibid., pp. 370–1.

19 Geoffrey Nowell-Smith, 'A note on "history/discourse"', in John Caughie (ed.), *Theories of Authorship* (London: Routledge, 1981), pp. 232–41.

20 Hans-Georg Gadamer, *Truth and Method*, trans. G. Barden and J. Cumming (New York: Seabury Press, 1975).

21 Jürgen Habermas, *The Structural Transformations of the Public Sphere*, trans. T. Burger and F. Lawrence (Cambridge, MA: MIT Press, 1989).

22 See Ning Ma, 'The textual and critical difference of being radical: reconstructing Chinese leftist films of the 1930s', *Wide Angle*, vol. 11, no. 2 (1989), pp. 22–31.

23 Chow, *Primitive Passion*, p. 9.

24 Ibid.

25 Walter Benjamin, 'Theses on the philosophy of history', in Hannah Arendt (ed. and trans.), *Illuminations* (New York: Schocken, 1969), p. 255.

12 Affecting legacies: historical memory and contemporary structures of feeling in *Madagascar* and *Amores perros*

Laura Podalsky

In the midst of recent discussions of the death of utopias and the crisis of the Left in Latin America,[1] a number of films demonstrate a similar preoccupation with the legacies of radical political projects and revolutionary militancy. Some, including *Tango feroz* (Marcelo Piñeyro, Argentina/Spain, 1993), *Alma corsária* (Carlos Reichenbach, Brazil, 1993) and the widely distributed *Que É Isso, Companheiro?/Four Days in September* (Bruno Barreto, Brazil/USA, 1997), are set in the 1960s and 1970s and explore various types of resistance, from the rebellion of a rock musician against the strictures of bourgeois normality in Buenos Aires, to the militancy of several Brazilian youths who join the guerrilla group MR8 and kidnap the US ambassador. Others, such as Alejandro Agresti's *Buenos Aires vice versa* (Argentina/Netherlands, 1996) and Beto Brant's *Ação Entre Amigos/Friendly Fire* (Brazil, 1998), are set in the present day and deal with the legacies of that period of revolutionary fervour. Without ignoring the larger social, political and economic changes that ensued, many of these films pay particular attention to the effects that the period had on personal relationships; in other words, they tend to focus on the personal cost of revolutionary ideals. In so doing, such films might be seen as attempts to reinscribe revolutionary projects in light of the dominant neoliberal paradigm in contemporary Latin America. By underscoring the naivety of the Left's utopian projects to create a more just and equitable society, the brutality of leftwing guerrilla groups as well as the rightwing military, and the way in which individuals were lost, literally and metaphorically, in collective struggles, the films might be said to delegitimize calls for structural change, thus strengthening the neoliberal project even as they seemingly criticize the alienating aspects of market logic.

Yet, as I shall argue, the way in which these films evoke and deploy emotion suggest an alternative reading. This will be shown through the analysis of two films set in the 1990s that address the 1960s and 1970s as subtext: Fernando Pérez's medium-length feature *Madagascar* (Cuba, 1994) and Alejandro González Iñárritu's *Amores perros/Love's a Bitch* (Mexico, 2000). Perez's film chronicles the deteriorating relationship between Laura, a woman who came of age during the early years of the

Cuban Revolution, and her teenage daughter Laurita, who appears increasingly disengaged from her surroundings in 1990s Havana. As part of its interlocking narratives of life in contemporary Mexico City, the better-known *Amores perros* features a homeless man who is trying to reclaim the family that he lost due to his involvement in a guerrilla group in the 1970s. While *Madagascar*'s dreamy and hollowed-out mise-en-scene attests to feelings of *desarraigo* or uprootedness, *Amores perros*'s inventive cinematography conveys a dread of impending violence that permeates everyday life. As detailed later, the films' emotional engagement with both the revolutionary past and the neoliberal present has much less to do with what is shown onscreen than with how the spectator is situated and how the films resonate with dominant notions of the past, the present, and the relationship between the two (for example, discourses about rising levels of urban poverty and violence in 1990s Latin America and the legacy of state-sponsored terror). In sum, these films are carrying out emotional work as well as, or *as part of*, their political work; it is this interface between affect, politics and history that I shall explore.

In the process, I engage with the work of Thomas Elsaesser who, along with Marcia Landy, has begun to reexamine the relationship between affect, history and the cinematic form, and to problematize the dominant tendency to denounce the evocation of emotion in historical films as a trivialization of the past.[2] Elsaesser's lucid and complex essay, 'Subject positions, speaking positions: from *Holocaust, Our Hitler* and *Heimat* to *Shoah* and *Schindler's List*', is particularly relevant for the issues under discussion because he speaks of what has often been seen as the limit case of all social trauma (the Holocaust) and of the political and social efficacy of filmic and televisual texts that try to address that traumatic past. Elsaesser suggests that attempts to deal with Germany's Nazi past have not been entirely successful in dealing with the issues of complicity, responsibility and guilt; and asks, 'what kinds of affect might possibly "unlock" numbness, apathy, indifference, and reconcile memory and hope, commemoration and forgetting, [and] mediate between pity, sentiment, and shame'.[3] Challenging conventional critical paradigms that oppose emotion to cognition with reference to films, including Steven Spielberg's *Schindler's List* (1993) and Claude Lanzmann's *Shoah* (1985), he argues that the evocation of affect in film (and television) can have a mobilizing effect, and invokes the German term '*Betroffenheit* which roughly translates as "the affect of concern" but in its root-meaning includes "recognizing oneself to be emotionally called upon to respond, act, react"'. Elsaesser goes on to explain that the term 'covers empathy and identification, but in an active, radical sense of being "stung into action"'.[4]

Clearly not all films evoke this 'affect of concern' or 'touch a point where the self itself knows and can experience otherness'; and Elsaesser suggests that the ability to do so depends upon 'the ambiguous or extreme subject positions [films] are able to sustain'.[5] He is speaking not only of what is presented onscreen, but also of the relationship established between the film and the spectator. He praises Marcel Ophuls's *Hotel Terminus* (1988) and Lanzmann's *Shoah* for 'fill[ing] the mind's eye and ear with voices and presences: they will forever speak of a history for which there is neither redemption or exorcism'.[6] At the same time, he argues that even as their multifaceted testimonials 'suspend preconceived narrative and explanations' and underscore the incommensurability of having any (number of) representative(s) stand in for those who were killed (that is to say, the inadequacy of any representation to account for what happened), neither of the two films 'threaten[s] the coherence of the viewer's identity'.[7] In this sense, they fail to revitalize the spectator's understanding of his/her engagement with the past, with the present as historical moment, or with the social body. Elsaesser contrasts the two documentaries with Joseph Losey's *M. Klein* (1976), a much more mainstream film about the Holocaust, 'carried along by the processes of fictional identification' between spectators and the central character that employs those very processes to force the spectator to acknowledge his/her own 'impotence [as well as] collusion and complicity' in historical processes like the one portrayed – in other words, to destablilize the spectator's subject position.[8] For Elsaesser, such mainstream fiction films have a particular advantage in potentially reshaping the spectator's cognitive understanding of history and historical processes and of his/her own role in those processes.

Although Elsaesser's attempt to complicate the dominant understanding of the role of affect in film responds to US and European critical traditions, his arguments have a special pertinence for recent Latin American cultural productions. Coming of age in the aftermath of the New Latin American Cinema, the politically and aesthetically revolutionary cinema of the 1960s and 1970s, Latin American film criticism (particularly as practised by US-based critics) had accepted the way in which radical filmmakers like Glauber Rocha, Fernando Solanas and Octavio Getino dismissed early Latin American cinema made between the 1930s and the 1950s as excessively emotional. Their call to *concientizar el pueblo* was understood as a push to make spectators think, to use their minds when they watched films, to confront them with 'reality' by disrupting mechanisms of emotional identification with fictional protagonists; by forestalling narrative closure and by replacing 'easy', escapist pleasures with thought-provoking audiovisual images, among other things.[9] If the appearance of Tomás Gutiérrez Alea's essay 'Dialéctica del espectador'/ 'Viewer's dialectic' (published initially in Spanish in 1982) and the work of scholars such as Ana López on melodrama from the early 1990s have complicated this paradigm, the relationship between affect, cognition, and Latin American film remains largely unexplored.[10] Debates have continued to erupt over the ability of particular films, novels, paintings, and so on to deal with the trauma and aftermath of the revolutionary movements and military dictatorships of the 1960s – especially over works that solicit the spectator's affective engagement through melodramatic conventions and sensationalizing tactics.

The following analysis of the role of affect in Iñárritu's *Amores perros* and Pérez's *Madagascar* attempts to problematize those critical traditions. Evoking distinct emotional responses and set in different places, these films have a great deal to say about contemporary urban life, about personal as well as social losses, and about the current generation of young adults caught between the politically charged, if corrupt, legacy of the 1960s and postmodern ephemera. Although neither is a historical film per se (that is, one set in the past), they are vitally interested in engaging the recent past and its affective, as well as its political, legacies. As films about the past set in the present, they offer provocative counterweights to the tradition of historical films about revolution specific to both Mexico and Cuba and to the ways in which those films deployed emotion. Classic Mexican films about the Revolution of 1910 like *Flor silvestre / Wild Flower* (Emilio Fernández, 1943) and *Río Escondido* (Emilio Fernández, 1947) often employed melodramatic conventions to stress the affective ties binding the subject to the nation-as-family. In contrast, Cuban films like *Lucía* (Humberto Solás, 1968) and *Primera carga del machete* (Manuel Octavio Gómez, 1968), about the Revolution of 1959 and earlier revolutionary movements, frequently used hyperbolic onscreen acting and disjointed camerawork to disrupt conventional identificatory mechanisms and to hail their audience as performative subject – citizens who must embody their commitment to the nation state inside and outside of the theatre.[11] As discussed in greater detail below, *Amores perros* and *Madagascar* break with these respective representational conventions and deploy affect quite differently to register the crises of the present in the context of perceived historical crossroads.

In exploring the way in which these films register contemporary social crises and resituate the past, this study will take a cue from Elsaesser and analyze their modes of address – in other words, how they engage the spectator, particularly in the affective realm. After an overview of *Amores perros*'s plot, basic themes, and historicizing thrust, I shall analyze the film's emotional charge and suggest that it has less to do with what we see onscreen (for example, the violence of the dogfights, the pained expressions of the characters) than with its cyclical narrative structure and its literal and metaphoric framing of the action. In terms of *Madagascar*, the film Pérez made just before his more acclaimed *La vida es silbar / Life is to Whistle* (1999), I will examine the emotional work carried out through its ingenious soundtrack and sparse mise-en-scene.

In analyzing two films about the past that are set in the present, this essay will depart from Elsaesser's proposal by exploring how affect participates not only in the construction of popular historical memory, but also in the articulation of what Raymond Williams called 'structures of feeling'. I will argue that whether or not they destabilize the subject position of the spectator and his/her relationship to history, the two films register an epistemological crisis wherein the past functions as the site of reckoning for contemporary social breakdown. Finally, I will discuss the degree to which these films strengthen and/or question the moral economy and historical sensibility underpinning the dominant neoliberal project. Thus, beyond its analysis of two important Latin American films, this essay attempts to rethink the so-called 'waning of affect' and the death of history in contemporary society.

Chronicling the occasionally intersecting lives of several residents of present-day Mexico City, *Amores perros* ostensibly has little to do with Mexico's turbulent past. The first episode ('Octavio y Susana') deals primarily with Octavio, a young man who gets involved in dogfighting as a way to escape his violent neighborhood and liberate his battered sister-in-law from his abusive brother. The second episode ('Daniel y Valeria') picks up characters seen briefly in the earlier episode and traces the personal and professional crisis of Valeria, a rich and beautiful model who is united with her married lover Daniel and then loses her leg in a car accident. The final episode ('El Chivo y Maru') examines the life of a tramp living off what he collects on the city streets and earns from contract assassination jobs. These are tales of tragedy, loss and degradation, about the transitory nature of love in a contemporary cityscape, where connections between human beings are slowly eroded in a dog-eat-dog world.

As with many Latin American films made since the 1980s, *Amores perros* pays great attention to the private sphere. These are intimate stories or, rather, stories about intimacy or the lack of intimacy, shown in the careful detailing of personal habits and mundane routines: where people sleep, what they watch on television, what they eat and whether or not they clean their fingernails. The interior spaces of homes – whether Octavio's modest, working-class home or El Chivo's broken-down hovel – are depicted as dark, hermetic, seemingly airless places rather than tranquil locations protected from the hustle and bustle of city streets. This is true even of Valeria's luxury apartment, located in a high-rise far above street level and adorned with modern art and a lavish photo spread of Valeria herself. Situated directly across from a huge billboard featuring Valeria in an advertisement for 'Enchant' perfume, the light-filled apartment seems to be a testament to her rising success in both personal and professional spheres. Yet during her recuperation from the accident, her home turns into a claustrophobic jail cell where she must come to terms with her changed situation in the world.

In these stories, the home is not an escape from the violence of the outside world, but rather the very site in which hostile actions and petty cruelties are carried out with excruciating familiarity. Although *Amores perros* opens with a fast-paced chase sequence with speeding cars, plenty of blood, and gunshots, the film quickly goes into reverse, returning us to an earlier moment in Octavio's home. It is there that the chain of events begins that leads, seemingly inescapably, to the public confrontation we have just witnessed. In this originary moment at home, Cofi, the family dog, escapes onto the street, Octavio's brother Ramiro cruelly berates his adolescent wife, Susana, for letting the dog out, and Octavio tries to defend his sister-in-law. For his troubles, he becomes subject to his brother's wrathful harangues and his mother's admonitions not to get involved. Taking place within the confines of their small kitchen, the family conflict is situated between scenes of a dogfight taking place in a nearby building. This sequencing creates an interesting parallel between the two 'combat zones' and characterizes Octavio and Ramiro as a pair of vicious dogs engaged in a meaningless battle to the death for the right to rule over an already disintegrating family home.

Yet, as much as *Amores perros* focuses on the dynamics of family intimacy, the interlocking nature of its three episodes and their common dog motif suggest that the film is an allegory depicting Mexico as a family in crisis – a trope traceable at least as far back as films and novels about the Revolution. While all three episodes discuss the disintegration of families, the first and last episodes pay particular attention to the Cain-and-Abel conflict between the brothers. In the first episode, Octavio and Ramiro's fights escalate from daily verbal clashes into physical beatings. Frenetic montage sequences – like the one ricocheting between shots of Octavio at Cofi's dogfights, Ramiro robbing pharmacies, and Octavio having sex with Susana to the driving beat of a hip-hop song ('Dime qué te sientes/Tell me what you feel . . .') – assault us with brutal acts and betrayals that belie myths about the cohesive nature of the Mexican (and Latin American) family in times of crisis. A later montage sequence, interspersing shots of Octavio and Susana making love on top of the dryer with others of Ramiro being beaten by a group of thugs contracted by Octavio, demonstrates the complete breakdown of brotherly love.[12]

The conflict between Octavio and Ramiro finds a parallel in the final episode where a man named Gustavo contracts El Chivo to kill his swindling business partner Luis, who is also his half-brother. The elevated economic status of Gustavo and Luis suggests that the decay of the Mexican family is not a result of growing levels of poverty as it occurs at all levels of society. The film may indeed be critiquing the moral bankruptcy and personal cowardice of Mexico's upwardly-mobile middle class as it mocks Gustavo's inability to get his hands dirty and kill his brother himself. And, indeed, there are hints of intra-class warfare breaking out as a result of escalating greed and competitiveness in El Chivo's earlier assassination of an industrialist. Yet, given the parallels it establishes in the first and third episodes, the film's critique goes beyond a particular class or social group and is not primarily a denunciation of the current economic situation. Rather, the film's critique is at once more diffuse and more specific, as can be seen in the final episode.

Here we find out that El Chivo's estrangement from his own family (and specifically his daughter, María Eugenia (or Maru), whose apartment he has been breaking into) was a result of his participation in a guerrilla group fighting to establish a more revolutionary and just society in the 1970s. Committed to his cause and jailed for his actions, El Chivo agreed to give up any claim to his wife and daughter. Rather than depicting his actions as heroic (as a sacrifice of personal security and happiness for a larger social good), *Amores perros* characterizes it as a solipsistic and futile act of personal hubris and political naivety. El Chivo/Martín himself renounces his political past near the end of the film in a phone message he leaves for his daughter: 'Back then I thought that I had to change the world before sharing it with you. . . . As you can see, I failed.'[13] As the final episode of the film, the story of this family breakdown is given special weight and a type of explanatory authority that casts the radical political struggles of the 1960s and 1970s and, more particularly, the reification of totalizing schemes of societal reform, as a major contributor (if not the source) of private and public decay and the breakdown of the Mexican family.

To a certain degree, the film's reworking of Mexico's radical past is somewhat analogous to that which occurred in classic films from the 1940s about the Revolution of 1910. By romanticizing revolutionary struggle just as the Mexican state initiated an industrialization process, a film like *Flor silvestre* (1943) helped entomb revolution as a necessary antecedent to contemporary modernization projects even as its melodramatic conventions became a conduit through which to articulate a generalized sense of longing characterized as the affective legacy of *past* losses (rather than as dissatisfaction with the transformation of contemporary socioeconomic structures). Whereas *Amores perros* dismisses revolutionary struggle outright, like *Flor silvestre* it ties uncertainties about contemporary life to past conflicts. Yet, Iñárritu's film is less interested in displacing concerns about contemporary society entirely onto the past than with utilizing its affective register to convey an epistemological crisis that has destabilized the subject's understanding of contemporary society and, perhaps, more importantly, his/her ability to make substantive proposals for a better future.

As suggested above, the way in which the film disconcerts the spectator has little to do with what is shown onscreen. The moments of explicit physical violence are startling and graphic, but often quite brief. Nor, I would argue, is the spectator overpowered by the faces of the characters contorted with physical pain or emotional grief (like those featured in the film's publicity). These are certainly affecting elements, but they do not sufficiently account for the type of emotional work performed by the film: this is done by its narrative structure and inventive use of offscreen space.

As discussed earlier, the interlocking stories make *Amores perros* a film about Mexican society as a whole. Each subsequent episode further develops a character or characters depicted only briefly in an earlier episode and, at the same time, gives us glimpses of what has happened to the main characters from earlier episodes. For example, while we see brief shots of Daniel (in his car with his family, or kissing his daughters goodnight) in Episode One, his story only becomes fully developed in Episode Two, which begins as the continuation of a television programme first seen in Episode One by Octavio and his friend, Jorge. In Episode Three we see brief glimpses of what has happened to Octavio, Susana and Ramiro after the car crash that ends Episode One. Rather than showing three discrete groups, the film suggests that everyone's life somehow affects everyone else's life and that Mexican society itself is spiralling down into a vortex of violence.

However, the significance of the film's narrative structure goes beyond establishing those thematic parallels, as the stories from each episode are not only interlocking, but circular. We see the same events more than once, either from the same perspective (for example, Octavio and Jorge in the car chase at the beginning of the film and at the end of Episode One) or from a different perspective (for example, the car crash from Octavio's perspective in Episode One and from Valeria's perspective in Episode Two). This narrative repetition of particular events has a different effect here than in Orson Welles's *Citizen Kane* (1941) or even Quentin Tarantino's *Pulp Fiction* (1994), to which many have compared the Mexican film. In *Amores perros*, this narrational technique not only transforms how we think about what we see (for example, what are the causes, what are the effects, who is responsible), but also substantively frames how we perceive those events on an emotional level. Most specifically, it allows us to anticipate – not only foresee, but also 'forefeel' – tragic events such as Valeria's car crash. The circularity or looping nature of the narrative infuses the spectator with an ongoing sense of dread: having seen the tragic car crash once, then twice, then a third time, the film conditions the spectator to be wary, to assume that another encounter with violence is just around the corner, or just around the edges of the next frame.

The looping structure also instils the feeling that there is no escape from tragedy and loss and that any belief in redemption is futile and naive. As the characters from earlier episodes reappear later on, the film initially suggests that they have survived both physically and emotionally the earlier confrontations, but quickly rips away that fantasy. In Episode Three, we see a seemingly reconciled Ramiro and Susana walking on the city streets only soon thereafter to witness Ramiro's death in a failed bank robbery. We find out that Octavio survived the car crash despite serious injuries, but his attempt to reunite with Susana after Ramiro's death and his dream of escaping with her to Ciudad Juárez are once again doomed to fail.

The way in which the film infuses the spectator with a sense of impending doom and lurking danger is greatly dependent on its artful play with the relationship between what is observable and what is not, or between different modes of perception. In a number of ways, the film draws a contrast between what we see and what we feel or 'know' through other senses. As suggested earlier, the horrifying effects of *Amores perros* are less the result of what we see onscreen than of what we intuit, and the way in which the film directs our attention towards what cannot be seen, but only detected by other means.

The film's mechanisms for building suspense depart from the classic paradigm outlined by Alfred Hitchcock, wherein a film shows something to the audience that the characters do not see or 'know about' (like the villain placing a bomb under a table) and thus pulls the spectator to the edge of his/her seat with the desire to 'tell' the characters what we know. Suspense works differently in *Amores perros*, which teaches us to anticipate coming violence or lurking danger without giving us a privileged view. For example, having seen the image of a bloody dog in the car in the opening sequence and then the initial moments of a dogfight, the spectator senses that Cofi's escape from Octavio's house in the next scene will only end in more violence. Something similar, but more diffuse, occurs with the scenes showing El Chivo watching a variety of people. Having seen that he is a man who will defend his dogs with a machete and having witnessed his ability to carry out a public assassination in the middle of a bustling street, the spectator learns to associate his watchfulness with impending danger. This, in turn, imbues the repeated scenes where he peers at his daughter, just as he visually stakes out the young businessman, with a sense of great unease.

One of the primary ways in which the film toys with the relationship between the knowable and the visible is through its ingenious use of offscreen space. In the sequence where Cofi escapes from the house, the camera presents a long-shot that remains on the doorway to the house even after Susana runs offscreen right to pursue Cofi. The shot's fixity frustrates our desire to travel with Susana, to see where Cofi is going. Having seen earlier evidence of injured and attacking dogs, the spectator can now only imagine what will happen next.

A more sustained example of the unsettling use of offscreen space occurs in the second episode, when Richie, Valeria's beloved Lhasa apso dog, becomes lost beneath the floor of her luxury apartment. Haunted by the periodic sounds of his muffled barks and scurrying feet over several days, Valeria eventually moves from worry to panic – an escalating emotional trajectory that threatens her relationship with Daniel. Her ability to perceive her dog's continuing predicament through auditory means alone leads her to imagine Richie suffering not only gradual starvation, but also being eaten by marauding rats. Lost in a dark and fathomless maze, Richie comes to symbolize all of Valeria's latent fears about the end of her modelling career and the uncertainty of her relationship with the still married Daniel. Through its deliberate manipulation of what we see and what we hear, the film manages to draw the spectator into Valeria's feelings of panic, suspicion and paranoia and, in the context of the larger film, position the unseen events occurring beneath the floor as a metaphor for the ongoing suffering and violence underlying society as a whole.

This essay has paid a good deal of attention not only to the major themes of *Amores perros*, but also to how the film makes us feel, because Iñárritu's work gets at 'structures of feeling'.[14] In his effort to understand culture as a process, and not as something already crystallized and visible in particular objects (for example, paintings, novels, films), Raymond Williams proposes the notion of 'structures of feeling' as a way to get at 'experiences, beliefs, consciousnesses, and sensibilities' that manifest themselves in emergent artistic productions in structured ways. Through this concept, he manages to forego conventional philosophical paradigms opposing thought to feeling.

Williams argues that structures of feeling are 'distinguishable from other social and semantic formations by [their] articulation of presence'.[15] In other words, he is interested in getting at currents of thought–feeling that have not already been named, classified, and boxed-up to serve a variety of aesthetic, social and/or political purposes. For example, he cites the work of Charles Dickens, Emily Bronte and others as having been important for registering generalized sensibilities that were dismissed by dominant Victorian ideology as deviations from the norm, limited to sectors of the population affected by poverty, debt or illegitimacy.[16] Williams is not arguing that the works of these authors articulate a working-class critique of the industrial change (which, according to Williams, emerges only later as an alternative ideology), but rather that, at a particular moment of history, those novels become a privileged register for streams of latent, unsedimented beliefs and feelings.

Iñárritu's film functions in a similar way. In other words, what is most powerful about *Amores perros* is not its slick, postmodern surface (for example, its driving soundtrack, stripped film stock, disjunctive cinematography), but rather the way in which it articulates contemporary structures of feeling about the true horror of contemporary society. Premiering in an age of escalating urban crime in Mexico City and of growing economic inequalities, *Amores perros* transmits the feeling that violence, loss and conflict are constitutive elements of everyday life, as illustrated by several scenes in which a shot of a violent act is directly followed by a closeup on a plate of food. This is a tale about the mundane – about people's pets and what they eat – not about state-sponsored terrorism, the ravages of current economic inequalities, political corruption, the breakdown of moral principles in a Catholic nation, or the artificiality of the media – though these are all touched upon. Without defending the film's 'realism', I am arguing that it evokes the dull ache of lived experiences, despite the fact that the film is quite ideologically and politically conservative.[17]

If the horrifying violence of *Amores perros* stirs up feelings of disgust, fear and horror, a film like Pérez's *Madagascar* works quite differently. It is a much quieter film, chronicling a young girl's affective 'disconnection' from her family and society as well as her mother's feeling that she has lost her ability to dream.[18] Unlike the stylistic flash and rapid pace of Iñárritu's film, *Madagascar* pursues a much more lyrical, contemplative aesthetic. Yet, like *Amores perros*, it is a story about a family on the verge of a breakdown set against the backdrop of a decaying cityscape: it too, is a personal story with social implications. Within the context of the family drama, both films question the meaning and legacy of the revolutionary projects of the 1960s and, most importantly, articulate structures of feeling. Within the context of Cuban cinema, *Madagascar* is a unique film for its preoccupation with the interior life of the subject and for its suggestion that psychic crises are linked to the process of instituting revolution as a collective struggle.

Pérez's film focuses on the world-weariness of Laura, a university physics professor, and, more particularly, the growing tensions between Laura and her daughter Laurita. At the same time as Laura is finding less and less satisfaction in her professional life, her relationship with Laurita is becoming more and more strained. Laurita shows little interest in school or her immediate surroundings, and dreams of travelling to Madagascar because, as she tells her mother, 'es lo que no conozco' ('I know nothing about it'). Her mania for rock music transmutes into a fixation with 'great' art and, later, into a devotion to evangelical Christianity. Her changing obsessions and disjunctive emotions flummox her mother, who admits in voiceover that she does not understand why Laurita sometimes cries and sometimes does not. Scenes showing Laurita's initial affective disengagement from her mother and surrounding social institutions (specifically her school and the nation-state) are followed by others where we see her sobbing uncontrollably as she listens to 'Con te partirio' ('It's Time to Say Goodbye') and peers at a painting in a museum. Laura herself continually teeters on the edge of hysteria as she repeatedly screams at her daughter, in ever less successful efforts to penetrate Laurita's self-contained, somewhat solipsistic demeanour and seemingly selfish disregard for wider social norms.

The film avoids 'diagnosing' Laurita's changing interests and wildly oscillating emotions, leaving any concrete explanation elusive. However, it does suggest that the tensions and affective disjunction present in Laurita's family are part of a larger dynamic. At several points in the film, we see groups of people chanting the word. 'Madagascar' – most notably in one sequence in which innumerable young adults stand with their arms outstretched on the roofs of apartment buildings throughout Havana. Pictured as crosses or as antennas, the people reach out for something unknown; their bodies are isolated, separate, but their words signal their common search for something beyond themselves and beyond their immediate surroundings.

To a certain degree, *Madagascar* locates this search as a generational issue felt most acutely by young adults – as visualized in the scene described above or as indicated in the final dedication of the film to the director's three children. However, the parallels it establishes between Laurita and Laura (who by the end have exchanged roles) as well as the presence of older adults, particularly Laurita's grandmother, chanting 'Madagascar', suggest that the 'problem' is not limited to a single age-group but permeates Cuban society as a whole.

In quite specific ways, *Madagascar* is a meditation on the lost promise of the 1960s and the uncertainty of the future in the early 1990s. Laura frequently muses on the failings of fellow university professors like Mercedes, who was to have been the greatest researcher ever in her field, yet who now merely repeats the same classes over and over again. As Laura ponders in voiceover: '¿Qué pasó? Nadie sabe lo que pasó' ('What happened? Nobody knows what happened'). Laura's growing disillusion with what has been achieved in the last thirty years is most evident in a scene in which she looks at an old photograph from the 1969 May Day celebration. Reminiscing with her mother about the fun she used to have with a friend (who later married an Italian billionaire and left the country), Laura's laughter abruptly stops when she is unable to locate herself in the crowded picture. Taking out a magnifying glass, she searches the photograph asking, '¿Dónde estoy yo? ¿Dónde estoy yo?, Dios mío' ('Where am I? In God's name, where am I?'). Framing the photograph in an extreme closeup through the distorting power of the magnifying glass, the film suggests that the self has been lost in the social and that the pursuit of greater equality overlooked personal fulfilment and, at worst, treated difference as deviance. Similarly, these themes are underlined in comic fashion in Pérez's *La vida es silbar*, when a teacher makes her young students recite the word 'I-GUAL-DAD' (e-qual-i-ty') again and again and again until they 'get it right'. Although *Madagascar*'s lyricism and elliptical narrative discourage a narrowly sociopolitical reading, its swipes at hollow revolutionary rhetoric are quite obvious as it defends Laurita's lack of interest in '"flags, emblems" or preaching about "conciencia"'.

The film attempts to capture and transmit the characters' alienation in two main ways: through the inventive use of asynchronous sound and a sparse mise-en-scene. Unlike *Amores perros*, which engages the spectator in a structure of feeling through the manipulation of offscreen space (that is to say, through what is not visible), *Madagascar* plays with what we do see and hear by 'hollowing out' both the sound and the image tracks. The film opens with a sequence that crosscuts between closeups of people on bikes riding through the streets of Havana and extreme closeups of Laura being examined by a doctor. Although Laura's voiceover accompanies the shots of her, only vague or muffled sounds of horns, voices and music are audible during the shots of people on the street. As a subsequent shot shows the doctor examining Laura's ear, the film seems to link the distorted sounds on the street with Laura's 'ailment', suggesting that we were perceiving the world as Laura does. At the end of the film, we return to the doctor's office where Laura's statement that 'everything has returned to normal' is belied by her subsequent comparison of herself to a violin that is out of tune and cannot quite catch on to what is being played, a musical metaphor that becomes central to *La vida es silbar*.

Our visual perceptions are just as important to drawing us into Laura's understanding of the world. Shot through a telephoto lens, the closeups of the cyclists in the opening sequence isolate the figures against a blurry foreground and background. Just like the emptied-out soundtrack, the images visualize Laura's sense of alienation as a feeling of distanciation from her contemporaries and of being out-of-touch with her surroundings. In other words, the opening sequence of the film plays with our sense of depth, a sense that is central to our understanding of reality and that is at once visual and auditory, to communicate the character's affective disjunction.

The film's arrangement of space is particularly important in this regard. As evident in a later sequence in which Laura is honoured for her contributions to the university in an open-air ceremony, the film presents Havana as a vacant wasteland and uses the mise-en-scene to unmask the celebratory language of officialist discourse during the so-called 'special period'. The final 'frozen' moment of this scene manages not only to underscore the absurdity of declaring triumphs ('cuando hay empeño, hay logros' / 'When there is effort, there is achievement') in the context of such obvious material devastation, but also to amplify Laura's feelings of alienation by laying over the sonorous notes first heard at the beginning of the film. The vacant, decaying spaces in *Madagascar* are important registers of the deterioration of material conditions of Cuban society at large, but the devastated homes and public plazas also function as metaphors for the psychic impoverishment of individuals.

The deployment of the ruined cityscape as metaphor of the contemporary crisis in Cuba can be seen in numerous contemporary films, including Pérez's own *La vida es silbar* (1999), Gutiérrez Alea and Tabío's *Fresa y chocolate / Strawberry and Chocolate* (1993) and even Wim Wenders' *Buena Vista Social Club* (1999).[19] However, the clearest resonance is the work of younger filmmakers like Enrique Alvarez (*Sed* [1991] and *La ola* [1995]), and more particularly, Jorge Luis Sánchez, who has served as Pérez's assistant director on a number of films including *Madagascar*. In his short documentary *El fanguito* (1990), Sánchez examines the persistence of poverty, racism and marginalization in contemporary Cuba through a series of interviews with residents of a slum on the outskirts of Havana and echoes the critique found in Sara Gómez's 1974 film *De cierta manera / One Way or Another*. The devastated cityscape becomes even more important in another of his shorts, *Un pedazo de mí* (1989), that presents interviews with a number of young adults (called *frikis*) who find solace in US and British rock music. The film uses its sparse mise-en-scene in inventive ways to capture the young men's sense of alienation and marginalization as they walk through half-finished apartment buildings or construction scaffolding on the streets of the city. Attesting to the economic hardships experienced by these young men, the mise-en-scene also speaks, in quite poetic ways, about their feelings of emotional isolation and abandonment and about the absence of affective ties to their own families or to the larger society.

To a certain degree, films like these might be seen as a response to contemporary economic conditions on the island and, more specifically, as an implicit critique of the increasingly visible disjunctions between urban renovation projects aimed at attracting more tourists and the increasing physical degradation of surrounding neighbourhoods.[20] At the same time, the lyrical representation of space in the work of younger filmmakers such as Sánchez, as well as in the more widely recognized films of Fernando Pérez, is evidence of something else: an emergent aesthetic interested in capturing not only people's thoughts about contemporary life, but also their emotional states, their sense of somehow being disconnected, out of synch – spatially and temporally disengaged – from their surrounding environment and from society itself. This feeling of *desarraigo*, of being uprooted and afloat, is best captured in *Madagascar* by Laura and Laurita's constant movement from one house to another. Their inability to find a stable home or, more generally, a place in which they feel at home, gestures towards the unsettled and unsettling sensibilities underlying Cuban 'reality'.[21]

While uprootedness has been a theme of numerous recent Cuban films, including *Miel para Oshún / Honey for Oshun* (Humberto Solás, 2000) and *Vídeo de familia* (Humberto Padrón, 2001), most of these works have linked that feeling almost exclusively to the issue of exile and to those living outside of the island or to those on the island who feel the loss of friends and family who live abroad. *Madagascar* is unique in the way that it posits this uprootedness (of which physical exile is one manifestation) as a constitutive element of the revolutionary experience wherein the individual has become unmoored during a restructuring process grounded in collective identity and solidarity. Its indictment of the Revolution is consequently much harsher than the critiques present in countless other Cuban films. Whereas it has become commonplace for Cuban films to poke fun at officialist discourses about revolutionary triumphs and to underscore what the Revolution has not yet achieved, *Madagascar* points to the Revolution's constitutive costs, to what may be the unavoidable loss of such commitment to the social good.

Rather than suggesting that *Madagascar* is an anti-revolutionary film, I am highlighting its humanism and the way in which its contemplative aesthetic and emotional work interpellate the spectator as a historical subject differently from other Cuban films. Cuban historical films have traditionally encouraged their spectators to see the Revolution of 1959 as the culmination of a long line of previous rebellions against injustice and to see themselves as the guardians of such a heritage. As Barnard has argued, an unfortunate consequence of this otherwise refreshing effort to 'sting' the viewer-subject into action has been to avoid contentious issues of contemporary society.[22] In contrast, *Madagascar* invites the spectator to 'tune in' to the affective dissonances of contemporary life for what they reveal about how any grand scheme of society must not disregard the notion of the individual.

I want to conclude this essay by returning to some of the issues brought up at the beginning, by presenting some final thoughts on how the emotional address of *Amores perros* and *Madagascar* responds to a sense of crisis about contemporary life and about cinema's ability to represent what is happening. In the aftermath of the 1960s, with the appearance of numerous dictatorships, growing levels of censorship, and ongoing financial difficulties, filmmakers learned to 'speak other languages' by going into exile and speaking to audiences outside the bounds of the nation, or by staying at home and either refraining from explicitly political critique or speaking through allegories or oblique references.[23] Even after the much heralded 'return to democracy', there were few fiction films that directly addressed the dictatorships of the 1960s to the 1980s. Part of the problem faced by filmmakers and other artists has been to represent what cannot be seen (the disappeared), or that which defies representation (torture). Another, even more thorny issue – particularly given the military's continuing political power in many countries even during democratic administrations – has been how to challenge spectators to engage in a process of self-examination about their own stake in the violence that took place[24] *as well as* in ongoing struggles over the myriad of issues left unresolved by the return to democracy. In other words, the rise of neoliberal paradigm and the relative paralysis of the Left have been accompanied by a representational crisis.[25] How does one talk about systems of oppression (such as widespread political corruption and neocolonialism) in the aftermath of the failed utopian revolutionary projects of the Left? How does one denounce growing economic inequalities without chasing the skirts of the latest neorealism? How does one talk about collective sensibilities and not telescope these into the struggles of seemingly 'representative' individuals? As suggested by Kathleen Newman, the quest to move beyond the moralizing of the traditional Left (and in cinematic terms, the New Latin American Cinema) and its embrace of facile cultural nationalism is particularly evident in the work of younger filmmakers.[26]

Directors like Iñárritu and the older Pérez (who is particularly engaged with the younger generation of Cuban cineastes) have responded by proposing an aesthetic of 'presence', where sociopolitical critique is secondary to altering our perceptions. *Amores perros* gestures towards what is visibly inaccessible and, at the same time, detectable. It registers an exhaustion with political debate and an extreme disenchantment with the paradigms of the Left even as the film seemingly criticizes the inequalities and ephemeralities of neoliberalism. *Madagascar* is less definitive in its rejection of the political legacies of the past, and yet forces us to address the affective price that has been paid for revolutionary change by hollowing out our perceptions and unmooring us from the immediacy of sensorial impressions, or common sense(s).

The films do not entirely unsettle the subject position of the viewer, at least not in the way theorized by Elsaesser. They do not shock the spectator into recognizing the inadequacy of his/her own moral economy or complicity in particular historical processes. Nor do they encourage the spectator to reimagine his/her relationship with the community. *Amores perros* in particular limits its articulation of the social to the recurrent metaphor of the family. While both suggest that the path to the future is uncertain (*Amores perros* closes as El Chivo walks off into a hazy, sun-cracked mudflat, and *Madagascar* as Laura and Laurita walk their bicycles into a tunnel), only *Madagascar* engages the spectator in the process of imagining a different future through the lines of identification it has forged between Laura and the spectator.

Nevertheless, in their affective mode of address, both films problematize the very knowableness of the present by disrupting and reorienting the spectator's perceptions: *Amores perros* by questioning the epistemological primacy of the visual realm, and *Madagascar* by playing with our sense of depth. The attempt by Iñárritu's film to recuperate the deep uncertainties it has articulated, and thus its complicity with the neoliberal paradigm, lies not in its gesturing towards past errors,[27] but rather, primarily, in its moral economy in its call to honour one's family, one's brothers-in-the-nation, as the basis of future redemption. Although *Madagascar* also highlights family breakdown, it does not draw the same metonymic connection between family and society. Its historical sensibility is also different and goes beyond its critique of the limitations of revolutionary projects. The past is made present in Pérez's film in its residual liberal humanism, a stance that clashes with the type of individualism promoted by neoliberalism (subject as constituted by the market) as well as with the Marxist formulations of Ché Guevara and Julio García Espinosa, who argued that the fullest realization of man would occur through a true commitment to the revolutionary process and the social body.

Acknowledgements

I am grateful to Claire Fox for commenting on an earlier version of this paper and to Kathleen Newman, who has witnessed the development of this project over several months and been instrumental in shaping my thoughts on contemporary Latin American cinema.

Notes

1 See Chilean social scientist Martín Hopenhyn's *No Apocalypse Now/No Integration: Modernism and Postmodernism in Latin America* (Durham, NC: Duke University Press, 2001), and US-based Argentine literary critic Francine Masiello's *The Art of Transition: Latin American Culture and Neoliberal Crisis* (Durham, NC: Duke University Press, 2001) among others.

2 This is the case even in the very thoughtful work of historian Robert Rosenstone, who himself criticizes his colleagues' traditional denunciation of the representation of history in film as oversimplistic. See 'The historical film: looking at the past in a postliterate age', in *Visions of the Past: The Challenge of Film to Our Ideas of History* (Cambridge, MA: Harvard University Press, 1995).

3 Thomas Elsaesser, 'Subject positions, speaking positions: from *Holocaust, Our Hitler* and *Heimat* to *Shoah* and *Schindler's List*', in Vivian Sobchack (ed.), *The Persistence of History: Cinema, Television and the Modern Event* (New York: Routledge, 1996), p. 172.

4 Ibid., p. 173.

5 Ibid.

6 Ibid., p. 174.

7 Ibid.

8 *M. Klein* focuses on a gentile who buys the art collections of Jews fleeing Hitler. Despite the character's 'morally suspect behaviour', the film encourages the spectator to identify with him up until the moment he is arrested by the Gestapo and loaded onto a 'train with all the Jews who have been rounded up', at which point 'the spectator want[s] to say . . . "But you've got the wrong man: he isn't a Jew" – until with a sudden shock one realizes that all the people on the train are "the wrong men"' and must acknowledge one's own 'impotence' and 'complicity'. Ibid., pp. 174–5.

9 Their own evocation of emotion was either operatic (as in the case of Rocha) or tightly contained within a larger rationalist argument (as in the slaughterhouse sequence *in La hora de los hornos/The Hour of the Furnaces* (1968)); in these ways, the films seemingly prevented their spectators from 'wallowing in emotion' and instead forced them to maintain a 'proper' aesthetic discourse.

10 Gutiérrez Alea was the first to underscore the need for both identification and distanciation. See 'Dialéctica del espectador', reprinted in *Hojas de cine: Testimonios y documentos del Nuevo cine latinoamerico*, Volume III (Mexico, DF: Dirección General de Publicaciones y medios, Secretaria de Educación Pública/Fundación Mexicana de Cineastas, AC/Universidad Autónoma Metropolitana, 1988); John King, Ana López

and Manuel Alvarado (eds), *Mediating Two Worlds: Cinematic Encounters in the Americas* (London: British Film Institute, 1993).

11 For an incisive analysis of Cuban historical films as well as viewing practices, see Timothy Barnard, 'Death is not true: form and history in Cuban film', and Marvin D'Lugo's discussion of the way in which Cuban films promote interpretive communities through 'dramatized onscreen audiences' in 'Transparent women: gender and nation', both in King, López and Alvarado (eds), *Mediating Two Worlds*.

12 The extradiegetic rock ballad playing in this later sequence (speaking of a lover's frailty and the need for honesty) provides an ironic counterpoint to what we see.

13 The film initially characterized El Chivo's past actions as criminal, not political, as we hear about them from Leonardo, the corrupt policeman, who tells another character that El Chivo placed a bomb in a commercial centre, kidnapped people, and assassinated two policemen.

14 Raymond Williams, 'Structures of feeling', in *Marxism and Literature* (Oxford: Oxford University Press, 1977).

15 Ibid., p. 135.

16 Ibid., p. 125.

17 Here I depart from Williams's theorization of structures of feeling that point towards its progressive potential.

18 For an overview of Pérez's work, see Beat Borter, 'Moving to thought: the inspired reflective cinema of Fernando Pérez', in Ann Marie Stock (ed.), *Framing Latin American Cinema: New Critical Perspectives* (Minneapolis, MN: University of Minnesota Press, 1997).

19 This exploration of the cityscape is not entirely new as it was a recurrent motif in the work of Tomás Gutiérrez Alea at least as far back as his 1968 classic *Memorias del subdesarrollo / Memories of Underdevelopment*. See Ana López, '*Memorias* of a home: mapping the revolution (and the making of exiles?)', *Revista Canadiense de Estudios Hispánicos*, vol. 20, no. 1 (1995), pp. 5–17.

20 After the end of the Soviet subsidies in the early 1990s, tourism once again, as in prerevolutionary days, became one of the central pillars of the Cuban economy. For a discussion of subsequent urban renovation projects, see Roberto Segre, *América Latina, fin de milenio: Raíces y perspectives de su arquitectura* (Havana: Artes y Literatura, 1990).

21 Cuban film critic Juan Antonio García Borrero calls 'the search for a certain intimate emotivity . . . another of the most recurrent characteristics of Cuban cinema in the 1990s' (my translation). See 'La utopía confiscada (De la gravedad del sueño a la ligereza del realismo)', in *La edad de herejía (Ensayos sobre el cine cubano, su crítica y su público)* (Santiago de Cuba: Editorial Oriente, 2002), pp. 169–94.

22 Barnard, 'Death is not true', pp. 235–40.

23 For a fine study of films made in Argentina during the military dictatorship (1976–83), see Sergio Wolf, 'El Cine del Proceso: Estética de la muerte', in Wolf (ed.), *Cine argentino: La otra historia* (Buenos Aires: Ediciones Letra Buena, 1992).

24 Almost without exception, films like *La historia oficial / The Official Version* have dealt with those who were 'witnesses' to the battles between guerrilla groups and the military. By encouraging their spectators to identify with these 'unknowing' bystanders, like *La historia*'s protagonist Alica, the films failed to promote any critical examination of each viewer-subject's own stake in the violence that took place.

25 For a discussion of these issues in relation to the USA and Europe, see the articles by Hayden White and others in Sobchack (ed.), *The Persistence of History*.

26 Kathleen Newman, 'Contemporary Argentine cinema', unpublished paper presented at 'Crossing Borders: Symposium on Latin American Film', Notre Dame University,

9–10 November 2001, and 'Democracy and film narratives: the legacies of the New Latin American Cinema', unpublished paper presented at the annual conference of the Society for Cinema Studies, Denver, 23–26 May 2002.

27 The film provides a warning about radical projects through the character of El Chivo, the former political militant, who is the only character able to recognize the detrimental effects of systemic violence on basic human relations.

Appendix: Articles and other items on world cinema in *Screen*, 1967–2004

Vol. 17 (1976)

Kristin Thompson and David Bordwell, 'Space and narrative in the films of Ozu', no. 2, pp. 41–73.

Edward Branigan, 'The space of *Equinox Flower*', no. 2, pp. 74–105.

Jonathan Rosenbaum, Letter responding to Thompson and Bordwell's essay in vol. 17, no. 2; and their reply, no. 4, pp. 121–4.

Vol. 22 (1981)

Rosalind Coward and John Ellis, 'Hong Kong–China 1981', no. 4, pp. 91–100.

Vol. 23 (1982)

John Ellis, 'Electric shadows in Italy: a retrospective of Chinese film', no. 2, pp. 79–83.

Vol. 24 (1983)

Robert Stam and Louise Spence, 'Colonialism, racism and representation: an introduction', no. 2, pp. 2–20.

Julianne Burton, 'The politics of aesthetic distance: the presentation of representation in *São Bernardo*', no. 2, pp. 30–53.

Mick Eaton, 'Another angle on anthropological film: a review of *Two Laws*', no. 2, pp. 55–9.

Teshome H. Gabriel, 'Teaching Third World cinema', no. 2, pp. 60–4.

Janet Hawken and Chaim Litewski, 'Exploitation for export: preview of *Pixote*', no. 2, pp. 66–70.

Sue Aspinall, 'One way—or another? Cuban cinema', no. 2, pp. 74–7.

Olivier Richon, 'Orientation' [photo-essay on Bombay film sets], no. 2, pp. 81–9.

Michael Chanan, Letter responding to vol. 24, no. 2, nos. 4–5, pp. 175–6.

Homi Bhabha, 'The Other question: the stereotype and colonial discourse', no. 6, pp. 18–36.

Vol. 26 (1985)

Julianne Burton, 'Marginal cinemas and mainstream critical theory', nos. 3–4, pp. 2–21.

Ella Shohat and Robert Stam, 'The cinema after Babel: language, difference, power', nos. 3–4, pp. 35–58.

Roy Armes, 'Black African cinema in the eighties', nos. 3–4, pp. 60–73.

Gerry Turvey, '*Xala* and the curse of neocolonialism', nos. 3–4, pp. 75–87.

Fernando Birri, 'For a nationalist, realist, critical and popular cinema', nos. 3–4, pp. 89–91.

Julio García Espinosa, 'Meditations on Imperfect Cinema . . . fifteen years later', nos. 3–4, pp. 93–4.

Sarah Montgomery, 'From one country to the next: interview with Dora Ramírez', nos. 3–4, pp. 96–100.

Rosie Thomas, 'Indian cinema: pleasures and popularity', nos. 3–4, pp. 116–31.

Vijay Mishra, 'Towards a theoretical critique of Bombay cinema', nos. 3–4, pp. 133–46.

Robert Crusz, 'Black cinemas, film theory and dependent knowledge', nos. 3–4, pp. 152–6.

Vol. 27 (1986)

Teshome H. Gabriel, 'Colonialism and "law and order" criticism', nos. 3–4, pp. 140–7.

Kobena Mercer, Report on Third Cinema: Theories and Practices, Edinburgh Film Festival 1986, no. 6, pp. 95–102.

Vol. 28 (1987)

Felicity Collins, 'A (sad) song of the body: review of *Song of Ceylon*', no. 1, pp. 78–89.

Carmen Huaco-Nuzum, 'Matilde Landeta: a pioneer Mexican filmmaker', no. 4, pp. 96–105.

Vol. 29 (1988)

Coco Fusco, 'Fantasies of oppositionality: reflections on recent conferences in Boston and New York', no. 4, pp. 80–93.

Perminder Dhillon-Kashyap, 'Locating the Asian experience', no. 4, pp. 120–6.

Vol. 30 (1989)

Ravi Vasudevan, 'The melodramatic mode and the commercial Hindi cinema', no. 3, pp. 29–50.

Andrew Higson, 'The concept of a national cinema', no. 4, pp. 36–46.

Zuzana M. Pick, 'The dialectical wanderings of exile', no. 4, pp. 48–64.

Vol. 33 (1992)

Paul Willemen, '*Bangkok–Bahrain* to *Berlin–Jerusalem*: Amos Gitai's editing', no. 1, pp. 14–26.

Annette Hamilton, 'The mediascape of modern Southeast Asia', no. 1, pp. 81–92.

Laleen Jayamanne, 'Sri Lankan family melodrama: a cinema of primitive attractions', no. 2, pp. 145–5.

Mary Ann Farquhar, 'The "hidden" gender in *Yellow Earth*', no. 2, pp. 154–64.

Bishnupriya Ghosh, 'Satyajit Ray's *Devi*: constructing a third-world feminist critique', no. 2, pp. 165–73.

Annette Hamilton, 'Family dramas: film and modernity in Thailand', no. 3, pp. 259–73.

Vol. 34 (1993)

Felix Thompson, 'Metaphors of space: polarization, dualism and Third World cinema', no. 1, pp. 38–53.

Martin Allor, 'Cultural *métissage*: national formations and productive discourse in Québec cinema and television', no. 1, pp. 69–75.

Carrie Tarr, 'Questions of identity in Beur cinema: from *Tea in the Harem* to *Cheb*', no. 4, pp. 321–42.

Vol. 35 (1994)

Amit Rai, 'An American Raj in Filmistan: images of Elvis in Indian films', no. 1, pp. 51–77.

Jacqueline Maingard, 'New South African cinema: *Mapantsula* and *Sarafina*', no. 3, pp. 235–43.

Laura Marks, 'A Deleuzian politics of hybrid cinema', no. 3, pp. 244–64.

Vol. 36 (1995)

Jose Munoz, 'The autoethnographic performance: reading Richard Fung's queer hybridity', no. 2, pp. 83–99.

Dimitris Eleftheriotis, 'Questioning totalities: constructions of masculinity in popular Greek cinema of the 1960s', no. 3, pp. 233–42.

Ravi Vasudevan, 'Addressing the spectator of a "third world" national cinema: the Bombay "social" film of the 1940s and 1950s', no. 4, pp. 305–24.

Stephanie Donald, 'Women reading Chinese films: between Orientalism and silence', no. 4, pp. 325–40.

Vol. 37 (1996)

Florence Ayisi and Carol Sydney, Conference Report: Africa and the History of Cinematic Ideas, London, 9–10 September 1995, no. 1, pp. 85–9.

Oscar Quirós, 'Critical mass of Cuban cinema: art as the vanguard of society' no. 3, pp. 279–93.

Yosefa Loshitzky, 'Travelling culture, travelling television', no. 4, pp. 323–35.

John Welchman, 'Moving images: on travelling film and video', no. 4, pp. 336–50.

Roland B. Tolentino, '*Inangbayan*, the mother-nation, in Lino Brocka's *Bayan Ko: Kapit sa Patalim* and *Orapronobis*', no. 4, pp. 368–88.

Vol. 38 (1997)

Hector Rodriguez, 'Hong Kong popular culture as an interpretive arena: the Huang Feihong film series', no. 1, pp. 1–24.

Julian Stringer, '"Your tender smiles give me strength": paradigms of masculinity in John Woo's *A Better Tomorrow* and *The Killer*', no. 1, pp. 25–41.

Lalitha Gopalan, 'Avenging women in Indian cinema', no. 1, pp. 42–59.

Roy Armes, Report on the Third Biennale of Arab Cinema, Paris, 21–9 June 1996, no. 1, pp. 84–7.

Jacqueline Maingard, 'Film studies in South Africa', no. 2, pp. 190–1.

Catherine Grant, 'Camera solidaria', no. 4, pp. 311–28.

Ismail Xavier, 'The humiliation of the father: melodrama and Cinema Novo's critique of conservative modernisation', no. 4, pp. 329–44.

Catherine Davies, 'Modernity, masculinity and Imperfect Cinema in Cuba', no. 4, pp. 345–59.

Dolores Tierney, 'Silver sling-backs and Mexican melodrama: *Salón México* and *Danzón*', no. 4, pp. 360–71.

Michael Chanan, 'The changing geography of Third Cinema', no. 4, pp. 372–88.

Vol. 39 (1998)

Lalitha Gopalan, Report on Conference on Tamil Cinema: History, Culture, Theory, Chennai, 15–19 August 1997, no. 2, pp. 196–200.

Nezih Erdoğan, 'Narratives of resistance: national identity and ambivalence in the Turkish melodrama between 1965 and 1975', no. 3, pp. 259–71.

Vol. 40 (1999)

Jyotika Virdi, 'Reverence, rape – and then revenge: popular Hindi cinema's "woman's film"', no. 1, pp. 17–37.

John Hess, 'No mas Habermas, or . . . rethinking Cuban cinema in the 1990s', no. 2, pp. 203–7.

Catherine Davies, 'Reply to John Hess', no. 2, pp. 208–11.

Aniko Imre, 'White man, white mask: Mephisto meets Venus', no. 4, pp. 405–22.

Vol. 41 (2000)

Catherine Grant, 'www.auteur.com?', no. 1, pp. 101–8.

Ravi S. Vasudevan, 'National pasts and futures: Indian cinema', no. 1, pp. 119–25.

Scott MacKenzie, 'A screen of one's own: early cinema in Québec and the public sphere 1906–28', no. 2, pp. 183–202.

Andrea Noble, Report on Latin American Cinema Conference: Theory and Praxis, University of Leeds, 29–30 June 1999, no. 2, pp. 238–41.

Vol. 42 (2001)

See Kam Tan, 'Chinese diasporic imaginations in Hong Kong films: sinicist belligerence and melancholia', no. 1, pp. 1–20.

Martin Stollery, 'Masculinities, generations and cultural transformation in contemporary Tunisian cinema', no. 1, pp. 49–63.

Andrea Noble, 'If looks could kill: image wars in *María Candelaria*', no. 1, pp. 77–91.

Yomi Braester, 'Memory at a standstill: "street-smart history" in Jiang Wen's *In the Heat of the Sun*', no. 4, pp. 350–62.

Vol. 43 (2002)

Esha Niyogi De, 'Modern Shakespeares in popular Bombay cinema: translation, subjectivity and community', no. 1, pp. 19–40.

Nezih Erdoğan, 'Mute bodies, disembodied voices: notes on sound in Turkish popular cinema', no. 3, pp. 233–49.

Vol. 44 (2003)

Shohini Chaudhuri and Howard Finn, 'The open image: poetic realism and the New Iranian Cinema', no. 1, pp. 38–57.

Alastair Phillips, 'Pictures of the past in the present: modernity, femininity and stardom in the postwar films of Ozu Yasujiro', no. 2, pp. 154–66.

Ning Ma, 'Signs of angst and hope: history and melodrama in Chinese fifth-generation cinema', no. 2, pp. 183–99.

Laura Podalsky, 'Affecting legacies: historical memory and contemporary structures of feeling in *Madagascar* and *Amores perros*', no. 3, pp. 277–94.

Dolores Tierney, Report on the 24th International New Latin American Film Festival, Havana, 3–13 December 2002, no. 3, pp. 333–6.

Vol. 45 (2004)

Asuman Suner, 'Horror of a different kind: dissonant voices of the new Turkish cinema', no. 4, pp. 305–23.

Index

Related titles from Routledge

Chinese National Cinema
Yingjin Zhang

What does it mean to be 'Chinese'? This controversial question has sparked off a never-ending process of image-making in Chinese-speaking communities throughout the twentieth century. This introduction to Chinese national cinema covers three 'Chinas': mainland China, Hong Kong and Taiwan. Historical and comparative perspectives bring out the parallel developments in these three Chinas, while critical analysis explores thematic and stylistic changes over time.

As well as exploring artistic achievements and ideological debates, Yingjin Zhang examines how – despite the pressures placed on the industry from state control and rigid censorship – Chinese national cinema remains incapable of projecting a single unified picture, but rather portrays many different Chinas.

ISBN 10: 0-415-17289-6 (hbk)
ISBN 10: 0-415-17290-X (pbk)

ISBN 13: 978-0-415-17289-9 (hbk)
ISBN 13: 978-0-415-17290-5 (hbk)

Available at all good bookshops
For ordering and further information please visit:
www.routledge.com

Related titles from Routledge

The Film Cultures Reader
Edited by Graeme Turner

This companion reader to *Film as Social Practice* brings together key writings on contemporary cinema, exploring film as a social and cultural phenomenon. Key features of the reader include:

- thematic sections, each with an introduction by the editor
- a general introduction by Graeme Turner
- sections: understanding film, film technology, film industries, meanings and pleasures, identities, audiences and consumption.

Contributors include: Tino Balio, Sabrina Barton, Tony Bennett, Jacqueline Bobo, Edward Buscombe, Stella Bruzzi, Jim Collins, Barbara Creed, Richard Dyer, Jane Feuer, Miriam Hansen, John Hill, Marc Jancovich, Susan Jeffords, Isaac Julien, Annette Kuhn, P. David Marshall, Judith Mayne, Kobena Mercer, Tania Modleski, Steve Neale, Tom O'Regan, Stephen Prince, Thomas Schatz, Gianluca Sergi, Ella Shohat, Jackie Stacey, Janet Staiger, Robert Stam, Chris Straayer, Yvonne Tasker, Stephen Teo, Janet Wollacott, Justin Wyatt.

ISBN 10: 0-415-25281-4 (hbk)
ISBN 10: 0-415-25282-2 (pbk)

ISBN 13: 978-0-415-25281-2 (hbk)
ISBN 13: 978-0-415-25282-9 (pbk)

Available at all good bookshops
For ordering and further information please visit:
www.routledge.com

Related titles from Routledge

Mexican National Cinema
Andrea Noble

Mexican National Cinema offers an account of the development of Mexican cinema from the intense cultural nationalism of the Mexican Revolution, through the 'Golden Age' of the 1940s and the 'nuevo cine' of the 1960s, to the renaissance in Mexican cinema in the 1990s.

The book moves from broad historical and theoretical context, particularly theories of nation, emergent discourses of 'mexicanidad' and the establishment and development of the Mexican industry, towards readings of key film texts and genres. Films considered include:

- Y tu mama también

- ¡Que viva México!

- La mujer del Puerto

- El Castillo de la pureza.

In each case, Andrea Noble considers the representation of nation inherent in these films and genres, placing an emphasis on the ways in which they intersect with debates in cultural history, particularly Mexico's quest for modernity.

Mexican National Cinema provides a thorough and detailed account of the vital and complex relationship between cinema and national identity in Mexico

ISBN 10: 0-415-23009-8
ISBN 10: 0-415-23010-1

ISBN 13: 978-0-415-23009-4
ISBN 13: 978-0-415-23010-0

Available at all good bookshops
For ordering and further information please visit:
www.routledge.com

Related titles from Routledge

Transnational Cinema, the *Film* Reader
Edited by Elizabeth Ezra and Terry Rowden

Transnational Cinema: the Film *Reader* provides an overview of the key concepts and debates within the developing field of transnational cinema.

Bringing together seminal essays from a wide range of sources, this volume engages with films that fashion their narrative and aesthetic dynamics in relation to more than one national or cultural community, and that reflect the impact of advanced capitalism and new media technologies in an increasingly interconnected world-system. The essays demonstrate that, in an era no longer marked by the sharp divisions between communist and capitalist nation states, or even "first" and "third" worlds, Europe and the U.S. must be factored into the increasingly hybrid notion of "world cinema."

The reader is divided into four sections:

- From National to Transnational Cinema
- Global Cinema in the Digital Age
- Motion Pictures: Film, Migration and Diaspora
- Tourists and Terrorists

When read in juxtaposition, these essays make clear that the significance of crossing borders varies according to the ethnic and/or gendered identity of the traveler, suggesting that the crossing of certain lines generates fundamental shifts in both the aesthetics and the ethics of cinema as a representational art.

Contributors: Homi K. Bhabha; Peter Bloom; Robert E. Davis; Jigna Desai; David Desser; Elizabeth Ezra; John Hess; Andrew Higson; David Murphy; Hamid Naficy; Diane Negra; John S. Nelson; Terry Rowden; Elana Shefrin; Ella Shohat; Ann Marie Stock; Patricia R. Zimmermann

ISBN 10: 0-415-37157-0 (hbk)
ISBN 10: 0-415-37158-9 (pbk)

ISBN 13: 978-0-415-37157-5 (hbk)
ISBN 13: 978-0-415-37158-2 (pbk)

Available at all good bookshops
For ordering and further information please visit:
www.routledge.com